William Faulkner in the Media Ecology

Southern Literary Studies

SCOTT ROMINE, SERIES EDITOR

William Faulkner in the Media Ecology

Edited by

Julian Murphet & Stefan Solomon

LOUISIANA STATE UNIVERSITY PRESS ■ BATON ROUGE

Published by Louisiana State University Press

Manufactured in the United States of America
First printing

Designer: Michelle A. Neustrom
Typeface: Brix Slab
Printer and binder: Maple Press

Library of Congress Cataloging-in-Publication Data

William Faulkner in the media ecology / edited by Julian Murphet and Stefan Solomon.

pages cm. — (Southern literary studies)

Includes index.

ISBN 978-0-8071-5948-4 (cloth : alk. paper) — ISBN 978-0-8071-5949-1 (pdf) — ISBN 978-0-8071-5950-7 (epub) — ISBN 978-0-8071-5951-4 (mobi) 1. Faulkner, William, 1897–1962—Criticism and interpretation. I. Murphet, Julian, editor. II. Solomon, Stefan, 1986– editor.

PS3511.A86Z98569526 2015

813'.52—dc23

2014033789

The paper in this book meets the guidelines for permanence and durability of the Committee on Production Guidelines for Book Longevity of the Council on Library Resources. ♾

To Noel Polk

Contents

Acknowledgments

The editors would like to acknowledge the assistance of the Australian Research Council and its support of the research project "William Faulkner between Cinema and Literature," which subsidized the conference out of which this collection has subsequently grown, as did a small grant from the Faculty of the Arts and Sciences at UNSW Australia. The Centre for Modernism Studies in Australia hosted the "Faulkner in the Media Ecology" conference at UNSW. The dean of the Faculty of Arts and Social Sciences, James Donald, and the head of the School of the Arts and Media, Andrew Schultz, deserve particular mention for their support.

All participants at the conference contributed to what was a uniquely convivial and productive event; several graduate students in the School of the Arts and Media were especially helpful in making the three days as smooth as could be imagined: Penelope Hone, Sam Dickson, Grace Hellyer, and Kate Montague.

During the passage from conference papers to a book of full scholarly essays, our path was smoothed considerably by the professionalism and courtesy of Margaret Lovecraft, acquisitions editor at LSU Press, and by the copyediting services of Susan Murray, whom every contributor would like to acknowledge for the outstanding quality of her work. We are also thankful to an anonymous press reader whose comments substantially aided us to make a better volume than we might have.

Sarah Gleeson-White's chapter, "Auditory Exposures: Faulkner, Eisenstein, and Film Sound," originally appeared in *PMLA* 128, no. 1 (January 2013), published by the Modern Language Association of America. The editors are grateful to the board of *PMLA* for permission to reprint the essay here.

Finally, we would both like to acknowledge the warm and unstintingly generous intellectual presence of Noel Polk, who very sadly passed away during the compilation of this volume, though he was the presiding genius of its foundation in sociable exchange. We both miss him enormously, and dedicate this volume to the incomparable services he tendered to modern Faulkner studies. Noel, your martinis were peerless.

William Faulkner in the Media Ecology

Introduction

JULIAN MURPHET

In the typically verbose prose prelude to the third act of his *Requiem for a Nun* (1951), William Faulkner condensed what he then understood to have been the material physiognomy of change—to Jefferson, Mississippi; to the South in general; and *universally* throughout modernity—that his life's work had taken upon itself to address. The potted history lesson made available in "The Jail (Nor Even Yet Quite Relinquish——)" is as thoroughgoing as any in Faulkner's texts, though it is true that such panoramic historical vistas appear here and there throughout the oeuvre; the accent here, however, is pronouncedly material and, in a word, *mediatory.* What the narrator of this dense and telescoped story of origins and destinies seems particularly at pains to impress upon us is the sheer extent to which "Jefferson" is the accumulated product of the mediatory vectors that crisscross it and turn its locality progressively inside out. We begin, naturally, with the railroads—the Redmond-Sartoris-Compson 1876 railroad,

> from Jefferson north into Tennessee to connect with the one from Memphis to the Atlantic Ocean; nor content there either, north or south: another ten years [. . .] and the railroad was part of that system covering the whole South and East like the veins in an oak leaf and itself mutually adjunctive to the other intricate systems covering the rest of the United States, so that you could get on a train in Jefferson now and, by changing and waiting a few times, go anywhere in North America.[1]

Here, with the figure of the veined oak leaf, technological mediation is ironically troped as "natural," leaving the reader to decide exactly what is "natural" about the fact that "now you could go to bed in a train in Jefferson and wake up tomorrow morning in New Orleans or Chicago; there were electric lights and running water in almost every house in town except the cabins of Negroes; and now the town bought and brought from a great distance a kind of gray crushed ballast-stone called macadam, and paved the entire street between the depot and the hotel" (634–35). A small regional town's destiny, in the America of electromagnetic propagation, coal locomotion, and the combustion engine, is to abandon its peculiar historic specificities to a relentless campaign of standardization and networked conformity: so much is a conventional truism in Faulkner criticism. But we would do well to attend to the precise terms in which this transformation is registered.

> Moving faster and faster: from the speed of two horses on either side of a polished tongue, to that of thirty then fifty then a hundred under a tin bonnet no bigger than a washtub: which from almost the first explosion, would have to be controlled by police. (635)

Fast linkage is an inevitable function of progress, but such speed catapults the local into the national, and elicits the compulsions of federal law. What mediates the social atoms of modernity simultaneously blurs them into an abstract generality, a soup of indifferent particles, stirred into homogeneity by materials drawn from elsewhere: extensions of a distant spreading center, spreading so wide and so far that it has ceased to be alien. Centralization is, indeed, a becoming-immanent of the very forces and materiel of mediation.

> [A]nd, now and at last, the last of silence too: the country's hollow inverted air one resonant boom and ululance of radio: and thus no more Yoknapatawpha's air nor even Mason and Dixon's air, but America's: the patter of comedians, the baritone screams of female vocalists, the babbling pressure to buy and buy and still buy arriving more instantaneous than light, two thousand miles from New York and Los Angeles; one air, one nation: the shadowless fluorescent corpse-glare bathing the sons and daughters of men and women, Negro and white both, who were born to and who passed all their lives in denim overalls and calico, haggling by cash or the instalment-plan for garments copied last week out of *Harper's Bazaar* or *Esquire* in East Side sweat-shops. (637)

What strikes Faulkner's narrator here is the irresistible "inversion" of a whole way of life by way of radio's waves and radiation, themselves the continuance by other means of the railways and the macadam roads. "America" emerges as just this abstract weave of systemic lines of force; the nation itself a concoction of commercial media techniques undreamed of by the Founding Fathers, and succeeding now thanks to the limitless capital invested in them, in pursuit of that repetitious formula, "to buy and buy and still buy," set fast in the social substance like the national DNA itself. Nor, however, will the vista draw its limits at the edges of national mediatic territoriality, for it is compelled still further, to touch upon the very outer limits of that geopolitical space for which "America" is now lodestar and impetus in the capitalist saturation of the global economy's war machine. The Second World War brings to view

> one nation, one world: young men who had never been further from Yoknapatawpha County than Memphis or New Orleans [. . .] now talked glibly of street intersections in Asiatic and European capitals, returning no more to inherit the long monotonous endless unendable furrows of Mississippi cotton fields, living now [. . .] in automobile trailers or G.I. barracks on the outskirts of liberal arts colleges, and the father and now grandfather himself still driving the tractor across the gradually diminishing fields between the long looping skeins of electric lines bringing electric power from the Appalachian mountains, and the subterrene steel veins bringing the natural gas from the western plains, to the little lost lonely farmhouses glittering and gleaming with automatic stoves and washing machines and television antennae. (638)

It is a veritable catalogue of the defining historic moments of technological mediation, this humanistic cry of loss and despair at "America's" evisceration of its own past—as if to say, and explicitly, that the terrible price paid for the speeds, conveniences, movements, and transactions of modernity is everything that the novel as a form has, historically, arrogated to itself as responsibility and property: knowable communities, defined individuals, durable relations, and dense structures of feeling. Which is why, of course, the telescoped prose sketch of Jefferson's becoming-American ends on an extreme close-up of that scarcely visible etching in the jailhouse window, literature's last allegorical gasp in the dreadful accelerations of the twentieth century. *There it is*:

> a fragile and workless scratching almost depthless in a sheet of old barely transparent glass, and (all you had to do was look at it a while; all you have to do now is remember it) there is the clear undistanced voice as though out of the delicate antenna-skeins of radio, further than empress's throne, than splendid insatiation, even than matriarch's peaceful rocking chair, across the vast instantaneous intervention, from the long long time ago: *"Listen stranger; this was myself: this was I."* (648–49)

And here, in the very depths of an overlabored pathos and in the hushed accents of threnody, we find the ultimate figural paradox—the grain of sand that casts us back upon the whole, involuted proem with eyes and ears worried to irritation by its presence. For at the climax of the narrator's catalogue of techno-mediated obviations of literature's specific function—here where the unblemished verbal historical trace calls us back to its authenticity—we are given a simile that is the exact inversion of the earlier "veins in an oak leaf": the "tender ownerless obsolete girl's name and the old dead date in April almost a century ago" (644) are compared directly to "a clear undistanced voice as though out of the delicate antenna-skeins of radio."

What on earth are we to make of this wholly unexpected figural chiasmus? If the new can be ironically troped as the "natural," does the old's metaphorization as a radio signal redouble that irony, or negate its negation? How does Faulkner's text *actually* handle the opposition between the (immediate) authenticity of "then" and the (mediated) inauthenticity of "now"? Clearly, if this instance is anything to go by, the opposition is never so stable as it appears, and is in fact to be caught in the act of deconstructing itself through the force of its own tropology: the only way to figure forth mediation is by way of a natural semaphore (the oak leaf); whereas, the most effective way of figuring the unmediated, "undistanced" voice of the living past, to make its "vast instantaneous intervention" aesthetically comprehensible, is to compare it to the radio voice itself, of which Adorno once noted that "[t]he absence of visible persons makes the 'radio voice' appear more objective and infallible than a live voice; and the mystery of a machine which can speak may be felt in atavistic layers of our psychical life."[2]

I draw out this extended illustration to make a much larger point, and to introduce this volume: Faulkner's oft-remarked antimodernity—his discomfort with the new in general, and his specific repertoire of complaints against the technological forms that it took—is secretly undone by a persistent figural feedback loop, in which the techno-mediatic-new inscribes itself indelibly into the available matrix of representational means for making the past present.[3] If the new media technologies of modernity trouble and disable much of the traditional vocation of literature, then they also make possible a renewed lease of life for its stubborn historical impulse. More than that, it seems urgent to insist that, for all of his intolerance toward the technologically mediated aspects of modern existence, Faulkner is committed, at the level of his style and tropology, to the "utopian dimension" of those very forces, as John T. Matthews has drawn out at significant length in the first chapter of his *William Faulkner: Seeing Through the South.* Writing of this peculiarly Faulknerian effect in *Pylon* (1935), Matthews notes:

> One of the hallmarks of modernity involves the body's extension by technology. As photography came to preserve the human image, and phonographs the human voice, modern technology begins to dream of supplementing the biological organism. *Pylon* signals this evolution in the constant intrusions of the air announcer's amplified voice, which transcends the limits of the human organ, but does so as eerily "disembodied." Technology, Faulkner foresees, will extend human presence, but only as it deconstructs it too. In the moment of fantasizing the liberating effects of technology in *Pylon,* there's something mesmerizing even about such disembodiment, whatever the menace, as if this, too, is a way to break the ties of a single body, to a single place. The utopian note comes through in the early description of the airport as "a mammoth terminal for some species of machine of a yet unvisioned tomorrow, to which air earth and water will be as one."[4]

Techno-mediation (here, the loudspeakers, the aeroplanes, and newspaper journalism) equips the novelistic imagination with proleptic visions of futurity, even as it underwrites the renovated techniques of historical fiction. But the critical thing to realize is that Faulkner's profound appreciation of techno-mediation's ambivalence as a social phenomenon affects the very substance of his art. No mere stenographer of this complication of regression and utopianism in the media's reshaping of a now global humanity, Faulkner rather pitches his very sentences at the instability at the heart of the process. The venerable art of novel writing is far from being untouched in its innermost essence by what everything from the railroads to television and the atom bomb—as a meta-medium of destruction under which "Man" is henceforth obliged to live out "his" dramas[5]—has done to the social environment that the novel would chart: to the contrary, that essence is itself altered, warped around a germ of the foreign element lodged at its sensitive core.

We are learning to reconsider this purportedly regional artist, happily wedded to his "little postage stamp of native soil," as one of the greatest artists of technological mediation in the literary tradition. Far from being simply the reclusive, private artist of the underdeveloped periphery, Faulkner turns out to have been as attuned to the waves and radiation of modernity's evolving media system as any to have taken up pen and ink against that system's predations upon what had once given value to social life: embeddedness, organic community, and historical depth. No abstract inveigher against the modern, Faulkner today appears sensitively, radically immersed in the materiality of the media ecology that defined the horizons of his cultural present. The various adaptations and mutations he instigated in the aesthetic substance of the novel as a form are illuminated by an attention to this sensitive immersion. He writes in *Sanctuary* (1931), that novel written for money, this bitter vignette of media colonization:

> The sunny air was filled with competitive radios and phonographs in the doors of drug- and music-stores. Before these doors a throng stood all day, listening. The pieces which moved them were ballads, simple in melody and theme, of bereavement and retribution and repentance metallically sung, blurred, emphasised by static or needle—disembodied voices blaring from imitation wood cabinets or pebble-grain horn-mouths above the rapt faces, the gnarled slow hands long shaped to the imperious earth, lugubrious, harsh, and sad.[6]

There can be no mistaking the critical accent of this passage in context; the mechanical substitution of a prerecorded or distantly broadcast musical sound track for a living tradition of song on the land is satirized with melancholy terseness. On the other hand, the passage indicates a deep awareness of the media ecology it consciously contests, such that the "competitive" electronic and mechanical sounds of mass mediation not only reshape the represented aural space, but also cast this novel back upon itself, its own matrix of production. If the new sounds are "emphasised by static or needle," then so too are these words, written into that aural space. The thought encourages a radical reconsideration of the book written virtually simultaneously with this one, *As I Lay Dying* (1932), as itself a "radio play for voices," alive with its own internal competition between stations and frequencies, with an underlying static hiss, and any number of telling vibrations of the writerly stylus in its groove.[7] Faulkner's assiduous experimentations with voice, genre, mode, sentence structure, and tense are lit up by the thought of his texts' ambient awareness of the now structural technological mediation and dissemination of information and culture. To write novels in such a situation is necessarily to adapt the very forms of that art to the conditions of possibility precipitated by it. If there are insistent contradictions between the conscious ideological messages emanated by his texts' explicit statements on techno-mediation, and the formal matrix in which those statements are embedded (itself composed of technical effects parasitic upon that very system of mediation), then that might provide a key to some of Faulkner's more notorious torsions at the level of style: his defects often enough attributable to underlying and irresolvable tensions in the imaginative infrastructure itself.

In any event, we are standing here at a crossroads in the interpretation and reputation of a writer often thought of as the United States' greatest novelist since Melville. We can sketch a broad-brush potted history of our own, concerning the fortunes of the various "schools" and tendencies to have mediated Faulkner to his students and readers—a partial and one-sided sketch, to be sure, but whose purpose is to bring to view the logic and rationale of the Faulkner proposed by this volume. We can immediately sequester the two historically dominant tendencies—the biographical and the ethical—as simply endemic to the way in which Faulkner has been routinely domesticated, and not likely to go away soon. What emerges upon their subtraction from the critical scene is a palimpsest of different emphases and theoretical paradigms not confined to the biographical subject or his works' presentation of character. An early French existentialist push was the first to associate Faulkner's work with a philosophical problematic; this vied, dialectically, with a more American preoccupation with the formal and New Critical properties of his novels. Myth-critical and religious interpretations characterized the period of Faulkner's full canonization in the 1950s; on the other hand, there emerged a radical attentiveness to the peculiar morphology of his syntax and style. In all of these early modes of attention, Faulkner was dished up as a "universal" artist whose regional affiliations and literary chrono-topography served as the given medium through which the abstract "truths" of his art were made manifest. Gradually, however, as area studies evolved and the actuality of his southernness became an entrenched article of faith, Faulkner was steadily transformed into a regional artist, whose unique knowledge of his native area of Mississippi was reckoned to have defined his aesthetics far more deeply than the "universal" Faulkner of yesterday could have appreciated. But by a paradox of historical coincidence, this particularist Faulkner emerged cheek by jowl with another one: Faulkner the modernist, now admitted to a pantheon of international artists defined at once by their reactions against the realist protocol, and their aesthetic distanciation of the mass culture of modernity. The next shift was similarly double: on the one hand, a prodigious sophistication of the historical frame of reference within which Faulkner's "southernness" was to have been construed (thanks to Joel Williamson in particular)—a thickening of the descriptive repertoire available for thinking "the South" in relation to the North, and for thinking the antagonistic relations of production threading through both; on the other, a reclamation of those tendencies in Faulkner's art that fell foul of the august high modern he had been constructed as being—specifically, his participation in the film industry, his stubborn attachments to material and popular culture, and his commercial activities as a writer. The 1970s culminated in a paroxysm of psychoanalytic brilliance, in John Irwin's tour de force reading of the "enduring core" of Faulkner's lifework; an achievement so unique as to have been a one-off consummation of sorts. Throughout the 1980s, a number of otherwise flourishing political schools of criticism were drawn to this fully established modern classic: Black studies clearly had a good deal to say about Faulkner's oeuvre, defined as it centrally was by a lifelong obsession with racial difference and discrimination; feminists were drawn to the perdurable matrix of sexist stereotypes and logics of presentation that orchestrated such paradoxical ideological effects (a sort of feminist misogyny) in his fictions; and queer studies discovered a good deal of disavowed homosexual desire in the novels and stories of a man whose imagination turned, repeatedly, on the homosocial bond, on intimate male friendship, and on hunting as a scene purged of the feminine. Yet since the early 1990s, the well of theoretical innovation has arguably run progressively drier (a phenomenon to be observed across the discipline, and by no means confined to Faulkner studies). The great achievements of this period have been: the establishment of an authoritative edition of the works (thanks to Noel Polk and Joseph Blotner); the enriched consolidation of a historical-materialist perspective in the works of John T. Matthews and Richard Godden (where Marxism rejoins New Critical sensitivity to syntactic and lexical details); the extended flourishing of a film-centered "pop" Faulkner (in works by Catherine Kodat, Joseph Urgo, Vincent King, and Peter Lurie); and the New Historical relocation of Faulkner's writing practices in relation to state discourses, legal statutes, philosophical jargons, and imperialism (see works by Ted Atkinson, Jay Watson, Thadious M. Davis, Taylor Hagood, and Charles Hannon). Otherwise, the bulk of Faulkner studies since 1990 has cautiously restricted itself, more or less, to the repetitive rehearsal of biographical stories in relation to "themes" plucked from the fiction, alongside the scattered contributions of race studies, regionalism, psychoanalysis, and other discontinuous critical paradigms to the interpretation of these now venerable works.

In this context of diminishing returns, media studies today invites scholars back to the scene of Faulkner's work, with the tantalizing promise of unearthed riches. For despite the intermittent attention paid to Faulkner's actual work in the film industry, and the increasing consideration of the extent to which "high" and "low" cultures are blended in his art, it is as if the very thought of media and mediation has stayed determinedly out of the frame of Faulkner criticism, at least until John T. Matthews's more recent work. When that thought is allied to the remarkably sophisticated theoretical endeavor of the leading media theorists of the last thirty years—to the work of Friedrich Kittler, Lev Manovich, Lisa Gitelman, David J. Bolter and Richard Grusin, Donna Haraway, N. Katherine Hayles, Anne Friedberg, and many others—then we have to hand a mature theoretical paradigm within which to recalibrate our understanding of this truly astonishing verbal artist. From this perspective, the definitive aspect of Faulkner's achievement is his formal and technical wrestling of the novel form in relation to an explosion and consolidation of an entirely novel "media ecology"—mechanical and electric, if not yet digital—in which the long-term fortunes of the published codex have begun to seem unhealthy, even improbable. Though it is no place here to develop this thought adequately, what seems most promising about this optic is that it both displaces the biographical subject as the locus of meanings—since now it is the media ecology itself dictating the terms in which aesthetic progress might be made—and simultaneously impresses the written work with marks and scars of that circumambient ecology. What a media-ecological approach makes possible is the notion of a transposition and displacement of technical properties between media, in the context of an opportunistic struggle for advantage between established and nascent media platforms. If the printed book necessarily suffers an absolute loss in the scale of social purchase and horizontal spread (from its high-water mark in the late nineteenth century), it nevertheless achieves "vertical" success in the hierarchy of cultural prestige across the media landscape, precisely by leeching from its relatively "naïve" new neighbors the determinate formal properties associated with their medial specificity, but which they are not themselves free to explore. If this were not the case, if aesthetic development in the verbal arts did not turn upon the lateral colonization of new media techniques, then literary history would have to remain hopelessly idealist, and would be helpless to explain such phenomena as effects of montage, granularities of voice, or depersonalization.

Faulkner's body of work is laden with extraordinarily fruitful opportunities to rethink modernism (a movement to which he was conscripted retrospectively) as so many adjustments to existing artistic institutions, in order to take the measure of newer media and keep them at bay. Some of those opportunities are explored in depth in the following collection of new essays on the subject of Faulkner's subjection to, and incorporation of, a media ecology to which he was, of necessity, extremely well attuned—seasoned veteran of the magazines, hired studio gun, celebrity, radio voice, television scriptor, record collector, aviator. In the interests of organizational logic, we have divided these essays into three sections. The first of these, "Memory and Mediation," considers the dialectical interplay between Faulkner's construction of a usable past, and the technological mediations through which America insists on itself and its cultural logic. John T. Matthews's opening essay makes a commanding bid for the various film adaptations of Faulkner's masterpieces made in the 1950s as sites of salient contradictions—Martin Ritt's adaptations take southern rebarbativeness toward the North as masks for a left-wing critique of Cold War America itself. Thus a "mediated" Faulkner adds a wholly new dimension to his modernism, a historically coeval development, since it provides it with a mobile political edge, one for which a residual realism is effortlessly absorbed into a more generous definition of modernist tactics. Catherine Gunther Kodat then offers a superlative meditation on the place of television—as media technology, social phenomenon, and aesthetic window—in Faulkner's aesthetic and social ideology. The intriguing consonance between a set of social expectations about black Americans and a set of aesthetic beliefs about television sets the stage for this original excursion into the mediated imagination of a great writer. In the third chapter, Stefan Solomon considers the propagative force of the telegram as an instance of the letter in the authorial unconscious, specifically in the vicinity of Faulkner's efforts in the short story form. If the great self-proclaimed humanist finds little good to say about the telegram as an electrically mediated and abbreviated mode of interpersonal address, nevertheless something about its logic installs itself at the boundary between the sayable and the nonsayable in his shorter fictions, dependent as they are upon the capitalist economics of the magazine sector of the publication industry. It is with a similar logic that radio waves accommodate paradoxical semantic vectors in the same stories; and film projection enters the field at an obtuse angle. Rounding off this opening movement, Donald M. Kartiganer provides a symphonic account of the multiple staves on which Faulkner's growing celebrity was played out as a media artifact. From the literary marketplace proper, through the broader and ecological "field of cultural production" (Bourdieu) in which the former is contained—and including photography, radio, television, the lecture circuit, prizes, magazine culture, newspapers, the newsreel and cinema screen, and so forth—Kartiganer tracks Faulkner's evolving and mutating mediatic persona. Not the least intriguing aspect of this argument is the case it makes for the very formal procedures Faulkner was applying to his novels as modalities of his celebrification.

Part 2, "Sound and Vision," focuses more pointedly on the various ways in which Faulkner has been found to have harnessed electronic and mechanical sound media in his verbal art, and the manner in which that sound track is affixed (or not) to a stream of visual information. It also attends to the medial specificities of photography as a persistent node of aesthetic force in Faulkner's literary labor. Jay Watson provides a synoptic overview of Faulkner's "sound art" through a consideration of the coeval (de)evolution of cinematic language upon film accession to the world of sound—the technical stabilization of a synchronized sound track. As Watson presents the matter, it is precisely early sound film's unevenness of synchronization, and the opportunities thereby opened up for contrapuntal and counterintuitive sound effects, that sheds the most revealing light on Faulkner's various sound effects:

a partial derangement of the sonorous texture of the novels, in line with non-synchronized moments, discorporated voices, and "terrific silences." Michael Zeitlin offers a provocative account of the dovetailed media energies of the "radio phenomenon" as analyzed by Theodor Adorno in the 1930s, and the libidinal investment in airplane scenography and story in Faulkner's fiction—itself another techno-mediation, but becoming increasingly autonomous in Faulkner's imagination, in the guise of the barnstormer or stunt pilot. New "psychic velocities" are untapped in the airplane material, velocities that seem to find their logical habitat in the light-speed transmissions of voice made possible by electronically amplified radio transmission and telephony. *Pylon* (1935) is the test case of a novel so thoroughly structured by these velocities, these mediations, that it seems plucked out of the Yoknapatawpha sequence and elevated to its own private space in the Faulkner universe. Sarah Gleeson-White's analysis of the "missed" encounter between Faulkner and Sergei Eisenstein provides a scintillating and active mediation between the author's perceived "hack work" for the studio system, and his serious literary work. It is in the projected sound track of Faulkner's work for the films that something comes to the surface whose consequences can be registered in the aesthetic substance of his highest masterpiece, *Absalom, Absalom!* Adapting Eisenstein's screenplay for "Sutter's Gold" in his own treatment, Faulkner discovers sonic energies and techniques highly unusual in the film industry, but with multiple applications to his literary work. Robert Jackson, meanwhile, unfurls a motley history of interpenetrating media institutions in his account of the "media surfaces" in which Faulkner's identity was played out in the 1930s and 1940s. Specifically, Jackson takes up the complex interface between architecture, film, music, and celebrity to speculate about a mediatized "skin" through which a public persona like Faulkner's was lived. Most importantly, *race* emerges as a function of that mediatized skin, and it is to this that Jackson relates the experiments in form that Faulkner undertook as a writer and a public persona: a networked and racialized technology of identity, constituted via surfaces of inscription and reproduction. Finally in this section, Sascha Morrell pursues that kind of thinking into the photographic nexus of desire and transformation that informs Faulkner's racial ideology and its aesthetic mediation. Relating Faulkner's experiments in dialectical photographical negation to earlier instances in the work of Melville and Hawthorne, and later revisions in the great novel by Ralph Ellison, Morrell adroitly charts a passage through

Faulkner's unstable racial topology by way of Hegelian maneuvers that are materially written into the texts. Morrell's Faulkner is abandoned to the mediatic play of photography's incessant negatives, its transubstantiations of that "tonal" identity whose reified images are "black" and "white."

In our final part, "Time and Space," we broaden the media-ecological framework to ask how the very Kantian categories of phenomenal perception—the temporal, the spatial—are fundamentally recalibrated by the emergence of machines of perception and sense-data storage, machines that *do our perceiving and remembering* for us. Mark Steven attends to the radical transformation of time in the modern period, first by the imposition of clocks in the calculation of the working day, and second by the instauration of a new temporal art that was minutely calibrated in the duration of its projection: film. If the mechanical and electronic unfolding of cinematic time brought unique critical attention to bear upon the individual, still photograms that subtended the flow of duration, then, Steven argues, Faulkner adapted that attention to his own syntactic materials as a literary artist. "Narratograms" function in his texts as the displaced temporal corpuscles of another art form that Faulkner scarcely recognized as such. Next, Peter Lurie asks us to consider the aching temporal paradoxes of indexicality in Faulkner's mature prose—specifically, the prose of *Go Down, Moses* (1942). What the archive painstakingly preserves as traces of the past, the cinema records automatically; this introduces to a verbal art form like the novel a torsion in the space of memory itself, stretched between two incompatible nodes—the written trace; the automatic print. This leaves in the prose itself evidence of a curious form of temporality, "backlooping," which Lurie posits as a unique Faulknerian tarrying with the altered media ecology, such that past, present, and future are melded into a single substance, alive with paradox and contradiction. As to the section's, and the book's, final chapter, this writer certainly knows better than to offer any kind of summary of the arguments of Richard Godden, proceeding as they do by way of an unparaphrasable double-optic: the meticulously analyzed lexical substratum, on the one hand, and the vast totality of the mode of production itself, on the other. Suffice it to say here that in this bravura performance, Godden finds the means to offer a fully mediated understanding of *As I Lay Dying,* where the dominant medium is the oldest of all—which is to say, *money,* and what Godden wants us to attend to is the radical material effects of a money economy on a once-pastoral way of life, effects that are parsed in the Faulknerian text as so many stylistic tics and lexical symptoms. It is a timely reminder that the entire media ecology of modernity is properly subsumed under the rubric of monetary equivalence, that medium in which all differences are dissolved and surplus value can appear.

NOTES

1. William Faulkner, *Requiem for a Nun*, in *Novels 1942–1954*, ed. Joseph Blotner and Noel Polk (New York: Library of America, 1994), 633. Hereafter cited parenthetically.

2. Theodor W. Adorno, *Current of Music*, trans. Robert Hullot-Kentor (Oxford: Polity, 2009), 47.

3. This is a topic I examine at much greater length in my forthcoming book on Faulkner's mediation of romance.

4. John T. Matthews, *William Faulkner: Seeing Through the South* (Chichester: Wiley-Blackwell, 2009), 61; quoting *Pylon*, in *Faulkner, Novels 1930–1935*, ed. Joseph Blotner and Noel Polk (New York: Library of America, 1985), 786.

5. The reference is to Faulkner's well-known 1950 speech in Stockholm and its zinger summation of the epoch: "There are no longer questions of the spirit. There is only the question: When will I be blown up?" (William Faulkner, "Address upon Receiving the Nobel Prize for Literature," in *Essays, Speeches and Public Letters*, ed. James B. Meriwether [New York: Modern Library, 2004], 119).

6. William Faulkner, *Sanctuary*, in *Faulkner, Novels 1930–1935*, ed. Joseph Blotner and Noel Polk (New York: Library of America, 1985), 257.

7. Lorine Niedecker would compose out of Faulkner's novel just such a "radio play for voices": see her radio adaptation of *As I Lay Dying* in *Collected Works*, ed. Jenny Penberthy (Berkeley: University of California Press, 2002), 343–60.

I

Memory and Mediation

Faulkner to Film in the Fifties

JOHN T. MATTHEWS

Repurposing Faulkner

Martin Ritt directed two film adaptations of Faulkner's fiction in the late 1950s: *The Long, Hot Summer* (1958), based mostly on *The Hamlet,* and *The Sound and the Fury* (1959). Both movies were produced by the legendary if infamous Jerry Wald, the ruthless Hollywood mogul immortalized in Budd Schulberg's novel *What Makes Sammy Run?,* and both were scripted by the wife-and-husband team Harriet Frank Jr. and Irving Ravetch.[1] It was evidently Ravetch and Frank who proposed to Martin Ritt the idea of adapting Faulkner's fiction to screen, and who got Wald to purchase the properties; but all four of them were already admirers of Faulkner's work. What makes their joint adaptations of Faulkner's texts so surprising is the extent to which the adaptors felt free to alter the originals. *The Long, Hot Summer* made radical changes to the material it drew from *The Hamlet* as well as from the short stories "Barn Burning" and "Spotted Horses"; these included making up new characters and overturning basic plot elements. The later movie, though presenting itself in the opening credits as "William Faulkner's *The Sound and the Fury,*" even more aggressively rewrote that novel of 1929, boldly reconfiguring the Compson family and adding scenes from Faulkner's recent novel *The Town* (1957).

Ritt, Ravetch, and Frank update and reset both originals in the late 1950s. In *The Long, Hot Summer* a down-on-his-luck newcomer named Ben Quick arrives in Frenchman's Bend and immediately begins to insinuate himself into Will Varner's good graces, with an eye toward the old man's fortune and his pretty daughter, Clara. Quick is a composite of Ab, Sarty, and Flem Snopes, while Clara Varner is a new character altogether. Varner presides over a modern commercial empire encompassing a large industrial farm along with realty and money-lending enterprises. Jody has become a happy-go-lucky son who has no appetite for business and prefers to spend his time cavorting with Eula, who is no longer his sister but his wife. *The Long, Hot Summer* retains its agrarian setting, and Quick, perhaps anachronistically in 1958, is offered a tenant-share contract by Jody. But the movie quickly establishes that the plantation is a modern *business*. Ben Quick eventually proves he has up-to-date marketing acumen, Varner anoints him his successor, and Ben wins the heart of Clara to boot. Unlike the novel, in which Flem's defeated opponents lie ruined or humiliated, the movie ends with even the displaced Jody reconciled and the entire family celebrating several rejuvenated and prospective marriages with Shakespearean glee.

Ritt's adaptation of *The Sound and the Fury* makes even more radical changes to the original. Jason Compson and his mother are rewritten as lower-caste newcomers to the Compson household who have arrived as the result of a second marriage for Mr. Compson. This Caroline Compson and her son are Cajun, and she shows up in Jefferson full of working-class resentment at having been a cook for fishermen in the Louisiana bayous her whole life. No longer related by blood, the child Jason has elbowed his way into the household and now, as an adult, takes pride in having reconsolidated it by capitalizing on the Compson name and making a success of himself as a merchant in 1940s and 1950s Jefferson. He takes credit for restoring the House of Compson to solvency and for disciplining as best he can its wayward holdovers. One unsettling development in the novel's story is the return of Caddy after two decades, her life ruined, seeking refuge in Jason's household and hoping for reconciliation with her daughter. Miss Quentin, a restive teenager in 1958 as in 1928, clashes with her stepuncle's authority, but instead of running off, she ends up submitting to it and remaining in Jefferson. This entails the even more unsettling development in the film of an actual romance between Miss Quentin (played by Joanne Woodward) and her now not-uncle (played by Yul Brynner). By the film's conclusion Miss Quentin and Jason seem headed toward domestic prospects not even this movie has the stomach to put on-screen.

The question of fidelity seems irrelevant to understanding what Ritt and his colleagues were doing, since plainly the makers of these movies were not trying to duplicate Faulkner's texts on-screen. *Summer* is generally considered a "good commercial film," as Ritt himself modestly put it, although Bruce Kawin complains that it turns *The Hamlet* on its head, making a novel deeply offended by greed into a rags-to-riches romance. *Sound and Fury* gets more thoroughly dismissed for reducing one of the greatest works of modern literature to a feeble fable of two misfits' longing for respectability in 1950s small-town America.[2] It was a box office failure, and even Martin Ritt admitted that he "made some mistakes" in filming it.[3] The deepest offense of the adaptation to its many detractors was the filmmaking team's refusal to try to reproduce the technical virtuosity of the novel. Yet Ritt was a serious, even earnest director, who believed movies worth making should be idea films; he went on to direct a number of important movies with liberal-left politics such as *Hud* (1963), *The Molly Maguires* (1970), *Sounder* (1972), *Conrack* (1974), and *Norma Rae* (1979).

Ritt's adaptations of Faulkner are conspicuously and thoroughly transformations, plainly less the result of defect than design (however possibly misguided). My contention is that we might better appreciate Martin Ritt's adaptations of Faulkner's texts as repurposings—repurposings that sought to adapt the recalcitrance toward national pieties in Faulkner's southern modernism to cloak Ritt's own critique of U.S. liberalism during the Cold War. Faulkner commanded the respect of Ritt, Wald, Frank, and Ravetch not only because he was a master of modernist style and form, although they all clearly did appreciate that, but also because his fiction chronicled the massive revolutions that produced national modernity over the first half of the century. From the 1920s through the 1950s, Faulkner's own writing described the collapse of an agrarian plantation order subtended by slavery and its descendant system of racial segregation; the evolution of former gentry and land-possessing elites into speculative financial elites; the rise of a modern liberal welfare state; the conflicts over expanded enfranchisements under a project of modernity; and the emergence of a global U.S. hegemon between World War I and the Cold War (the subject of Faulkner's *A Fable* in 1954). Ritt's determination to translate Faulkner to screen rested on his confidence that Faulkner's cultural and social value did not inhere exclusively in the formal features of his modernism. In this respect, Ritt demonstrates how Hollywood preserved the capacity of modernist art to speak to the conditions of modernity *through* its subject matter precisely as the U.S. literary establishment sought to save high modernism by putting it into the museum. Modernism by the 1950s was being canonized by the New Critics and New York intellectuals as the sanctification of aesthetic technique, the modernist work typified by its virtuoso experimentalist form and its purported elevation above mass media and popular audiences.

By contrast, Martin Ritt's purposes with modernist texts like Faulkner's and Hemingway's depended upon a quite different relation to modernism. As James Bloom has been the most recent to demonstrate, in his study *Hollywood Intellect,* the film and entertainment colony was where intellectual life flourished outside the academy during this period, and the purposes to which modern literature was put there contrast sharply.[4] I contend that the films of Faulkner's fiction made by Ritt, Frank, and Ravetch suggest an alternative appreciation of modernism, one that reads the modernist work as much for its representational capacities as its technical virtuosity, and that takes the modernist text's principal value as a critical narration of the project of modernity. From this standpoint, "Faulkner" constituted a set of properties whose high value had to do with their complex reflection on their own moments of modernity, and their potential for adaptation to persisting conditions in the 1950s.

Media Ecology

Julian Murphet suggests a genealogy for this academic consensus in the 1950s by examining the scene of modernism's emergence. In his book *Multimedia Modernism,* Murphet demonstrates how the appearance of new media forms between 1880 and 1914 altered the environment for literature and necessitated its engagement with them. Technologies of representation like photography, the phonograph, and eventually the movies created competition for literature, and its response involved what Murphet characterizes as a double move of convergence toward such media and differentiation from them. "The new media system" tended to be industrial and technological: it "represented in its essence and throughout all its modes a new stage in the capitalist mode of production, a stage which it was decisive in consolidating: monopoly capitalism, imperialism, finance capital, the new possibilities of the assembly line; and their ramifications in mass politics, mass culture, commodification and everyday life."[5] Furthermore, the moment of literature's exposure to a new industrial and market climate corresponded to the transformation of social and economic interests among the bourgeoisie, a transformation that divided into two orientations: on the one hand, a "sinking class" of the bourgeoisie retained their ties to the gentry, whose fortune proved to be in decline; on the other, "a new and aggressive faction of the middle class" reassigned its loyalties from the residual upper classes to the creative energies of the working classes, mass culture, and mass production.

Modernist art fought for a renewed legitimacy on such a terrain by "borrowing" and internalizing the subject matter and aesthetic modes of the new media, and in so doing sought to demonstrate its unique ability to master them. The consequence of such absorption of industrial and technological media was the "overvaluation of 'technique' as an aesthetic imperative" (30). Precisely by imitating the most menacing features of its competitors, modern literature bid to vanquish them. So, for example, "nothing is less amenable to filmic remediation than literature's technical borrowings from the film medium" (36): "the novel technically 'did cinema' better than the naturalist screen" (33). By adopting the status of the new media system as material, literature eventually preserved its immaterial essence—as inimitable technical virtuosity. The work of modernist art as specially autonomous, standing across the great divide from mass culture (as Andreas Huyssen so indelibly put it, for better or worse),[6] was a status consolidated in the 1950s, under the pressures of renewed movements of political entitlement, artistic kitsch, scientific culture, military industrial dominance, finance capitalism, and Cold War consumption. Thus the "purity" of the work of art, its attainment of "quality and value," is achieved by means of the differentiation of each art from every other, and by the artwork's presumed indifference to material conditions.

Lawrence Schwartz's familiar account of how Faulkner's reputation was in large measure made in the United States during the Cold War illustrates this broad outline of the strategic reading of modernism in the 1950s. As Schwartz points out, the New Critics insisted on judging art by its technical virtuosity, not its content, a position that reflected the identification of literature with a distinct poetic language and that held avant-garde modernism as the acme of aesthetic formalism and autonomy in the face of degraded industrial culture. Modern literature's capacity to create "opposing sel[ves]" to bourgeois modernity (as Lionel Trilling put it) helped install writers like Faulkner as aesthetic moralists, for both the New Critics and the New York intellectuals. Moreover, the technical virtuosity of modernist art created in the United States made it especially useful as a symbol of democratic ways in the 1950s: "Inherent textual difficulties made [Faulkner's] prose even more valuable in the Cold War, as a symbol of resistance to Fascism and to delimited individual freedom, and as a symbol of the importance of stylistic innovation and personal perceptions over socially conscious art."[7]

Disregarding such deployment of Faulkner to the Cold War front as an avatar of American individualism, Ritt, Frank, and Ravetch examine more closely the presumptions of liberal democratic progressivism: their new versions of Faulkner's stories dramatized a managerial class forming bonds with an ambitious working class while it jettisons dynastic elites but also ignores fundamental structural injustices. These movies worry about the advance of modern commercial and materialistic mentalities; their "Hollywood modernism" puts questions of property, ownership, and saturation by market considerations on display, arguably making visible the very condition of literature in the 1950s that academic treatments suppressed.

Fables of the Modern Plantation

Both of Ritt's Faulkner movies make use of the novels' plantation settings to suggest its continuing relevance in the 1950s as a site of economic, social, and political conflict. In Faulkner's originals, the plantation order appears by the 1920s as a discredited system but one that still shapes mentalities and even economic and social opportunities in the South and beyond. The Compsons of Faulkner's *The Sound and the Fury* confront the end of the leisured gentry class created by slave-driven commercial plantation agriculture, even if the customs of privilege for moneyed white males continue to operate as a virtual reality for decades in the South. In *The Hamlet,* Faulkner begins his tale of poor white ascent by surveying the ruins of the Old Frenchman Place, Yoknapatawpha County's massive original plantation, and, as it turns out, one that still provides a template for the dreams of wealth, property, and style entertained by a master of the market like Flem, who we may remember ends up as president of the Merchants' and Farmers' Bank of Jefferson, and the owner of a house he makes over to look like Mount Vernon. Movies like *The Birth of a Nation* and *Gone with the Wind* revivified the plantation as a screen for fantasizing the reorganization of white male power and selective capitalist renewal, making it fun to picture continued inequality in national life.

The plantation also persisted in reconfigured form as a functioning system of economic production and political imagination through the century.

Charles Aiken recounts how the southern plantation morphed into a modern system of large-scale agricultural production after the Great Migration and the Great Depression, with the development of new methods for consolidating landholding, controlling capitalization, and ensuring cheap labor.[8] Tennessee Williams's *Cat on a Hot Tin Roof* reflects this persistence, for example, Big Daddy having turned the plantation he inherits into a commercial empire at mid-twentieth century. Jessica Adams, Houston Baker, and others have described the survival of the plantation as the basis for "modern" penitentiary labor farms, their preservation as profitable tourist attractions, and their utility as U.S. labor "machines" exported to sites beyond the U.S. South.[9] Fordlandia, Henry Ford's spectacular experiment in 1928 to create a total plantation facility in Brazil for the production of rubber, exemplified the enduring social and economic application of the fantasy. Moreover, while Ritt was redoing Faulkner texts like *The Hamlet* and *The Sound and the Fury* as movies picturing the reconstitution of patriarchal families, Faulkner himself was writing novels in the 1950s like *The Town, The Mansion*, and *The Reivers* that mapped continuities between the plantation and succeeding forms of speculation and "free" market trade: between slavery and peonage, prison farm and proletariat, planter and banker.

Given the persistence of the South's identification with resistance to modernization, its association with what Leigh Anne Duck has called a "chronotope" of social and cultural backwardness, the plantation functions as a privileged site through which to imagine limited shifts in regimes from those dominated by ancestral elites to those powered by mercantile speculation and consumption.[10] With a kind of historical parallax, Ritt's remakings in the 1950s of Faulkner in the 1930s seem at face value to posit an unfolding story of liberal progress. Ritt, blacklisted in 1952 for refusing to name names of alleged leftist associates, lost his career at CBS, where he had directed weekly live dramas. He resurrected his professional life first as a teacher with the Actors' Studio in New York City, and then as a film director in Hollywood. He insisted that all worthwhile films dealt with social problems and that the prevalence of "liberalism" in Hollywood fostered the medium's generally progressive attitudes: "a great artist will always tell as much of the truth as he can. And it's my deep feeling that the greatest truth is in the liberal tradition."[11] Ritt made his way into Hollywood from his more leftist convictions in the 1940s and found a congenial if surprising critique of Cold War liberalism in Faulkner. (Though he was the son of Russian immigrants, Ritt went to college in North Carolina, where he developed an interest in the South. Few directors, in fact, set more of their films in the region than Ritt.) Ritt saw that Faulkner's unresolved stories of the violent conflicts triggered by the South's modern economic and social revolutions might give him cover for critiquing Cold War fantasies according to which the project of U.S. democracy permitted the peaceable enfranchisement of outcasts and negotiated smooth transitions between regimes of capitalism.

Martin Ritt turns Faulkner's phlegmy frog into a blue-eyed prince. *The Long, Hot Summer* recounts the arrival of Ben Quick, played by Paul Newman, in Frenchman's Bend after accusations of barn-burning elsewhere. Ben bears Ab Snopes's criminal history and evinces Sarty's conscience, but he is driven by Flem's ambition. Played by Orson Welles, Will Varner rules over a 1950s-style principality, with mentions of sizable landholdings, relentless profiteering, and command of the personal, economic, and social lives of everyone in sight. His son, Jody, chafes under the outsized expectations Will has for him as the old man's successor, confessing at one point that he has no stomach for business, and preferring instead to chase all over the lavish family mansion the pretty Lee Remick, who plays his wife, Eula. Varner's daughter, Clara, a schoolmistress in town, awaits a man who will respect her mind and character, as well as satisfy her sexually. Quick surveys the opportunities here, and by the end of the movie he has been brought into the Varner family as an effective son to Will, an older brother to Jody, and the husband-to-be for the won-over Clara, convincingly played by Joanne Woodward. Along the way, Clara must shuffle off the devotion of a fay genteel suitor, while Jody must prove his mettle as a suitable coheir at least. Despairing of keeping up with Ben, Jody sets fire to the Varner barn with the intention of killing his father, whom he has trapped inside. But Jody relents and releases Will, only to discover that he has inadvertently demonstrated just the anti-Oedipal spark Varner had been hoping for. At the end we're looking at one big happy family, renucleated around the newcomer.

One principal narrative of *Summer*, then, fantasizes a new era of entrepreneurial prosperity and consumer democracy. Ben Quick, unlike Faulkner's Flem Snopes in *The Hamlet*, ultimately proves to be a menace to no one as he advances. This required some rewriting of Faulkner, to be sure; one example involves Flem's notorious rejection of Mrs. Armstid's plea for the return of her money in the novel. In the movie, the aggrieved housewife gets nowhere with Jody, but then Ben steps in, cheerfully refunds her thirty dollars (apparently adjusted for inflation), and instructs his coproprietor that this is how you establish good customer relations. There's little resistance in the movie to Quick's mostly gentle rise either. Ratliff has shrunk as a moral opponent; he's no longer a narrator, and his wry humor is distributed among several onlookers. Ritt stages a fantasy that the practices of modern capitalism might settle easily on earlier ones now fumigated of their historical malodor.

The film version of *The Sound and the Fury* also wants to imagine the tonic effects of taking in outsiders to a once-closed society. An amalgamated foreigner, Jason-as–Yul Brynner must be accommodated as an effective foundling who brings new energies to an inbred community. As in *Long, Hot Summer,* the "decayed gentry" (as Will Varner calls them) are fated to oblivion, here represented by the dissolute new character "Howard" Compson, a composite of father Jason and son Quentin. Elsewhere, the future is materializing in town—in prosperous stores and well-appointed schools. On its surface, Ritt's *The Sound and the Fury* suggests that southern values of honor, family pride, and determination in the face of prejudice may serve as the basis for a renewed bourgeois domestic order. In the film, Jason doesn't turn the Compson place into a boardinghouse; he restores it as a family seat, his impending marital alliance with Miss Quentin auguring a future of small-town middle-class ascendancy.

Perhaps the most sustained fantasy of social progress in these two movies arises from women's demands for greater equality. Clara Varner in *Summer* and Miss Quentin in *Sound and Fury* both make strong assertions on behalf of ending women's subordination. Clara surprises her beau by informing him, "there's no sense in pretending girls don't think about sex. They do."[12] But she lets Ben know that mere sexual satisfaction is "not *nearly* enough! I'm a human being. Do you know what that means, Mister Quick? I set a price on myself—a high, *high* price. You may be surprised to hear it, but I've got quite a bit to give, things I've been saving up all my life—things like love and affection and understanding and jokes and good times and good cooking! I'm prepared to be the Queen of Sheba for some lucky man—or at the very least the best wife anybody could hope for!" (80).

Miss Quentin likewise tells Jason that she will demand "respect and affection" from any man who wins her heart. The Frank and Ravetch scripts had to graft these contemporary elements onto Faulkner, but the logic of expanding social modernization warrants such extrapolation. Each modern woman is in effect new to the story, the sharp-tongued schoolteacher Clara an invention altogether and Quentin now a self-possessed woman committed to staying in Jefferson. Both female leads were played by Joanne Woodward, whose greater age than her characters' quietly reinforced a sense that the movies were thinking of women in the 1950s through the stories of the last generation's girls.

A similar fantasy seems to structure Ritt's view of racial progress. Ritt strongly supported racial equality, going on to make *Sounder* and *Conrack*, both generally received as well-meaning portrayals of racial uplift, however limited some found their apparent white liberal assumptions. The issue of race relations in the South attracts no explicit attention in either *The Long, Hot Summer* or *Sound and Fury*, yet both reveal an unmarked fantasy about the achievement of desegregation at the moment of the 1950s civil rights movement. Repeatedly in both movies crowds in Frenchman's Bend and Jefferson are portrayed as racially mixed: blacks and whites mingle on porch galleries, on sidewalks and in streets, as members of audiences for street performances, even at the carnival. Although such mixture would not have been impossible historically, the unremarked ordinariness of it here suggests that Ritt was projecting a social fantasy. Such a view corresponds to *Sound and Fury*'s revisionist treatment of the Gibsons, too. Dilsey, played by Ethel Waters, and the rest of her family gain dignity beyond what the novel accords them; they speak "standard" English, their performances avoiding racial stereotype, but also threatening realistic effect.

Ritt's films so conspicuously *strain* as they stage narratives of liberal democratic modernity that their status as fantasy begins to show. All of the narratives of expanded enfranchisement that I have indicated in Ritt's adaptations so far—the ascent of immigrant and working-class individuals to middle-class security; the rise of African Americans to stations of equal social dignity and liberties; the exercise of equal entitlement by women—get exposed as ludicrous fancies. Both of Ritt's adaptations, I am arguing, stumble over the director's suspicion that confidence in a liberalizing Cold War America is an ideological fantasy that deserves to be deconstructed. These films of Ritt's in the late 1950s crack up because they recognize liberal optimism as a Cold War front.

Although space constraints prevent me from developing this analysis fully, I will illustrate a few moments in both films during which Ritt confronts the premises and trajectory of his films' own conceits. Martin Ritt's later films came increasingly to spotlight a tension between liberal and more radical protest of American social, economic, and political advantage and its repressive defense. *Hud* (1963) excavates the corrupt roots of modern materialism on the western frontier, while *The Molly Maguires* (1970) very nearly endorses violent labor terrorism against capitalist exploitation. Moreover, Ritt's take on 1950s Cold War America as a contradiction of its own ideals would have been reinforced by Faulkner's own new fiction during the decade. *A Fable* (1954) attempted no less than to identify the origins of the Eisenhower era's military-industrial complex in the global financial and military machinations of the Great War, while the two Snopes novels that later appeared, *The Town* (1957) and *The Mansion* (1959), contain some of Faulkner's most intemperate mockery of the national mistaking of free marketry for freedom. Faulkner goes so far in the last of these Snopes novels to imagine a full-fledged communist antidote, Eula's daughter, Linda Snopes Kohl, who marries a modernist sculptor, a Jewish Communist she meets in Greenwich Village, with whom she fights with the Loyalists in the Spanish Civil War. Widowed, Linda returns to Mississippi to found a school for black children.

Ritt's adaptations of Faulkner tend to upstage their narrations of modernity because they find progressive liberalism inadequate to the task. In the instance of racial recognition, the entitlement of workers and immigrants seems to augur little for the progress of African Americans. When the black servant Lucius, for example, shows Ben Quick to his new bedroom at the Varners', Quick marvels to him about its size: "I had five sisters and a brother and a father and a mother and an old lady aunt—and all together we slept in a room half this size." Lucius responds, "Same as my family." "Well, look at us now, Lucius," exults Ben. But for all the fellow feeling, what you see when you do look at them is not the similarity of their status, but the discrepancy of their progress. Earlier in *Summer,* Clara and the black child Jewel drop off the soiled rug to Quick at his cabin. The scene advances the romance between Quick and Clara, and it does so significantly by charging their attraction with class tension. The movie will persuade Clara that she can wed her future to a man with obscure origins but the right stuff. But this scene also frames the comparative marginalization of race in the transactions of advancement. The three characters compose a family portrait of those seeking expanded rights in the postwar nation, but the black figure, still a child, stands mutely and impassively low down in the corner, awaiting instruction and the gratification of his appetite as an afterthought, which comes as a handout from a white benefactor. Obliviousness to black political agency in the late 1950s South constitutes a blind spot in white liberalism, Ritt seems to apprehend, something on the order of the desegregation that magically has already happened in the movie's fantasy of 1950s Jefferson.

In the case of the emancipation of women, the female protagonists may register their growing refusal of paternalistic rule, but neither film imagines any revision of social institutions. On his ride into Frenchman's Bend with Clara and Eula Varner, Ben Quick notices that everything seems to belong to Varner, so he jokes as he gets out of the car, "You two girls belong to Varner?" Eula "snort[s] with laughter, 'We two girls most particularly belong to Varner!'" (8). But the mentality of commodified possession survives challenge—recall how Clara says she sets a "high, *high* price on herself," and ends up choosing as her suitor the very individual who most successfully rejuvenates standing social and economic ways, who already once had been decreed by Will as the man Clara *must* marry, and who becomes the old man's new son, his new-man. In *Sound and Fury*, Miss Quentin clearly intends to build on the romantic foundation laid down between her and her stepuncle. Once Miss Quentin's uncle and surrogate father, the movie's Jason now has emerged as her coconspirator in the pursuit of legitimacy, though of the sort that will preserve his power over her.

Jason stubbornly makes his way into a family in need of resuscitation; he identifies the fatherless Miss Quentin as a kindred spirit, one prepared to repudiate the Compson past in the person of her returned mother (whose ways she soon sees are hopelessly outdated and irrelevant to the independent womanhood she craves). In a startling moment in the film, Jason seizes Miss Quentin and gives her a long, hard kiss. The hand that grasps her neck soon drops away, as the movie transforms Jason's rage at the planter gentry's social eclipse in the novel into an espousal of white bourgeois ascendancy.

In the film's last scene, Jason explains to Quentin how he has surreptitiously sponsored her path to self-reliance. Marveling at her newly manifest self-possession, he muses, "Girls, first they're nothing, then all of a sudden they're everything." Although he seems, awkwardly, to be talking about girls' sudden emergence as women, Jason's abrupt observation also suggests the conundrum facing the ideology of liberal expansionism: the incorporation of newcomers into the polity requires a kind of fantasy in which the status quo responsible for exclusion in the first place is opened at a stroke to those who want in: nothing to everything. At the end of *Sound and Fury*, Quentin's voice-over narration includes a resolution to stay in Jefferson. For all her newly won independence, her closing sentence threatens to cancel it out: she thinks of Jason, "You're not done with me yet." Her future lies in being completed as a man-made woman. The fantasy of liberalism involves captives still choosing to live in their former prisons, only with the doors unlocked.

That Ritt was thinking of American democratic liberalism in the context of U.S. Cold War hegemony may be glimpsed in one detail Ritt adds in his making of *The Sound and the Fury*. When the carnival comes to town, Ritt brings it into the foreground. The novel's man in the red tie becomes a New Yorker named Charlie Busch, who falls in love with Miss Quentin, but whose fecklessness leads him to sell her out when Jason offers him money to go away. The outfit Charlie works for is identified as the Pan American Carnival Corp. As it is being set up, the manager spies Luster driving Benjy around town, and strikes a deal with this black local to get a first family sort, however unwittingly, to advertise the Yankee circus by being paraded in a sandwich board. Given U.S. efforts to secure Latin American loyalties in the era of Soviet competition, Ritt's quiet reference seems telling, all the more so the year before Castro's revolution.

Modernism's Subject Matters

Ritt could test notions about the continuing advance of modernity in projects like these because all of them took the essence of modernist works of imagination to be the representation of modern transformations. Operating in a sphere of cultural production apart from the literary academy, they treated Faulkner as a great chronicler of modernity, not only as a virtuoso of technique. In one of the two short publicity pieces Wald wrote for *Sound and Fury*, he says that the responsibility of a film adaptation of a literary work is to capture the "spirit, rather than the letter" of the original.[13] The formal structure of *Sound and Fury* was changed because the movie "had to tell the story in the present," so "it had to find another method of narration" (132).[14] In doing that, Frank and Ravetch were actually following Faulkner's own lead in adapting his modernist text.

Faulkner had himself, after all, returned to *The Sound and the Fury* fifteen years after its publication in 1929 to compose an update that became a de facto new fifth section. Its entries follow out the lives of the characters subsequent to 1929, along the lines of their *stories*. Faulkner's appendix suggests that continuations of his original work of art could be made in the domain of its subject matter apart from its modernist method. In fact, such a working principle is already reflected in the organization of the novel itself. "April Eighth, 1928" is not formally innovative in any remarkable way. Instead, everyone notices how the conventions of realist fiction are resurrected by Faulkner as the ending to a work with a quite different beginning. That is, Faulkner's synthesizing or absorptive kind of modernist aesthetic refuses to sacrifice story to technical virtuosity. As the reader moves through *The Sound and the Fury* sequentially, a compressed history of multimedia modernism unfolds. First we encounter the most purely cinematic narration in English, organized by flashback, crosscutting, complex parallel editing, eye-bound point of view, the fetishization of gaze without sound (the "dumb-show"), and so forth.[15] Over the next two sections, consciousness begins to get reassembled, conventions of personhood reappear, the effect of embodied, spoken voice emerges in Jason's monologue, and linear narrative returns (Jason retelling his story "harshly recapitulant"). The novel, as Faulkner suggested, starts looking like four treatments of the same story. In section 4, we have a method of narration that has succeeded in absorbing and mastering the technical effects of the new media: Shegog's voice gets reproduced once in "standard" literate English and once graphophonically in dialect; several parallel narratives spool out simultaneously but without ever entangling or breaking; omniscient narration returns, though permanently compromised by the effects of point of view; and descriptive language regains some confidence, however wary it must be of the new regime of the im-mediate eye (inscribed in the text in cautionary nonverbal form). *The Sound and the Fury* is the novel that swallowed the movies.

Such an act of absorption anticipates the nature of Faulkner's modernism. Faulkner's aesthetic practices a kind of modernism that is never embarrassed by its realist roots, does not get permanently stuck competing with or distinguishing itself from other media technologies, and conducts a kind of "modern" storytelling that avails itself of modernist techniques without fetishizing them.[16] It remains for later evaluative logics in the 1950s to recruit Faulkner to a kind of modernism defined essentially by technical virtuosity and the presumed autonomy achieved by the predominance of aesthetic effect. Outside the academy, Ritt engineers a kind of Hollywood modernism, a realism that reflects on its own narrative and points to its own limitations. The interference Ritt can permit has to come in the form of a front—a realistic entertainment that celebrates democratic stability and progress, but that stumbles into depths of implausibility, conspicuous performativity, and the manifest violation of their originals.

Media Made: *Mad Men* Takes a Page Out of *The Sound and the Fury*

Toward the end of the second season of *Mad Men,* advertising executive Don Draper travels to Los Angeles on business and discovers a new horizon of pleasure. He's taken up by a young woman named Joy, who introduces him to her cosmopolitan jet-set family, then seduces him. He awakens the next morning to find his bedmate reading: "What are you reading?" he asks. "William Faulkner," she says, turning the cover of *The Sound and the Fury* to him. "Is it any good?" Don asks. "*Sex* is good," she says, "this book is just OK." Joy does not seem the likeliest reader of this novel anyhow. She seems to be giving it a try for the sake of a syllabus (Joy mentions she has learned about Faulkner in an American literature survey at Pembroke, the former women's college at Brown University).

Don complies with this indifference to subject matter. At the end of the episode, Don receives a phone call and fumbles for something to write down the address he's being given. Joy's book comes to hand, and Don jots the information on the last page of the volume, then tears it out. The sheet he repurposes is the last page of the appendix: the listing of black characters that ends with "They endured." Although the civil rights movement has been noticed even by Madison Avenue, Don and his cohort seem interested only in what black people might now be able to buy. By 1962, of course, many significant events in the desegregation movement had already occurred, and earlier in this very episode the ad men of Sterling Cooper watch news footage of James Meredith's attempt to enroll at the University of Mississippi, identified as occurring in "Oxford." For Don the last page of *The Sound and the Fury* is not unreadable, just unread. Whatever the novel might have to tell him about racism and the South, Don is uninterested. Matthew Weiner makes us wonder about the price paid when academic institutions in the 1950s decided that modernist works of literature were essentially indifferent to political and social life and began producing new consumer elites like Joy who read them unmoved, and new productive elites like Don who don't read them at all.[17]

NOTES

1. Frank and Ravetch also wrote the script for the movie made from Faulkner's last novel, *The Reivers* [1969], although that was directed by Mark Rydell.

2. In a paper presented at the Southern Studies Forum in September 2011, "Jason Compson as Cajun Saint," Thomas Inge elegantly rehearsed the brief against the Ritt adaptation of *Sound and Fury*. I acknowledge his generosity in allowing me to consult a copy of his paper.

3. Patrick McGilligan, "Ritt Large," in *Martin Ritt: Interviews*, ed. Gabriel Miller (Jackson: University Press of Mississippi, 2002), 116.

4. James Bloom, *Hollywood Intellect* (Lanham, MD: Rowman Littlefield/Lexington, 2009).

5. Julian Murphet, *Multimedia Modernism: Literature and the Anglo-American Avant-garde* (Cambridge: Cambridge University Press, 2009), 20. Hereafter cited parenthetically.

6. Andreas Huyssen, *After the Great Divide: Modernism, Mass Culture, Postmodernism* (Bloomington: Indiana University Press, 1986).

7. Lawrence H. Schwartz, *Creating Faulkner's Reputation: The Politics of Modern Literary Criticism* (Knoxville: University of Tennessee Press, 1988), 199.

8. Charles S. Aiken, *The Cotton Plantation South since the Civil War* (Baltimore: Johns Hopkins University Press, 1998).

9. See Jessica Adams, *Wounds of Returning: Race, Memory, and Property on the Postslavery Plantation* (Chapel Hill: University of North Carolina Press, 2007); and Houston Baker, *Turning South Again: Re-thinking Modernism* (Durham, NC: Duke University Press, 2001).

10. Leigh Anne Duck, *The Nation's Region: Southern Modernism, Segregation, and U.S. Nationalism* (Athens: University of Georgia Press, 2006).

11. Gabriel Miller, *Martin Ritt: Interviews* (Jackson: University Press of Mississippi, 2002), 120. Hereafter cited parenthetically.

12. Irving Ravetch, Harriet Frank Ravetch, and Michael R. Frank Ravetch, *"Hud"; "Norma Rae"; and "The Long, Hot Summer": Three Screenplays* (New York: New American Library, 1988), 49. Hereafter cited parenthetically.

13. Jerry Wald, "Faulkner & Hollywood," *Films in Review* 10, no. 3 (1959): 131.

14. Martin Ritt acknowledged that leaving out Faulkner's prose may have been too much of a sacrifice finally, since in that novel language is "the star of the story" (Miller, *Interviews*, 115), but neither he nor Frank and Ravetch seem much concerned about altering the method of storytelling to suit the narratives they were now trying to tell. Walter Metz, in fact, gives *Sound and Fury* special credit for one technical innovation of its own, in according a voice-over narrative to a woman, with all its protofeminist formal implications (see Walter Metz, "Signifying

Nothing?: Martin Ritt's *The Sound and the Fury* as Deconstructive Adaptation," *Literature Film Quarterly* 27, no. 1 [1999]: 21–31).

15. Kawin was the first to demonstrate the novel's reliance on cinematic techniques, particularly on montage in its opening two sections (Bruce Kawin, *Faulkner and Film* [New York: Ungar, 1977], esp. 18–21). Kawin develops this line of analysis in "The Montage Element in Faulkner's Fiction," in *Faulkner, Modernism, and Film*, ed. Evans Harrington and Ann J. Abadie (Jackson: University Press of Mississippi, 1979). Two chapters in this volume address cinematic matters in *The Sound and the Fury*. In "The Unsynchable William Faulkner: Faulknerian Voice and Early Sound Film," Jay Watson identifies elements primarily in the first section of the novel that he argues correspond to two features of early film: the slippage in the synchronization of speech and image, and the semantic use of silence. In "William Faulkner's Mediated Time: Capitalism, Cinema, Syntax," Mark Steven considers *The Sound and the Fury* as staging the progressive section-by-section disciplining of literary temporality and sensory experience under the increasing regulative authority of modern narrative and capitalist production—Benjy's section preserving vestigially the pure temporality available only in literature, Quentin's and Jason's succumbing to the doom of clock time as bourgeois productive regularity.

16. Julian Murphet's paper at the "Faulkner and the Media Ecology" conference (UNSW, Sydney, 2011), "My Mother Is a Graphophone," structures Faulkner's meditation on the implications for literature of a new electronic medium like the radio, as mediated by the liminal or transitional third position indicated by the phonograph, a mechanical precursor of the electrified radio, permuting instructively the passage between premodern and modernizing national and gender regimes.

17. I am aware that Don Draper earlier gets introduced to Frank O'Hara's poetry, that he reads aloud from one of the poems, "Mayakovsky," as he muses over the poem's reflection of his own uncertain identity, and that he sends a copy of the volume of O'Hara he reads from, *Meditations in an Emergency*, to Anne Draper, the widow of the army buddy from whom he steals his identity. Don is a receptive reader of O'Hara's difficult poems about contemporary New York City; these speak to Don as subject matter through their experimental technique. This is precisely what has been precluded in academic Cold War readings of American modernists like Faulkner.

What Is Television For? (or, From "The Brooch" to *The Wire*)

CATHERINE GUNTHER KODAT

I take my text from the second book of Blotner, chapter 72, paragraph 5. It is mid-November 1958, and William Faulkner is at Princeton University, where, for a five-hundred-dollar fee (about four thousand dollars in today's currency), he is serving out the second half of a visiting writer's appointment. The arrangements at Princeton are rather different from those at Virginia, where Faulkner had been writer-in-residence for the entire 1957 and 1958 spring semesters. His agreement with Princeton had already seen him on campus for two weeks in March, and this weeklong November visit would close out the contract. Most of the heavy lifting had happened during the spring, when Faulkner conducted thirty-five "undergraduate interviews" and eight "group sessions," but the fall was hardly easier: six solid days of student meetings in an office in the library, with as many as thirteen individual appointments on a given day.[1] Then, too, there were the social obligations, often difficult for Faulkner but typical of this sort of thing. Saxe Commins, Faulkner's editor at Random House and a longtime Princeton resident, had died of a heart attack in July, but his widow, Dorothy Berliner Commins, nevertheless hosted two events at her home when Faulkner was in town, one of them a cocktail party whose invited guests were mostly members of the Institute for Advanced Study (IAS)—among them the institute's director, the legendary physicist J. Robert Oppenheimer.

Blotner writes that Oppenheimer "had elicited Faulkner's sympathy in the loyalty controversy which had swirled up around him" in 1954, after the Atomic Energy Commission, acting in the McCarthyist spirit of day, revoked its top secret security clearance from the man who had headed the Manhattan Project but whose wife and brother had belonged to the Communist Party in the 1930s. In July 1955 *Harper's* had published the essay "On Privacy," in which Faulkner deplored how a "pioneer in the simple science of saving the nation like Doctor Oppenheimer" had been "harassed and impugned . . . until all privacy was stripped from him."[2] Faulkner mentions Oppenheimer twice in the essay, and this public expression of compassion for one of Princeton's most celebrated residents may have been what prompted Dorothy Commins to plan the party. Faulkner, however, seems not to have been particularly keen to meet Oppenheimer, much less anyone from the IAS. "I don't understand their world," he complained to his hostess before the event, and indeed he spent most of the evening silently sitting "in a corner by himself, answering with yeses and noes when someone attempted a conversation with him" (2:1704–5). Then Oppenheimer—"a shy man himself in some ways," Blotner writes,

> walked across the room and joined Faulkner. "I saw your story 'The Brooch' on television, Mr. Faulkner, and I enjoyed it," he said. "I wonder what you think of television as a medium for the artist."
>
> [Faulkner's answer] was a short one. "Television is for niggers," he said, and there was little more to the conversation. (2:1705)

And there you have it: Faulknerian bad behavior in the implosive, self-destructive mode, of a particularly distasteful sort. What could he have been thinking? Why would such a seemingly simple question draw such a vituperative response?

While I am not the first to try to answer these questions, it is a little surprising how few have preceded me in the effort, given that Faulkner's outburst lands feet first on two topics of abiding interest in the scholarship (Faulkner and race, Faulkner and the culture industry)—topics that still generate good discussion today. Blotner, of course, does have something to say, and while his reading is not entirely satisfactory, it does cover a lot of bases. Dorothy Commins, he tells us, felt that Faulkner "meant that television was not a medium for the artist but rather one for entertaining a mass audience with a low level of appreciation," an observation that actually amplifies the offensiveness of Faulkner's remark by rendering its racist core in seemingly neutral language. Commins's pop psychology afterthought—"the answer [also] indicated a lack of breadth which [should be] blamed on the stultifying effect of [Faulkner's] native environment"—seems mostly an effort to contain the damage. Blotner himself decides that "the truth" of Faulkner's motivation in responding so nastily to Oppenheimer's friendly question lay in the intersection of the author's past failures as a writer—"like motion pictures, television was not his medium, and he was not particularly comfortable either writing for it or watching serious attempts at art on it"—and present discomfort as a celebrity: "he was in a situation which . . . produced boredom and resentment, and he . . . struck out" (2:1705). Blotner thus ushers race into the discussion via Commins's remarks mostly so as to quietly escort it back out by effecting a clear separation between "television" and "nigger": the first word references something actual, a problem in Faulkner's past, while the second, however deplorable, should be understood metaphorically: an unguarded expression of pique, a measure of the distress of the moment and little more. In his reading of Faulkner's teleplays of "The Brooch" and "Shall Not Perish" (Oppenheimer had seen the former on the *Lux Video Theatre*'s April 2, 1953, CBS broadcast), William Furry also briefly discusses the Oppenheimer exchange, adopting and slightly extending Blotner's first point: while "clearly dismissive of the medium," Faulkner's public display of contempt "may have masked a private frustration for his own failure with commercial television."[3] Furry is right to suspect Faulkner of protesting too much, even if he, no less than Blotner, wants to keep the focus on television and off race.

Frederick R. Karl and Richard Gray, the other two scholars who have written about Faulkner's outburst, take exactly the opposite tack: much less interested in television than in "nigger," they adopt a hard line on Faulkner's language. After rehearsing Commins's and Blotner's explanations, Karl concludes that "no explanation obtains except that [Faulkner] fell into the white man's most obvious retreat, using the Negro as someone so much lower in caste that the retort becomes unanswerable."[4] Placing the comment in a wider context of Faulknerian speech habits, Gray finds "Faulkner's frequent use of the word 'nigger' . . . disquieting."[5] The word, he notes, "is used in an apparently uncritical way," and even though Faulkner sometimes seems mainly "out to shock" a northern interlocutor with his diction, "more often than not the prejudice" expressed in the word "seems instinctive" (38). No less than Blotner's and Furry's, then, Karl's and Gray's interpretations of the retort are framed in contextual appeals to Faulkner's past experience, though here the salient history is not the failed effort to write for the movies or television but the failed intervention in the civil rights movement. For by November 1958,

Faulkner's hard-earned reputation as a courageous white southern friend of desegregation and civil rights had taken quite a beating. Faulkner landed the first punch himself when, on March 5, 1956—three months into the Montgomery bus boycott—he published "A Letter to the North" in *Life*, offering the entirely unasked-for (and, for supporters of civil rights, thoroughly uncongenial) advice "to the NAACP and all the organizations who would compel immediate and unconditional integration: 'Go slow now'" (*ESPL* 87). That same month saw the appearance in the biweekly magazine the *Reporter* of an interview conducted with London *Times* writer Russell Warren Howe, in which Faulkner expressed solidarity with white "Mississippi against the United States even if it meant going out into the street and shooting Negroes"; his insistence, later in the interview, that segregation was "wrong" and "untenable" did little to blunt the threat of violence detected by many readers in his confessed willingness "to make the same choice Robert E. Lee made" (Blotner 2:1591). Faulkner spent a good chunk of the rest of 1956 trying to clean up the ensuing mess, with little success: his letter to the *Reporter* characterizing his comments as "statements which no sober man would make, nor, it seems to me, any sane man believe" (*ESPL* 225) was met by a respectful but firm reply from Howe that "all the statements attributed to Mr. Faulkner were transcribed by me from verbatim shorthand notes of the interview" (Blotner 2:1601). And to James Baldwin's excoriating "Faulkner and Desegregation," published in the fall 1956 issue of *Partisan Review*, Faulkner made no public reply whatsoever. One year later, his response to the crisis in Little Rock was only slightly less clumsy than the performances in *Life* and the *Reporter*. His four-paragraph letter to the editor of the *New York Times* opens on a daring note ("The tragedy of Little Rock is that it has at last brought out into the light . . . the fact that white people and Negroes do not like and trust each other, and perhaps never can" [*ESPL* 230]) but quickly takes cover under the much-recycled, by then near-moribund prose of the Nobel Prize speech—prose that, in the letter's bombastic peroration, actually seems more a criticism than an endorsement of the federal government's decision to enforce *Brown*.[6]

These four readings of Faulkner's outburst, despite their different emphases, actually all derive from the same interpretive procedure: Blotner, Furry, Karl, and Gray split Faulkner's sentence down its spine, dividing it in half so as to argue for one of its two nouns as the governing interpretive term. What has not yet been attempted is a reading of Faulkner's retort taken intact, which is what I offer here. My approach involves focusing less on what "television" or "nigger" might have meant for Faulkner than on what that small though quite complex word "for" is doing in the sentence. It doesn't take long for the realization to sink in: "television is for niggers" simultaneously articulates two distinct assertions about the relationship between television and black Americans, one cultural—television is a denigrated art for a denigrated people—the other political: television is a champion of the disenfranchised and dispossessed. These claims have in turn a complex double relation to each other, and it is only in examining the terms of this double relation—this in many ways unreconciled two-ness—that we can begin to take the measure of Faulkner's outburst. Without doubt, television's uncanny capacity to embody and transmit the "warring ideals" of postwar life—those increasingly acute, and acutely felt, contradictions of modern American capitalism—was becoming quite clear by 1958.[7] Of course, television is not a folk; it possesses neither soul nor consciousness nor agency, even if its startlingly rapid colonization of key aspects of American life and culture quickly led to denunciations of it as a kind of living alien force, an invasive, electronic mind- and body-snatcher. Yet it is precisely television's capacity to make almost shockingly obvious how, in the words of Jacques Rancière, "a 'medium' is not a 'proper' means or material" but rather "a surface of conversion, a surface of equivalence," and to do so in ways that raise pointed questions about what connections might (or might not) obtain between equivalence and equality, that make it such an aesthetically troubling medium for the artist.[8]

Furry's 1996 discovery of the teleplays for "The Brooch" and "Shall Not Perish" (also written for *Lux Video Theatre*, and broadcast on February 11, 1954) in the archives of the J. Walter Thompson advertising agency at Duke University remains important; his careful reading of the many changes Faulkner made in adapting these stories for television is highly suggestive, though I do not address them in any detail here. While Furry notes that "no letters or office memos between Faulkner and the *Lux* producers detailing the terms of their relationship have turned up" (124), information pieced together from other sources seems to indicate that Faulkner's work for *Lux* was extremely lucrative (he received $2,500 for the two teleplays—about $20,500 in today's currency [125, 138]) and quickly dispatched: advance publicity for "The Brooch" claimed that the teleplay had been written by Faulkner himself in forty-eight hours.[9]

Already small beer as literature (in his 1948 story list for Robert K. Haas, his first editor at Random House, Faulkner himself called it "Topical, not too good"),[10] the patriotic and sentimental "Shall Not Perish" makes for excruciating reading as a teleplay—the less said about it the better, frankly, and since it was not the broadcast seen by Oppenheimer, we can set it aside.[11] "The Brooch," first written in 1930 or 1931 and published in *Scribner's* in 1936 after several rejections and much revision, is obviously second-drawer Faulkner, but its grim, back-looping narrative of maternal malice, spousal betrayal, and suicide is not without interest. Yet the story bears little resemblance to the sappy, conventionally chronological teleplay, in which a good girl from the wrong side of the tracks prevails against her old meanie of a mother-in-law once her husband finally locates his spine. Jack Gould, the television critic for the *New York Times*, savaged "The Brooch," calling it a "synthetic" and "diluted" "soap opera," "a maudlin paean to young love." Acknowledging that Faulkner faced certain challenges in making a story with mature, disturbing content pass video code muster, Gould nevertheless asserts that "even under the television industry's purity code there was no reason for Mr. Faulkner to capitulate so completely to the video mores." Or rather, there was a reason, and it wasn't a good one: Gould insinuates that Faulkner "succumbed" "with eagerness" to "television's taboos" because the author himself, no less than the manufacturers of Lux Toilet Soap, was determined to cash in on his name. "Of all great American writers Mr. Faulkner undoubtedly is as entitled as any to enjoy a few of the materialistic pleasures which the fees paid by TV make possible," Gould observes.

> The small financial reward attendant to his literary efforts long has been a disheartening matter of record. If now he wants to whip out a few pot boilers for the video screen, his admirers may regret it but they will understand. At least no harm is done to his acknowledged artistic accomplishments of the past.
>
> But it is dismaying to find an author of Mr. Faulkner's stature and the producer of the Lux Video Theatre indulging in what amounts to literary sleight-of-hand. The advance fanfare over "The Brooch" obviously was an attempt to capitalize on Mr. Faulkner's justly-earned fame: yet what the audience saw was substitute merchandise not of the quality advertised.[12]

Even more dismaying for Gould are the consequences of a sell-out like Faulkner's for the future development of television as, precisely, a medium for the artist. "It is to the Faulkners that literally hosts of writers look for some inspiration and encouragement to do battle against puerile restrictions that so often in television gag the inquiring mind and the articulate voice," Gould writes. "If he intends to work further in TV, Mr. Faulkner must remember that his position carries with it certain inevitable responsibilities. He only betrays a new and promising medium if he accepts the theory that he will reserve his meaty stuff for other media and condone any literary hash for video."

In the final paragraph of "On Privacy"—the very essay in which he had expressed his solidarity with Oppenheimer in seeking "to preserve that privacy in which alone the artist and the scientist and humanitarian can function" (73)—Faulkner had scolded America for not yet having found any place for the artist, "him who deals only in things of the human spirit, except to use his notoriety to sell soap or cigarettes or fountain pens or to advertise automobiles and cruises and resort hotels, or (if he can be taught to contort fast enough to meet the standards) in radio or moving pictures where he can produce enough income tax to be worth attention" (75). It's widely agreed that "On Privacy" was written primarily in response to Robert Coughlan's splashy, two-part, unauthorized profile of Faulkner, published in the fall of 1953 in *Life*. It seems to me more than a little likely that Gould's review of "The Brooch," published just five months before the *Life* profile, was another goad. It can hardly be a coincidence that soap appears among the items an artist's "notoriety" can sell: the broadcast of "The Brooch" concluded with a dressing-room "candid" with Sally Forrest (the actress cast in the role of Amy Boyd, the plucky wife), in which she describes herself as "one of the millions of people who admire William Faulkner and consider him to be one of the truly great writers of our time." She continues:

> I feel it a particular honor to have appeared in Mr. Faulkner's first television play, which he wrote especially for the Lux Video Theatre.
>
> I'm grateful to Lux for the opportunity and grateful to Lux for another reason, too.
>
> Having made as many pictures as I have, and lived in Hollywood as long as I have, I can heartily recommend Lux Toilet Soap. A beautiful complexion is important to every woman—perhaps most of all to those of us who have to face cameras for a living—and that's why I depend on Lux for my complexion care. Why don't you? (Furry 178)

Adding Faulkner's experiences with the telecast of "The Brooch" to our contextual frame for reading "On Privacy" brings nearer to the surface of that essay a previously submerged defensiveness in Faulkner's tone. It also makes newly apparent the shock Faulkner must have felt to hear Oppenheimer himself (who, in truth, is really something of a bit player in "On Privacy") bring up a major source of the bitterness and, I think, not inconsiderable shame that informed the writing of that essay—where, interestingly enough, it's radio and moving pictures, not television, that Faulkner fingers as the most lucrative media options for the artist eager to "produce income tax" but unwilling to sell only his notoriety. This was perhaps because television's connection to salesmanship already was so overdetermined by 1955 that it went without saying. After all, it was the wish to safeguard television's unprecedented reach as an advertising medium that accounted for the mostly self-imposed network censorship condemned by Gould as a block to significant artistic expression: no network wanted to risk losing viewers through challenging or possibly offensive programming. As Melvin Ely has shown, it was in part the threat of an organized, highly public boycott of Blatz Beer, corporate sponsors of the short-lived (but long syndicated) *Amos 'n' Andy* television show, that led officials at CBS to take seriously NAACP complaints about the show from the moment the civil rights organization contacted them.[13]

I mention *Amos 'n' Andy* not so as to open a discussion of the representation of blacks in early television—that work has been done well by others, and I could do no more here than simply repeat it—but rather to develop our discussion by bringing further into the light a little-noted aspect of television programming's widely recognized contributions to the civil rights movement. Both J. Fred MacDonald and Sasha Torres have written persuasively about how television coverage of key developments in the civil rights movement—starting with Little Rock, which Taylor Branch has termed "the first on-site news extravaganza of the modern television era," and continuing through to the March 7, 1965, "Bloody Sunday" attack on Selma's Edmund Pettus Bridge—conveyed a sense of national urgency unachievable in any other medium.[14] What Torres describes as "the necessity of the imbrication of television with race trouble: on the one hand, race and racial conflict fed the medium's enormous appetite for visual spectacle; on the other, the mere fact of television's coverage served paradoxically to render racism visible in new ways, and to new audiences" (17) is not likely to have escaped Faulkner's notice. Faulkner himself may not have been watching much television in 1957, but by then the TV was on for five hours a day in 85 percent of American households; market penetration in the South, long "retarded as a consumer of television," had finally been accomplished; and the coverage of Little Rock was "unrelenting: NBC led with John Chancellor's reports from Arkansas every night for a month" (MacDonald 66; Torres 20). Many white southerners—not all of them segregationists—blamed television itself for turning the civil rights movement from a local problem into a national crisis, "inflaming" "Negro unrest" by supplementing the live broadcasts of distressingly violent responses to peaceful protests with steady coverage of the issue in documentaries and talk shows like *Issues and Answers* and *Face the Nation*. Almost certainly, Faulkner heard some of this talk; his letters to *Life* and the *New York Times*, as well as the 1956 essay "If I Were a Negro," published in *Ebony* magazine, bespeak an effort to redirect the national discussion of civil rights out of television and back into print, where he felt more firmly in control. And in fact there is considerable truth to the claim that television and the civil rights movement helped establish each other as legitimate forces in American life, though that truth goes well beyond television's reliance on conflict, "liveness," or spectacle to boost ratings.

For Samuel Ichiye Hayakawa, television's irreplaceable contribution to the civil rights movement lay in its power to directly address America's "nigger"—the poor, the badly educated, the segregated—and not only with vivid visuals of protests aimed at securing voting rights and equal access to education. Called on to deliver the opening address of the August 1963 International Conference on General Semantics at New York University and taking television and race as his topic, Hayakawa (then an English professor at San Francisco State, later a U.S. senator) observed that television had several "peculiar facts" as a medium that made it especially appealing to blacks. Partly because "it bypasses literacy," television "spread with greater rapidity among the poor than the rich in the United States, among the uneducated than among the educated. . . . The poor and the uneducated being numerous in the Negro community, television spread with special rapidity among Negroes."[15] By providing entertainment in the home, television also allowed southern blacks "to avoid the indignities of the ill-kept, humiliating, separate balconies of the segregated movie houses" (398). The final, crucial fact to be considered was television's high cost of production. As we have seen, it was this need to please advertising sponsors so as to make manageable its steep economies of scale that led Gould to bemoan television's aesthetic mediocrity, but Hayakawa read the situation otherwise. The fact that "all television programs are addressed pretty much to the whole community," he claimed, means that "whatever the television set says to white people, it also says to Negroes" (398). For Hayakawa, television was "profoundly democratizing" mostly because of its advertising:

> Here, for example, is a television commercial telling what fun and excitement children can have if they can persuade their parents to bring them to such-and-such an amusement park. The commercial does not bother to explain that they need not come if they are Negroes. Here is another commercial inviting the family to hop into the car and drive just twenty-five minutes from downtown to Woodland Acres, the beautiful new residential development, where three-bedroom ranch-type homes are now open for inspection. It does not tell you that if you are Negro, these homes are not for you. Here is an advertisement telling you to order this new, sparkling soft drink with the thrilling new flavor. It doesn't tell you that if you are Negro, you will have to drink it standing on the sidewalk outside the cafe.
>
> Now imagine that you are a Negro teen-ager, to whom the television set, with messages such as the foregoing, has been his constant baby-sitter and companion ever since he can remember. If you are this Negro teen-ager, you have spent more hours of your life in front of the television set than you have spent in school, according to the statistics given by audience research surveys. You do not know what your elders know, namely, which advertisements to heed and which to ignore as not being addressed to you. You only know that the friendly, friendly television set is always saying to you, "You are an American. You are entitled to eat and drink and wear what other Americans eat and drink and wear. You must think about the same political and world problems that other Americans think about. You are a member of this national community of Americans." (399–400)

In describing how political action arises as a consequence of this naïve response to televisual lures to consumption, Hayakawa proposes a view of the medium's contribution to the civil rights movement that accounts for both readings of Faulkner's outburst. It also steers fairly closely to Jacques Rancière's theory of the politics of aesthetics as being rooted less in an artwork's explicit (or implied) political "message" than in its formal capacity to alter the "distribution of the sensible" (*partage du sensible*) such that "new landscape[s] of the visible, the sayable, and the doable" come into imaginative being.[16] This is not to say that television advertising is art. It is, however, to begin to clear a space for considering television's potential as a medium for the artist by locating that potential precisely in *all* the ways that "television is for niggers" and, in turn, by highlighting how an understanding of medium as a means for expressing equivalence—advertising as politics, politics as spectacle, form as flow—has come to inform contemporary aesthetic practice.

Lest this discussion come to seem too theoretical or obscure, let me conclude with a brief reading of a scene from *The Wire*, the critically-acclaimed television series that ran for five seasons on the for-profit but subscriber-supported Home Box Office network. Much of the series' success grew from its ambitious and, in my view, successful effort to present what the show's creator and chief writer David Simon has called a "television novel" on contemporary American themes: the costly failures of the war on drugs; the collapse of urban industry and the corresponding disappearance of the blue-collar middle class; the heartrending inadequacies of public city schools; the implosion of the daily newspaper business—all of them adjunctive to the series' single overriding theme, the fate of the city of Baltimore. The population of Baltimore is 64 percent black, and a great deal has been written about the role of race in the *The Wire*, where forty-two of the eighty-four featured actors are blacks cast in roles ranging from police department chief to state senator and including teachers, drug lords, addicts, street punks, schoolroom strivers, detectives, and ministers. A proper discussion of this single issue in the show is beyond the scope of this chapter, but we can get a sense of how *The Wire* takes the linking of television and race as key to its art by a quick look at what has come to be known as the "Chicken McNuggets" scene in the second episode of the first season. D'Angelo, Wallace, and Poot, all young men in the employ of drug kingpin Avon Barksdale, are seated on a castoff couch in the center courtyard of the McCulloh Homes housing project, which functions as an open-air drug market. D'Angelo keeps a supervisory eye on the surrounding brisk trade while the younger Wallace and Poot share a lunch of Chicken McNuggets.

Impressed by both the tastiness and convenience of the Chicken McNugget, Wallace expresses his admiration for the man he imagines must have created it: "Motherfucker got the bone all the way out the damn chicken. Til he came along nigger's just been chewing on drumsticks and shit, getting they fingers all greasy. He said, 'Later for the bone. Let's nugget that meat up and make some real money.'" When Poot wonders whether in fact the inventor of the Chicken McNugget was paid for his work, Wallace replies with certainty that he must be "richer than a motherfucker." This prompts a scornful response from the older D'Angelo: "Nigger, please. The man who invented them things, he's just some sad-ass down at the basement of McDonald's, thinking up some shit to make some money for the real players." When Poot objects—"Naw, man, that ain't right."—D'Angelo goes off:

> Fuck right. It ain't about right, it's about money. Now you think Ronald McDonald gonna go down that basement and say, "Hey Mr. Nugget. You da bomb. We're selling chicken faster than you can tear the bone out. So I'm gonna write my clowny-ass name on this fat-ass check for you." Shit.
>
> And the nigger who invented them things still working in the basement for regular wage thinking of some shit to make the fries taste better, some shit like that. Believe.

Poot looks chastened, but Wallace does not back down. "Still had the idea though," he replies.

There are three aspects of this scene I want to emphasize. First, the use of the word "nigger" to describe both the admiring Wallace and the creatively entrepreneurial (if, it's implied, also duped) "Mr. Nugget." The word here continues to signify the downtrodden and despised, but it signifies something more: a talent to imagine, and to make, something new and different out of common, everyday material, and a grudging but nevertheless real respect for that talent. The scene readily acknowledges that the respect may proceed from incorrect or insufficient information (as is the case for Wallace) and that the talent may wind up being exploited (as happens to D'Angelo's hypothetical Mr. Nugget), but that acknowledgment is not, it seems to me, intended as unalloyed condemnation or dismissal. Second, we should attend to the scene's bluesy, simultaneous sounding of two discordant notes: *both* a bitter emphasis on the bottom line as the ultimate determinate of worth—"it ain't about right, it's about the money"—*and* a dogged insistence on intrinsic merit: "Still had the idea though." Third, consider the Chicken McNugget itself: Trash tricked out as nourishment, pretty much the epitome of everything that's wrong with contemporary America, the Chicken McNugget nonetheless serves as the vehicle for Wallace's reverie of ingenuity, invention, and justly lavish compensation. The entire scene—set in an open-air drug market and underscored with diegetic sound blending notes of domesticity and despair (the piping voices of playing children, the murmured exchanges of drug dealers and their clients, the muted but insistent rhythm track of a boom box)—is something of a crystallization of the aesthetic credo of *The Wire.* That credo is equal parts formal and sociological: a belief that to explore the equivalences between the drug trade and capitalism, between fighting crime and committing crime, between commerce and art is also, even necessarily, to reveal how equivalences do not add up to equality. Thus *The Wire* demonstrates how television is a medium "for" the "nigger."

It seems to me that, in Faulkner's view, television was not just "for" "niggers": it *was itself* "nigger," the "sad ass" in the basement of the postwar American media ecology, ginning up money for the "real players"—not only the studio executives and producers but also writers like Faulkner himself, who, at least in the estimation of the *New York Times*'s Jack Gould, stood for media segregation by maintaining, either explicitly or implicitly, that between work produced for television and the modernist novel there could be no aesthetic equality. Certainly that view seems to inform "On Privacy," where Faulkner strongly implies that "things of the human spirit" will never find expression in commercial media. Throughout the 1950s, Faulkner made a point of stressing his disdain for television, though never again (at least not publicly) in the violent terms he used with Oppenheimer. But as we all know, Faulkner had a lifelong tendency to misrepresent himself and his habits, so it should come as no surprise that this supposed World War I flying ace spent more than a few hours of the last year of his life parked in front of the tube at the home of his Oxford neighbors Jim and Dutch Silver, watching his favorite television show, *Car 54, Where Are You?*—a comedy set in a Bronx police precinct that, at its premiere in 1961, was the only show of its type to employ black actors in recurring roles (Blotner 2:1812; MacDonald 76). It is undoubtedly true that television's potential as a medium for the artist and the crucial role black America has played in making that potential a reality were things Faulkner was unable to see—though it's nice to think it's something that he would have been willing to watch.

NOTES

1. Joseph Blotner, *Faulkner: A Biography*, 2 vols. (New York: Random House, 1974), 2:1609, 1704. Hereafter cited parenthetically, giving volume and page number.

2. William Faulkner, "On Privacy (The American Dream: What Happened to It?)," in *William Faulkner: Essays, Speeches, and Public Letters*, ed. James B. Meriwether, updated (1965; New York: Modern Library, 2004), 70–71. Hereafter the volume edited by Meriwether is cited parenthetically as *ESPL*.

3. William Furry, "Faulkner in a Haystack: The Search for William Faulkner's Television Adaptations of 'The Brooch' and 'Shall Not Perish,'" *Faulkner Journal* 16: nos. 1–2 (Fall 2000/Spring 2001): 136. Hereafter cited parenthetically.

4. Frederick R. Karl, *William Faulkner: American Writer* (New York: Weidenfeld and Nicolson, 1989), 988–89.

5. Richard Gray, *The Life of William Faulkner* (1994; Oxford: Blackwell, 1996), 38. Hereafter cited parenthetically.

6. "Against that principle which by physical force compels man to relinquish his individuality into the monolithic mass of a state dedicated to the premise that the state alone shall prevail, we . . . may have to represent that last community of unified people dedicated to that opposed premise that man can be free by the very act of voluntarily merging and relinquishing his liberty into the liberty of all individual men who want to be free" (*ESPL* 231).

7. W. E. B. Du Bois, *The Souls of Black Folk*, ed. Henry Louis Gates Jr. and Terri Hume Oliver (New York: Norton), 11.

8. Jacques Rancière, *The Future of the Image*, trans. Gregory Elliott (2003; New York: Verso, 2007), 75.

9. Michael Millgate, *The Achievement of William Faulkner* (1966; Athens: University of Georgia Press, 1989), 50. Furry claims that Faulkner "dashed off" teleplays of both "The Brooch" and "Shall Not Perish" during a trip to New York City early in 1953, citing as evidence a March 31 letter to Else Jonsson (125, 138). However, Blotner's footnote to a February 22 letter to Jonsson, in which Faulkner writes that he "will make a television play of one of my stories this week" (346), indicates that Faulkner was working not on "The Brooch" or "Shall Not Perish" but on the adaptation of the "Old Man" section of *The Wild Palms*. Though the phrasing is ambiguous, Millgate seems to believe that the adaptation of "Shall Not Perish" was written in 1954, again on a tight schedule before the February 11 broadcast. For the letters to Jonsson, see Joseph Blotner, ed., *Selected Letters of William Faulkner* (New York: Random House, 1977), 346–47.

10. Blotner, ed., *Selected Letters of William Faulkner*, 274.

11. Though given the hiding he got in the *New York Times* for his teleplay of the "The Brooch," it seems odd that Faulkner, offered a second chance to prove himself, would produce such a poor script—an improbability that indirectly lends credence to Furry's theory that the adaptations of "The Brooch" and "Shall Not Perish" were written at the same time.

12. Jack Gould, "'The Brooch' on TV: William Faulkner Runs Afoul of Video's 'Code' and Comes Off Second Best," *New York Times*, April 12, 1953, X11.

13. See Melvin Patrick Ely, *The Adventures of "Amos 'n' Andy": A Social History of an American Phenomenon* (1991; Charlottesville: University of Virginia Press, 2001), esp. chap. 10.

14. Taylor Branch, *Parting the Waters: America in the King Years, 1954–63* (New York: Simon and Schuster, 1988), 223; J. Fred MacDonald, *Blacks and White TV: Afro-Americans in Television since 1948* (Chicago: Nelson-Hall, 1983); Sasha Torres, *Black, White, and in Color: Television and Black Civil Rights* (Princeton: Princeton University Press, 2003). Hereafter these works are cited parenthetically.

15. S. I. Hayakawa, "Communication: Interracial and International," *ETC: A Review of General Semantics* 20, no. 4 (December 1963): 397. Hereafter cited parenthetically.

16. Jacques Rancière, *Dissensus: On Politics and Aesthetics*, ed. and trans. Steven Corcoran (New York: Continuum, 2010), 149.

A Little Boy and an Idea

"Two Soldiers" and "Shall Not Perish"

STEFAN SOLOMON

In the penultimate chapter of William Saroyan's popular sentimental novel *The Human Comedy* (1943), the aging telegraph operator, Mr. Grogan, receives notice that the brother of his employee has been killed during the Second World War. Struggling to digest the portion of the message he has so far typed out, Mr. Grogan has a heart attack. When Homer Macauley, the telegraph messenger, arrives at the office, he discovers the dead Mr. Grogan and the half-typed message addressed to his mother, and, we are told, "[w]ithout even reading the words of the telegram, Homer knew the message, and yet refused to believe it." Although a friend reassures him that his brother may simply be hurt or missing, Homer asserts that his boss's death was the direct result of hearing the rest of the telegram, which if typed, would have confirmed the fatality: "He didn't type it, but he *heard* it."[1] Although he has been mortally wounded, at the end of the story, a returning soldier, one of the deceased's closest comrades, advises Homer to tear up the telegram and "throw it away" because "it's not true."[2]

Here, the telegram is "not true" because it cannot archive the dead in the same way that the surviving soldier is able to, in the memories he will reproduce for the bereaved Macauley family, that glimpse of their son's final moments alive. Like Melville's scrivener, Mr. Grogan is "sped to death," not simply by the death of Homer's brother, but by the steady aggregation of telegraphed obituaries that it is his duty to faithfully transcribe. This final telegram, like its predecessors, cannot expand on the dead soldier's brave exploits, both because it compresses his life span into a minimal number of characters, and because it does not constitute a living memory of the soldier himself, or indeed of anything. Here at its worst, as Theodor Adorno writes, the telegram offers "mutilated language condensed to carry the maximum information," which, "combined with the urgency of delivery imparts the shock of immediate domination in the form of immediate horror."[3]

The following essay, a case study of two of Faulkner's less-esteemed short stories, begins with the telegram for a number of reasons. First: because the telegram is itself a beginning, appearing to usher in a suite of analogue media that would dominate both communications and cultural outputs by the end of the nineteenth century. In thinking through Faulkner's representations of a particular media ecology in 1943, it is also worth considering the "archaeological"[4] position of those media, and how their relations were formed through uneven developments across time and space, though not necessarily in a linear, progressive manner.

Second: because critical attention to the fortunes of different media, both in the content and form of Faulkner's work, provides a means to interpret the changing nature of the author's own medium, literature. It pays to remember that the written word was one among many media at the turn of the twentieth century, and so the presence of its new compatriots (or rivals) in short stories, novels, and plays written thereafter certainly bears consideration.

Third: because Faulkner's oeuvre contains many references to the telegram (perhaps even more than it does to sonic or visual media), often in an overtly contemptuous tone. Indeed, the telegram emerges on many occasions in Faulkner's writing, from Horace Benbow's inability to master the form in *Flags in the Dust,* to Gavin Stevens's aptitude in *Intruder in the Dust,* as well as its various manifestations in the short stories, including "An Artist at Home" and "Pennsylvania Station," in which Mrs. Zilich "didn't know she had ten words without counting the address."[5] These mostly hostile perspectives on the telegram perhaps signal a more general distrust of modernity that appears in many guises over the course of Faulkner's career. But more than simply acceding to such conventional misgivings, we would do well to consider why the humble telegram is so often taken to task, and how such consistent opposition might even betoken a certain authorial anxiety about the fate of the written word.

In Faulkner's short story "Shall Not Perish," published in the same year as Saroyan's novel, the younger of the two Grier boys is just as incredulous as Homer Macauley when his family receives word in the mail of the death of their twenty-year-old, Pete: "'I know what it is,' Mother said. 'But I can't open it. Open it.' 'No it ain't!' I hollered, running. 'No it ain't!'"[6] The deathly message in question, paraphrased as "*A ship was. Now it is not. Your son was one of them,*" is unbelievable for the narrator, initially because he represses its contents, but then later because he reinterprets the meaning of the Western Union telegram, that "little pale envelope that didn't even need a stamp on it" (SNP 101). Ultimately, the telegram fails the deictic task of pinning his brother down "at some single spot on the earth," allowing for the possibility that he "still *is* everywhere about the earth, one among all the fighters forever, *was* or *is* either" (SNP 104). Part of the telegram's inadequacy here lies in its tendency toward syntactical contraction, ellipsis, and the mot juste, and so the contempt toward that particular form of writing seems consistent with the majority of Faulkner's disparaged telegrams. But at the same time, we might be tempted to say that the compulsory abbreviations of the telegram themselves allegorize the craft of short story writing, which is itself dependent on the author's adroitness with a minimal number of words.

A historical correspondence will reinforce the formal equivalences here: only four years after Samuel Morse had sent the first telegram in the United States, Edgar Allan Poe published his review of *Twice-Told Tales* (1842), Hawthorne's collection of short prose narratives, endorsing the same lexical frugality required of the telegram writer. On Poe's reckoning, the craft of the short story author was highly demanding, insofar as each work could contain "no word written, of which the tendency, direct or indirect, is not to the one pre-established design."[7] The same was still true for the short story a century later, and even today, where it regularly takes on the air of an "organic unity," and participates in a restricted economy of words, which "means in practice" that it runs "anything between five hundred and fifteen thousand words, or between one and forty average printed pages."[8] Of course, these boundaries are perhaps more rigidly set by the editors of literary magazines, in which space is often at a premium, and it was such a publication that prevented "Shall Not Perish" from finding immediate exposure. As Joseph Blotner observes, the *Saturday Evening Post* rejected it out of hand, stating that it was "overwrought and artificial." And in fact, after three attempts at revision, the *Post* still refused to publish the piece.[9]

Despite his proclivities for the verbose, Faulkner, like Poe before him, insisted that the short story represented the privileged mode of narrative construction, especially for its enticements toward precision. At the University of Virginia in 1957, he told students that with a novel "you can be more careless. You can put more trash in it and be excused for it." By contrast, in the short story, Faulkner insisted that "[a]lmost every word has got to be almost exactly right,"[10] and for that reason it was a form second only to poetry. If, as Leslie Fiedler once wrote, Faulkner "had no special talent for sustained narrative" but was rather "short-breathed in nature,"[11] then it was here, in the short story, that the author would test most sharply the ability of the written word.

On the one hand, then, Faulkner derides the nonliterary short form of the telegram, while on the other (and throughout his oeuvre), he endorses the short story form. Yet however the telegram's formal tendencies—which necessarily incline toward concision—may invite comparison with short narrative modes, there are definite distinctions between the first, brought into being by the "big business" of war and, later, of the stock market; and the second, which had vastly different genetic origins.[12] And at least for its author, this is the supremacy of prose fiction, which positions itself as distinct from other (commercial) media, with "Shall Not Perish" proceeding through a gallery of media objects, and mostly dismissing their discrete achievements.

For the telegram is only the first of a number of media adversaries in Faulkner's story, its truncated and "mutilated language" motivated by "the urgency of delivery," summoning other media that are less forthcoming in their affiliation with writing. Because Pete Grier's life and death are "condensed" into three (reimagined) fragmentary sentences, committing almost nothing of either to communal memory, and failing even to determine his final resting place, the need arises for the narrative to investigate the similar claims of other media. Indeed, in the media exemplars at the level of the story's content, this is precisely what takes place. In addition, the story offers itself as a type of meta-ecological category that harbors those media within itself and attempts to supersede each of them. For example, where telegrammatic words consistently founder in Faulkner's fiction, the short story stakes its claim to restore lexical authority, and in so doing asserts itself against other, nonliterary, cultural artifacts.[13]

With this in mind, the reaction against the inexact telegram in "Shall Not Perish" as the authoritative herald of death represents not only one character's refusal to accept the end of another's life but also, as refracted through the short story, a less obvious literary engagement with other media that profess supremacy as archival means. For, in "Shall Not Perish," just as Pete's legacy persists in a number of intermedial traces, so too does the logic of the story operate, the narrative impelled episodically by its "fascinations" with media objects increasingly dissimilar to itself—the telegram, followed by the radio, paintings, and then film. Though the media themselves should not occupy inherently fascinating positions in 1942, when each has a good deal of history, the narrative perspective of the young Grier boy permits of an appropriate modicum of fascination as the story works its way through this litany.[14] With the appearance of each, there is a certain sense of anxiety abiding within the form of the story, which seems to urge it onward to examine the claims of various media to do that at which the short story itself claims to excel—to memorialize its fading object with the precision required of Poe's "pre-established design," where "almost every word has to be almost exactly right."

But this tale of intermedial convergence and competition begins earlier, with the first of three Grier family stories, "Two Soldiers" (1942). As Faulkner would tell Harold Ober in 1944, when explaining his motivation for writing it, not all media were equal to the task. "I like it," he wrote,

> because it portrays a type which I admire—not only a little boy, and I think little boys are all right, but a true American: an independent creature with courage and bottom and heart—a creature which is not vanishing, even though every articulate medium we have—radio, moving pictures, magazines—is busy day and night telling us that it has vanished, has become a sentimental and bragging liar.[15]

And so, as Faulkner has it, although literary humanism can hold fast to the "true American," the little boy otherwise advances toward a vanishing point within every other "articulate medium"—he is no longer represented and has therefore ceased to exist. Faulkner's humanist convictions are symptomatic of what Régis Debray has diagnosed in modern attitudes toward technology, where some are "quick to define culture as the entirety of those functions that offer resistance to technology, in the same way life resists death."[16] And yet, Debray insists, this belief neglects "that fated solidarity of design which inscribes man in machine at the very threshold of our humanities or liberal arts."[17] One may designate something called "culture" as the theoretical antidote to technology's rapacious drive, but to do so would be to remain blinkered to culture's implication within the mechanized world. Coupled with the human being—another object reputedly removed from the machine—the cultural artifact is perceived as ontologically separate from the technological sphere. In Faulkner's story, however, the very content suggests that the form is not so much the corrective to "every articulate medium," but merely one carrier among many.

Crucially, the media that stand accused in Faulkner's letter all make indexical claims of one kind or another (telegram aside), each declaring its own veracity by reproducing a trace of the subject itself, severally as voice or image. In appropriating some element of their subject, the media of mass reproduction listed here—"radio, moving pictures, magazines"—are paradoxically capable of making that subject appear to have "vanished," or to warp it so far out of shape that it becomes a "sentimental and bragging liar." The "cultural" bulwark against this onslaught is, as Faulkner has it, the literary narrative (irrespective of the fact that his short stories are first published in the pages of magazines), which applies a softer touch to its subject and harnesses its "courage and bottom and heart" by way of representation, without actually needing to reproduce those values as images or sound bites. As the medium whose capabilities allow it only to represent rather than record its subject matter, literature for Faulkner comes to assume its place as the rightful cenotaph to the vanishing "true American." It is especially apt for this task because it denounces the overtly deictic, affording its readers more liberty of interpretation—in "Shall Not Perish," Pete Grier "still *is* everywhere about the earth" because neither his voice nor image have been captured, and so he is spared that "death-in-life" signaled by those more indexically able media.[18]

Indeed, the short story itself shares with the narrator that tortured relationship with rival media—the threat to the "little boy" of my title is also the threat to literature, where both carry the anxiety of being outstripped by a more proficient mode of representation but perhaps repress the barely concealed presence of those other discursive sources that have reconstituted them both. That is to say, irrespective of the story's spirited disavowal of "radio, moving pictures, magazines," it is explicitly informed by those media, and in allegorizing its own imperiled place in the cultural landscape, gestures toward a more dialectical recuperation of advanced communications technologies.[19]

Speaking to a class at the University of Virginia in 1957, Faulkner would describe the disparity between "Two Soldiers" and its manqué, "Shall Not Perish," as follows:

> The first story had to do with one of the most interesting of all conflicts, all human conflicts. To me, it's the boy trying to reconcile, to learn in order to accept the adult world he will have to cope with, and I believed more in the story about the little boy and his brother who got drafted than I believed in the idea that I tried to make into another story, the sequel to it.[20]

After all, he insisted, he was "simply not an idea man," and was "not really interested enough in ideas to take even my own too seriously."[21] After the gentle pathos of "Two Soldiers" came the strident abstractions of "Shall Not Perish." And, if commercial viability is any sort of barometer of technical merit, the former yielded its author one thousand dollars, and the latter only twenty-five dollars, and that after many revisions.[22]

The absence of critical success for "Shall Not Perish" is perhaps understandable when considered as the lesser sequel to an earlier, and already unsuccessful, story. Redoubling the sentimentality of "Two Soldiers," "Shall Not Perish" strangely abandons the younger Grier boy's southern dialect, and seems to turn unambiguously toward the patriotic "idea," marking it as a relative failure. Faulkner himself echoed this law of diminishing returns when in 1948 he wrote to Robert Haas regarding the inclusion of both works in the forthcoming *Collected Stories* (1950). The first he approved with a single word—"YES"—while on the second he hesitated, referring to it as "[t]opical" and "not too good."[23] Most critics have readily acceded to Faulkner's assessment of the second story, and many have often applied it to the first, too. But, as I have briefly mentioned, such occlusions of the story from discussions of Faulkner's best writing constantly neglect its most fascinating aspects. For, even if the narrator simply mouths an abstract and unthinking "idea," then it is by no means immaculately conceived, but manifests as a composite of stimuli within a particular discourse network[24]—comprising popular film and news media, radio (perhaps Roosevelt's "Fireside Chats"), and the telegram—and hence the more sententious writing Faulkner himself detects in "Shall Not Perish" is also a tonal shift that may usher in the network from whence it came.

In truth, the "idea," that impalpable object of contemplation that is too "topical" and not worth taking "seriously," first rears its head in "Two Soldiers." More specifically, it emerges on that date of infamy in December 1941, when Pete and his brother hear about the attack on Pearl Harbor over Old Man Killegrew's radio. Every night since that fateful broadcast, Pete "would lay there, a heap stiller than if he was asleep, and it would be something, I could feel it coming out of him, like he was mad at me even, only I knowed he wasn't thinking about me, or like he was worried about something, and it wasn't that neither, because he never had nothing to worry about."[25]

The radio waves, flowing imperceptibly through Pete Grier, are now "coming out of him" as "something," a by-product incomprehensible except in the simplest of terms. It is in this sense that the young narrator resolves the ensuing filial tension, stating that he "knowed it was the wanting to go to the war that had worried him and kept him awake, and now that he had decided to go, he wasn't worried any more.[26] And yet his conviction isn't shared by his mother, who likewise knows that Pete has "got to go" to war but doesn't understand why. Like her mother before her, who let her son, Uncle Marsh, venture to the French front line simply because "he had to go," Mrs. Grier doesn't expect to ever know why Pete wants to enlist.

Pete justifies his decision, declaring that "I jest ain't going to put up with no folks treating the Unity States that way,"[27] but this rationale only seems to obviate access to something more pervasive and entrenched: a more holistic network of discursive influences whose collective force translates itself belatedly onto the page of the short story. Specifically, Pete's objection to the Japanese attack on Hawaii emerges from the "fellow in the radio talking," volume up "as loud as it would run."[28] Furthermore, Pete is only able to interpret the information communicated by the radio because, unlike his brother, "he had done finished the Consolidated last June and he knowed a heap."[29] It is important in this story that the radio acts in concert with the consolidated schooling system, for the one is a medium that compresses distance, contracting the world to "village dimensions,"[30] while the other represents the abandonment of local rural schools for larger, centralized educational complexes.[31] The combination of a spatially consolidated pedagogy with a spatially consolidating medium results, for Pete, in a superior spatial awareness, the ability to differentiate between the Pacific Ocean and "that Government reservoy,"[32] Sardis Reservoir.

As the discursive goad that encourages Pete to fight for his country, the radio itself returns in the sequel to "Two Soldiers," when the narrator reconsiders his nightly excursions to Killegrew's in light of military developments after "Pearl Harbor and Manila." Now, he says, "Pete don't make one to listen to it. Nor do I. [. . .] Mother and Father and I don't need a little wooden box to catch the voices of them that saw the courage and the sacrifice" (SNP, 104). In an earlier, rejected draft, Faulkner wrote this passage in another way: "it is as though, on that instant when Pete was not, he became not naught but all, circumambient with that circumambience from which the radio's tongueless wood snares its voice. . . ."[33]

In this abandoned sentence, rebuffed because it was deemed inappropriately verbose, the narrator tries to redeem Pete from those radio waves on which he was borne to the Pacific Theater several months before. The siren's song was enough to lead him over the water but is not allowed to gain any purchase on his voice as an object primed for mass distribution, which itself is truly a kind of technologically crippled form of "circumambience." The technophobic strain that began with the telegram is continued here, at the very site of what the narrator supposes is Pete's attempted dismemberment at the hands of the mass ornament. In this way, radio in the story speeds Pete toward death, for it is the very same "wooden box" at Old Man Killegrew's that had attracted Pete to the war in the first place. While both the narrator and the author of the story he narrates attempt to repudiate rival media and technologies in "Shall Not Perish," there is no point in his life at which Pete Grier is not technologically constituted.

The origins of Pete's fascination with the war effort are explicitly mediated and, by virtue of Jefferson's isolation, can only be so. While the younger Grier boy attempts to remove his wartime idols—"them that saw"—from the rapacious economy of the "wooden box," this is the very same object that produces those reified virtues, "the courage and the sacrifice." Where Pete's brother considers the radio to fall short in its representation of the overseas conflict, it is, instead, the very source of what Mrs. Grier determines to be an unknown quantity—it represents the unrepresentable, by indexing the voice of the dead.

Radio professes to bear the indexical trace of the human voice, thus claiming to "know" because it *is* also the thing it merely represents. But in actual fact, the medium stands at one remove from the vocal capture that Pete's brother fears. Radio's electromagnetic propagation doesn't actually hold "the existential trace or impression left by an object,"[34] in the same way that photography—and later, cinema—bear that trace as light rays reflected from the really existing object make an impression on the photograph or photogram. But the initial sound recording of the voice certainly attests to the object's onetime presence in "some single spot on the earth," and radio subsequently makes pretenses to possess that same ability.

Bernard Stiegler has long argued that all human memory "is originally exteriorized"—that is, it has always relied on external, artificial aide-mémoire as its condition of possibility. And yet there is something materially and temporally specific about the exteriorization of memory when we consider the industrial development of what Stiegler terms mechanically advanced "mnemotechnologies."[35] To this end, he has speculated about the disjunction between written and mechanical media, where the first requires that its audience possess the same skill—literacy—as the author, while the second does not demand that the viewer, for instance, knows how to operate a film camera. This, Stiegler argues, rehearses the relation between producer and consumer that defines industrialized society, and it ushers in a separation between human beings and memory that requires a certain technical competency to reconcile the two.[36]

Some suspicion of this disparity, we might say, informs the young Grier boy's decision that the radio is a vessel inadequate for hosting his brother's memory. As the narrator of the story, he is naturally wary of other modes of representation that make the same elegiac pretenses that he does, but in a seemingly more complex manner. This is especially so in the case of the radio, the medium that speaks as with the authority of a person (even the president), and mystifies—at least to a young boy—its means of transporting voices across oceanic expanses. Again, as with the telegram, the frustration with, or objection to, other media here allegorizes the divergence between literature and mechanical media and so transmutes its author's own fear of the obsolescence of his craft. But however the narrator (and Faulkner) appear to remonstrate, at least some media are afforded a worthy place in the story, because it is chiefly by their mnemotechnological faculties that Pete remains in public memory.

And so, even in their disavowal of the wooden box, it is perhaps only natural that the Griers replace the radio communiqués from Old Man Killegrew's with the messages of other, older media—most obviously via the obituaries in the *Memphis Commercial Appeal.*[37] The telegram mutilates the written word because its necessarily deathly message is unfortunately circumscribed by exigency, and the radio captures voices with such precision that it seems as though they are voiced from inside its wooden casing. On the other hand, the "mass ceremony" afforded by the newspaper obituary—which at least provided "the pictures and names of soldiers and sailors from other counties and towns in Mississippi and Arkansas and Tennessee" (SNP 102)—reassures the Griers that their imagined community "is visibly rooted in everyday life."[38] The newspaper endows the dead with a greater number of words, written in the obituary section which, unlike the telegram, regularly sets one death alongside many others.

And yet, even though Pete is featured in the pages of the daily paper, the inability of that medium to convey anything of his intimate life in turn constructs his afterlife as an unarticulated object in "Shall Not Perish." Once more, Mrs. Grier confesses (this time to Major de Spain) that her eldest "knew why, even if I didn't, couldn't, never can. So it must be all right, even if I couldn't understand it. Because there is nothing in him that I or his father didn't put there" (SNP 109). Even if the genealogically transmitted "idea" is hard to define, de Spain asserts that its genetic relay determines that Mrs. Grier must know what it is: "What you and his father gave him. You must know what that was." And yet she appears to equivocate, suggesting simply that "it must have been strong to have lasted through all of us. It must have been all right for him to be willing to die for it after that long time and coming that far" (SNP 110). Mrs. Grier reasons that the family bloodline is the conduit for whatever it is that impels her kin to commit to the defense of country in the face of death, but the exact contents of that enduring objective remain inscrutable to her. Indeed, for Mrs. Grier, it is familial relations—rather than economic or cultural—that defines Pete's raison d'être, the "idea" that Faulkner held accountable for his story's poor reception. By way of contrast, Major de Spain (who has also lost a son in the war) contends that this idea, if it once had value in the American imaginary, had devolved over the past eighty years, such that Pete "didn't even have a dream. He died for an illusion. In the interests of usury, by the folly and rapacity of politicians, for the glory and aggrandisement of organized labor!" (SNP 108).

De Spain's assessment sounds a little closer to the truth. However, while Mrs. Grier urges "courage and honor and sacrifice" (SNP 108) and her interlocutor dismisses those values, perhaps both ignore the variety of mnemotechnologies that have contributed to the central animating "idea" that impels young men to defend their nation. It is not simply a matter of "the subservience of misled workingmen for the demagogues who misled them," nor is it enough to say that the idea "must be all right, even if I couldn't understand it" (SNP 108). Rather, what this debate seems to imply by omission is the influence of the media that circulate throughout the remainder of the story, the acknowledgment of which would supply the dialectical force with which to reconcile de Spain's and Mrs. Grier's contradictory positions.

Indeed, as though to propose "media" as the external answer to what was "put there" (SNP 109) in Pete, the story abruptly turns its attention elsewhere. Mrs. Grier and her son leave de Spain's house to return home, pausing at a gallery along the way.[39] It contained "pictures from all over the United States, painted by people who loved what they had seen or where they had been born or lived enough to want to paint pictures of it so that other people could see it too." Among other subject matter, these were "pictures of men and women and children who were the same people that we were even if their houses and barns were different and their fields worked different, with different things growing in them" (SNP 110–11). In the regional gallery, painting is motivated by "love," and it is this ethic, the narrator tells us, that allows him to draw comparisons between the inhabitants of Frenchman's Bend and citizens elsewhere in the country. If Mrs. Grier believes that the ineffable idea is carried along hereditary lines, then the painted canvas flattens out and unfetters this design, such that it takes on the scope of the sun's rays, "stretching all the way across America from the Pacific ocean," the narrator says, "like a big soft fading wheel" (SNP 111).

With its geographically diffuse collection of paintings, the gallery itself makes the curatorial gesture of gathering and arranging them such that each picture is viewed in relation to the entire collection. In this way, like the obituary faces from "Mississippi and Arkansas and Tennessee" and the faraway voices that are nevertheless inside the radio, the gallery also reduces the nation to "village dimensions." And yet there are also crucial differences between the gallery's collective tendency and the experience of community and connectivity garnered from reading a newspaper or listening to a wooden box. Unlike those that precede it in the narrative, the gallery satisfies the Grier boy's assumption that an older medium can adequately represent the lives of tenant farmers without needing to "catch"—or pretending to catch—the indexical traces of its objects of study. Where radio snares the voice, the folk painting makes no indexical claim of ownership. The framed pictures may reduce the heterogeneity of rural life to a comfortable, flat similarity, in much the same way that commercial radio tends toward the homogeneity of its particularized product, yet, like the short story, they do so as a purely representative gesture.

The intricacies of this indexical enterprise are explored further in the next scene, which invokes an earlier cinematic episode in the narrator's life, of "a continued picture, a Western; it seemed to me that it had been running every Saturday afternoon for years" (SNP 112). Every weekend, the Grier boys, along with their father, and sometimes mother, would go "to sit there in the dark while the pistols popped and snapped and the horses galloped and each time it would look like they were going to catch him but you knew they wouldn't quite" (SNP 112). Montage, here in one of its classical manifestations in the chase sequence, orders desire by terminating each alternating shot of the film's hero and villain at their points of maximum intensity.[40]

But when Grandpap accompanies the family to the theater, he isn't hard-wired to these formal cues and confuses the screened matter with his own dream-images of the Civil War, becoming roused from his slumber when a pack of horses look set to jump "clean out of the screen and go galloping among the little faces turned up to them like corn shucks scattered across the lot" (SNP 113). Reacting in much the same manner as the witnesses to the Lumiére Brothers train pulling into La Ciotat Station in 1895, Grandpap flees the scene, shouting: "'Cavalry!' Then he was on his feet. 'Forrest!' he said. 'Bedford Forrest! Get out of here! Get out of the way!'" (SNP 113).[41] While Pete reacts with hysterics, and his Father responds with embarrassed rage, Mrs. Grier rationalizes the outburst to her family—whatever spectatorial competency Grandpap lacks, he makes up for in courage, as a vessel for that seemingly sourceless fount of bravery that has endured through at least three major conflicts, what Major de Spain essentializes as the "dream": "He wasn't running from anybody!" she says; "He was running in front of them, hollering at all clods to look out because better men than they were coming, even seventy-five years afterwards, still powerful, still dangerous, still coming!" (SNP 114). If, in the earlier story "Dry September" (1931), Minnie Cooper also had to be escorted from the picture show because, ultimately, the images of happy couples on screen were for her too far divorced from the Real, then for Grandpap it is the opposite, and the medium of indexical proportions become a concrete continuation of the Confederate dream.

The Grier boys, better habituated to the logic of film—and the peculiarities of its editing—find their grandfather's reaction risible. However, though they might have attained an awareness of the separation between reality and the screened image, the brothers are perhaps less aware of the effect of filmic montage on their intimate lives. An inconclusive chase sequence in each installment not only entices the Grier boys to revisit the cinema every weekend but also governs the content of their intervallic discussions, and of their desires. As the star and his antagonist repeatedly trade blows, "the pistols popped and snapped and the horses galloped and each time it would look like they were going to catch him but you knew they wouldn't quite, that there would be some more of it next Saturday and the one after that and the one after that, and always the week in between for me and Pete to talk about the villain's pearl-handled pistol that Pete wished was his and the hero's spotted horse that I wished was mine" (SNP 112). The filmic montage here directly produces desire—desire to know the outcome of the chase, but also desire for the object ("that I wished was mine") and for the series itself, to which they incessantly return. The montage of the western serial here takes up the suspense-inducing aspects of the original technique and deploys them so as to heighten audience emotion in a bid for further investment in its ongoing franchise. In this way, the serial film functions so as to propel the experience of diegetic montage out into everyday life. Not only is there an alternation of villain and hero on this Mississippi screen, but the serial's weeklong interlude is also an exhortation to the young spectators to suture its narrative gaps with the conversational promise to attend "next Saturday."[42]

Faulkner had witnessed many such serials in his childhood and adolescence. After 1910, Oxford's Opera House first began screening films, and he was often accompanied twice weekly to the moving pictures by his own brothers, Murry and John. Although the siblings would see enough westerns "to realize that all scenes were taken at the same place and under virtually identical circumstances," they still "provided a vast new field of incredibly attractive entertainment."[43] Becoming accustomed to recurring content hadn't diminished film's apperceptive shocks for Faulkner and his brothers in its early days, but with the advent of sound cinema and the ossification of a formerly astonishing technique into its predictable deployments in the service of narrative, commercial motion pictures would seem to move toward a point of no return. By the early 1940s, as the Grier boys of Faulkner's short story eagerly anticipated the next installment of their continued picture, the once-radical and "shocking" technique of filmic montage had hardened into a form that was its opposite. The reification of montage would ultimately transport the technique from its dialectical origins into the service of capital, finally defanged of its radical potential.

Facing the alien surface of the silver screen, Grandpap is unable to satisfactorily grieve for a cause that is very much lost. The Grier boy, however, in grieving for his lost brother, cannot flee, but must negotiate with the onslaught of "articulate media" in the world that attempt to make of him "a sentimental and bragging liar" as he constructs his psychic cenotaph to Pete. At his mother's urging, he is able to simply "weep," without the need to reason with the cause of the casualty as de Spain does, and so the narrative contours of that grief appear to replicate only the inherited sentiments his mother herself has appropriated. And yet the narrator's grief also seems to inhabit a different, nonmaternal register, albeit unconsciously. For, as he tells us at the beginning of the story, "we allowed ourselves one day to grieve, and that was all. Because it was April, the hardest middle push of planting time" (SNP 102). The deliberate reference in the story to Eliot's *The Waste Land* also addresses itself to "the burial of the dead," and it, too, exposes itself to a confluence of voices and media, mixing "memory and desire" as the very process of the narrator's self-creation.

But more than simply harboring this poetic component, the memories on which the narrator's grief depends are founded even more explicitly on the constellation of other media that work their way into his worldview. Even as the boy tries to disavow them—or at least to favor folk painting's sincerity over cinema's illusion of movement—his resistance to mechanical media especially is a resistance to that which composes the majority of his adolescent experiences, and which is in this way the abiding aide-mémoire for the legacy of his dead brother. The obscured "idea" encoded within Pete Grier is a product, in part, of Old Man Killegrew's radio, and so in this way, perhaps his death *does* "make one to listen to it." More than simply "catching the voices" of the vanishing "true Americans," each medium in "Shall Not Perish" becomes unconsciously an exteriorized form of intimate memory, performing a mnemonic function that is nevertheless repudiated by its benefactor. For the short story form, too, those unsounded influences of rival media must be resisted, and yet in that resistance, they ineluctably come home to roost.

NOTES

1. William Saroyan, *The Human Comedy* (London: Faber and Faber, 1951), 213.

2. Ibid., 222.

3. Theodor W. Adorno, "The Schema of Mass Culture," trans. Nicholas Walker, in *The Culture Industry: Selected Essays on Mass Culture*, ed. J. M. Bernstein (London: Routledge, 2001), 96.

4. See Jussi Parikka, *What Is Media Archaeology?* (Cambridge: Polity, 2012), for a comprehensive introduction to this concept.

5. William Faulkner, "Pennsylvania Station," in *Collected Stories* (New York: Random House, 1995), 621.

6. William Faulkner, "Shall Not Perish," in *Collected Stories* (New York: Random House, 1995), 101. Hereafter cited parenthetically as "SNP."

7. Edgar Allan Poe, review of *Twice-Told Tales*, by Nathaniel Hawthorne (1842), in *Graham's Magazine*, May 1842, reprinted in *Essays and Reviews*, ed. G. R. Thompson (New York: Library of America, 1984), 572.

8. Martin Scofield, *The Cambridge Introduction to the American Short Story* (Cambridge: Cambridge University Press, 2006), 4.

9. Joseph Blotner, *Faulkner: A Biography*, one-volume ed. (Jackson: University Press of Mississippi, 2005), 436.

10. Faulkner, *Faulkner in the University: Class Conferences at the University of Virginia, 1957–1958*, ed. Frederick Gwynn and Joseph Blotner (New York: Vintage, 1959), 207.

11. Leslie A. Fiedler, "William Faulkner: An American Dickens," *Commentary* 10 (1950): 385.

12. Differences of origin aside, Siegert argues that the uniform "transmitting capacity" of the telegram produced its own "symbol economy"—expressionism (see Bernhard Siegert, *Relays: Literature as an Epoch of the Postal System*, trans. Kevin Repp [Stanford, CA: Stanford University Press, 1999], 182).

13. In a letter to Cowley, Faulkner wrote: "Telegrams are a casual business here; the office in town telephones them out and if you are not there to answer the phone, nothing else is done about it unless the operator happens to meet or pass you in the street and happens to remember to tell you a telegram came for you two or three weeks ago; did you get it?" (Faulkner to the President of the American Academy, December 31, 1948, in *The Faulkner-Cowley File: Letters and Memories, 1944–1962* [New York: Penguin, 1978], 139).

14. I am using "fascination" here in Tom Gunning's sense of the term. Following Viktor Shklovsky and Martin Heidegger, Gunning asks us to consider the renewed fascination for the old within a "dialectic of astonishment," whereby wonder, worn down into habit, can reemerge as wonder just when "rational explanation seemed to have triumphed." In "Shall Not Perish," the narrative itself is fascinated with older media and technologies, and its sense of bewilderment at something as old as the telegram redoubles the Grier boy's own wide-eyed preoccupation with the effects of various media (Tom Gunning, "Re-Newing Old Technologies: Astonishment, Second Nature, and the Uncanny in Technology from the Previous Turn-of-the-Century," in *Rethinking Media Change: The Aesthetics of Transition*, ed. David Thorburn and Henry Jenkins [Cambridge: MIT Press, 2004], 43).

15. Faulkner to Harold Ober, May 29, 1944, in *Selected Letters of William Faulkner*, ed. Joseph Blotner (New York: Random House, 1978), 184.

16. Régis Debray, *Media Manifestos: On the Technological Transmission of Cultural Forms*, trans. Eric Rauth (London: Verso, 1996), 116.

17. Ibid.

18. As an example of media's transformative power, Laura Mulvey has written of the deceptive nature of the filmic image, in which the indexical trace, professing contact with the Real, is nevertheless distorted in nature: "In the cinema organic movement is transformed into its inorganic replica, a series of static, inanimate, images, which, once projected, then become animated to blur the distinctions between the oppositions. The homologies extend: on the one hand, the inanimate, inorganic, still, dead; on the other, organic, animate, moving, alive. It is here, with the blurring of these boundaries, that the uncanny nature of the cinematic image returns most forcefully and, with it, the conceptual space of uncertainty: that is, the difficulty of understanding time, and the presence of death in life" (Laura Mulvey, *Death 24x a Second: Stillness and the Moving Image* [London: Reaktion, 2007], 52–53).

19. And yet, despite these tantalizing aspects of the first Grier family story, "Two Soldiers" was never well received. In a recent effort to reinterpret the piece, Shawn Miller has illustrated its collective critical dismissal (see Shawn E. Miller, "Returning to Faulkner's 'Two Soldiers,'" *Southern Literary Journal* 44, no. 2 [Spring 2012]: 38–50).

20. William Faulkner, "John Coleman's Writing Class: 25 February 1957," *Faulkner at Virginia*, ed. Stephen Railton, n.p., http://faulkner.lib.virginia.edu/display/wfaudio01_2#wfaudio01_2.17.

21. Ibid.

22. See Blotner, *Faulkner: A Biography*, 436, 452.

23. Faulkner to Haas, [late Sept. or early Oct. 1948], in *Selected Letters of William Faulkner*, ed. Joseph Blotner (New York: Random House, 1978), 274, quoted in Miller, "Returning to Faulkner's 'Two Soldiers,'" 39.

24. Kittler designates the "discourse network" as the matrix of "technologies and institutions that allow a given culture to select, store, and produce relevant data" (Friedrich Kittler, *Discourse Networks, 1800/1900*, trans. Michael Meteer, with Chris Cullens [Stanford, CA: Stanford University Press, 1990], 369).

25. Faulkner, "Two Soldiers," in *Collected Stories*, 82.

26. Ibid., 84.

27. Ibid., 83.

28. Ibid., 81.

29. Ibid.

30. Marshall McLuhan, *Understanding Media: The Extensions of Man* (London: Abacus, 1974), 326.

31. Calvin Brown, *A Glossary of Faulkner's South* (New Haven: Yale University Press, 1976), 58.

32. Faulkner, "Two Soldiers," 81.

33. Blotner, *Faulkner: A Biography*, vol. 2 (London: Chatto and Windus, 1974), 1100.

34. Tom Gunning, "Moving Away from the Index: Cinema and the Impression of Reality," *differences: A Journal of Feminist Cultural Studies* 18, no.1 (2007): 30.

35. Bernard Stiegler, "Memory," in *Critical Terms for Media Studies*, ed. W. J. T. Mitchell and Mark B. N. Hansen (Chicago: University of Chicago Press, 2010), 67.

36. See ibid., 77. In Faulkner's fiction, however, illiteracy doesn't always preclude the comprehension of the written word as a type of mnemotechnology. At the end of the titular story of *Go Down, Moses*, Molly Worsham Beauchamp asks the editor at the Memphis newspaper if he plans to publish the story of her deceased, dishonored son; even though it may harm his posthumous reputation, Molly requests that all of the details of his death be included in the piece. And, when the editor reminds her that "you couldn't read it, Aunty," she insists that she can still look at it (Faulkner, *Go Down, Moses*, in *William Faulkner: Novels, 1942–1954: Go Down, Moses, Intruder in the Dust, Requiem for a Nun, A Fable*, ed. Joseph Blotner and Noel Polk [New York: American Library, 1992], 280).

37. See Theresa M. Towner and James B. Carothers, *Reading Faulkner: Collected Stories* (Jackson: University Press of Mississippi, 2006), 56. There is a similar notion of the obituary in "Knight's Gambit": "the weekly *Yoknapatawpha Clarion* bearing the reproduced photograph and the brief obit already too familiar yet still cryptic as Sanscrit or Chinese—the countryboy face not really old enough yet to be a man's photograph, the uniform still showing the creases of the quartermaster shelves, the place-names which those who had created that face and flesh apparently in order that it might die in agony there, had never even heard of before, let alone pronounce" (William Faulkner, "Knight's Gambit," in *Knight's Gambit* [New York: Vintage, 1978], 239).

38. Benedict Anderson, *Imagined Communities: Reflections on the Origin and Spread of Nationalism* (London: Verso, 2006), 35–36.

39. This was probably the Mary Buie Museum, which opened in Oxford in 1939 (see Towner and Carothers, *Reading Faulkner: Collected Stories*, 59).

40. See David Trotter, *Cinema and Modernism* (Oxford: Blackwell, 2007), 52.

41. This fictional incident may have inspired Faulkner's brother Murry to write of their similar thoughts of the silent westerns shown in Oxford: "My brothers and I used to wonder what would have happened to us and the rest of the enchanted audience if the movie folks had gotten mixed up one time and let the cowboys blast out of the dust cloud first with the Indians chasing them. Probably we would have run out of the Opera House" (Murry C. Falkner, *The Falkners of Mississippi: A Memoir* [Baton Rouge: Louisiana State University Press, 1967], 50).

42. For a comparable analysis of the contemporary implications of the television serial on memory, which attends to diegetic and nondiegetic narrative strategies to engage the audience, see Jason Mittell, "Previously On: Prime Time Serials and the Mechanics of Memory," in *Intermediality and Storytelling*, ed. Maria Grishakova and Marie-Laure Ryan (Berlin: De Gruyter, 2010), 78–98.

43. Falkner, *The Falkners of Mississippi*, 50, 52.

Faulkner as Celebrity

DONALD M. KARTIGANER

> It is my ambition to be, as a private individual, abolished and voided from history, leaving it markless, no refuse save the printed books. . . . It is my aim, and every effort bent, that the sum and history of my life, which in the same sentence is my obit and epitaph too, shall be them both: He made the books and he died.
>
> —WILLIAM FAULKNER to Malcolm Cowley, 1949

The epigraph might appear to nip this essay in the bud, certainly in terms of the writer as not merely the bearer of personal celebrity resulting from public response to achievement but also, as my argument will try to demonstrate, the writer as the strategic agent of that celebrity. The oft-quoted, bald statement to Malcolm Cowley is, however, perfectly consistent with one of the major claims that Faulkner's high modernist predecessors and contemporaries were making as part of their effort to create a distinctive celebrity for themselves, namely, the elimination of the author from the literary work. While seeming to offer a lofty conception of the literary product, as if the work could appear immaculately from nowhere, the claim led back to an equally lofty conception of the maker, reborn as an inaccessible, unmoved mover, in Stephen Dedalus's words: "like the God of the creation . . . paring his fingernails."[1]

The phenomenon of celebrity has always embraced a negotiation, to use a neutral term, between an individual's merit and the fame that accrues to that individual. An ongoing question is whether merit and fame can exist in commensurate proportions, or must an inequality always obtain: fame insufficient to or in excess of achievement, or fame as the Warholian reward for simple presence, supported by no achievement whatsoever—with all these possibilities potentially in flux owing to the shifting tides of taste. Literary celebrity has been seen as a relatively new form, an eighteenth-century product of the transition from various forms of patronage to the judgment of a literary marketplace in which cultural and economic capital are locked in conflict, each one claiming independence of or control over the other, even as the reality suggests a dynamic of interacting forces, culture and commerce seeking an interdependence that sustains the value of the one and accommodates the necessity of the other.

The critical perception of Western literary modernism in the first half of the twentieth century has gone through two major phases in its understanding of celebrity. One is the insistence that major literature and major writers have operated outside the marketplace, with its emphasis on popular, commercial success. Indeed, one of the indicators of the value of such literature is its indifference to any criteria other than its achievement, according to authoritative judgment, as significant utterance.[2] Recently, critical attention has focused more comprehensively on the market and the ways in which it participates, for good or ill, in the life of those cultural products that, despite their authors' extraliterary pronouncements—and often in the formidable demands on readers they make—may be far more dependent on, and more actively involved in, the world of market forces.

Given the elaborate work of Pierre Bourdieu in the "field of cultural production," it has become apparent just how complex the relationship is among all the agents in the "field": the producers, the production, the promotion, the audience, and all the social, economic, material, and symbolic factors that fuel them, along with the larger "field of power" within which "the literary and artistic field is contained."[3]

My approach in this essay is to look at Faulkner and celebrity from the perspective of the producer of the art product. In doing so, I am following especially Aaron Jaffe's *Modernism and the Culture of Celebrity*, which focuses primarily on authorial agency in the modernist effort to create a distinctive form of celebrity, one in which a group of writers fashioned a preferred literary ethos, assembled a cadre of writers who practiced it, and set aside, explicitly or implicitly, a much larger group of writers who did not, or at least did not according to the accompanying criteria.

The strategy of this self-selected group of writers was twofold. On the one hand, there was what Jaffe calls the "upstream" direction: the creation of what, according to their own lights and the lights of readers capable of reading and understanding or at least appreciating it, was major literary work, characterized by "originality, [technical] mastery, and scarcity."[4] All three were necessary. The relative slimness of T. S. Eliot's *The Complete Poems and Plays*, for example, is owing not merely to his various day jobs, but to a strategy of promotion and circulation: poems must be fit and few. On the other hand, there was a "downstream" direction, the "secondary literature labors" (Jaffe 3), a major effort of promotion and circulation quite inconsistent with the values of the declared ethos—one of whose watchwords was to reject completely the promotional practices of the mass market and its primary goal of financial profit.

Regardless of the inconsistencies, a major effort of promotion and celebrity-formation was taking place. Switching metaphors, this was the left hand of modernism, safely hidden from the right although seemingly much busier, that indulged in the writing of introductions, prefaces, critical essays and manifestoes, memoirs and autobiographies, often with strategic promotional effect in mind. Overseeing all was the loose cohesion of the fabled few, the chosen: anointing each other as "representative" of the truly "new," corresponding with—complementing and complimenting—each other, collecting each other in what Jaffe calls "polemical anthologies" designed not to sample a genre or survey a historical period but to set forth a literary and critical program. The thrust of this elaborate promotional effort was to establish a celebrity of modernism.

While the two hands of celebrity never quite meet, another claim, less a contradiction than a paradox, was the insistence on—indeed it was one of the major criteria of what literary art should be—the impersonality of the work: the disappearance of the historical, biographical artist, that very artist whose name, at the same time, was being celebrated into adjectival status. The truth of the paradox lay in the artist's reappearance in the work, but no longer in what is usually meant by his or her identity: a reappearance, that is, not so much *in* the work but *as* the work. As Jaffe puts it, the writer became at once "dispossessed and enhanced, resolved with authorial selfhood damned at the same time as the mark of the author is sacralized" (54).

The supreme example of this, as Jonathan Goldman emphasizes in *Modernism Is the Literature of Celebrity*, is James Joyce's *Ulysses*. Here we read the writer disembodied into a supreme authoritative voice, seed of the work and its fruit, an instance of complete mastery. The writer is indeed a species set apart, as modernist dismay with mass-produced art implied, but in fact the artist *as* the work has no real existence anterior to it. Rather, Goldman writes, the artist is "created simultaneously with the text."[5] At this point the autonomy of the text takes on mystical dimensions—what Jaffe calls the "bogus sublime" (9–10)—the desired effect of which is to remove the work further from the world of the reader while still claiming to exercise a serious rendering and critique of that world. The work encloses and is enclosed by its creation. It urges on the reader the force of its face value while resisting interpretation of it. In part this is because of the difficulty of understanding it (in some ways the most celebrated quality of the modern), but also because of the gap between style and narrative, the sense that the narrative "reality" comes to us already appropriated, distilled before the reader takes hold of it. Adding to this is the sense, as Goldman argues, that "meaning [is] unrelated to the diegesis—the events and characters that compose the narrative" (13). It is as if readers were guests at a rite from an exotic alien culture rather than consumers of a product, free to discern and judge.

In *Ulysses,* Goldman writes, "Leopold Bloom 'knows' about 1904 Dublin (diegetic) but does not 'know' he is cast as a modern Odysseus (extradiegetic)" (61) journeying through it, wholly inscribed in a Homeric epic the particulars of which Joyce identified in a guide that he circulated to potential reviewers of the novel. Similarly, if on a lesser scale, in Faulkner's *As I Lay Dying,* Addie and Darl and Dewey Dell and Vardaman do not recognize the epic breadth of their bizarre journey, nor completely comprehend the extraordinary rhetoric gifted to them that constantly drifts back to a voice deeply *as* yet not *of* their created being.

In the course of such splitting of the narrative from its execution, the work becomes writer and interpreter incarnate, challenging readers to appreciate before understanding, to lift their level of attention to a new dimension of the work as icon: numinous, other than themselves. For an example of such respect, even reverence, we need go no further than Faulkner himself: "You should approach Joyce's *Ulysses* as the illiterate Baptist preacher approaches the Old Testament: with faith."[6]

This elevation of the literary text to virtually otherworldly status is, of course, its great limitation for many readers. Recognizing the promotional strategies coexistent with that elevation may make it more approachable or less, a sign of modernism's acknowledgment of the necessities of the real world in which it has to circulate, or a sign of its hypocrisy, in which it claims independence of market forces even as, by making inaccessibility and a breach between the action of a work and its larger meaning the touchstones of excellence, it makes use of precisely those forces.[7]

I want to digress for a moment in order to try to exemplify what celebrity, in its most intense forms, can be. Celebrity may be manufactured by self-promoting individuals and by institutions invested in that celebrity. Regardless of the process, however, there can be, even in the more familiar versions, a heightening of experience that in fact is moving in what look like magical ways. Perhaps this is what Leo Braudy is getting at when he writes: "The ease with which we allow ourselves to be absorbed by such images, the desire to be that way ourselves, confirms that the essential lure of the famous is that they are somehow more real than we and that our insubstantial physical reality needs that immortal substance for support."[8] If we ignore that element, that "immortal substance," I think we lose an important dimension of our subject, although in my example I invoke images that may have an exponential edge on even our most iconic writers.

There's a well-known story that when Marilyn Monroe went on a U.S. State Department tour of Korea to entertain American troops, she said to her husband at the time, Joe DiMaggio, following one of her shows, "Joe you never heard such cheering!" To which he replied, "Yes, I have."

Never having seen Marilyn Monroe in person, I turn to DiMaggio. For those who are too young or too remote from this U.S. celebrity, DiMaggio was to baseball what Monroe was to cinematic beauty, and both were to the mystery of celebrity. My example, however, is not a story of cheers at one more exhibition of celebrity performance, but a strange, even momentous, reversal, and an ensuing shock that reverses again in a kind of supreme acknowledgment of the original mystery.

It was 1951, in what proved to be DiMaggio's last year as a player, and he was enduring the great athlete's decline—age thirty-seven—all in a single season. My brother and I were once again at Yankee Stadium for a night game and saw DiMaggio make a mistake, not an error of the body, but a mental lapse, which was even more rare, almost unheard of. The Detroit Tigers were in town, and with one out in the seventh inning of a tied game, and a man on second base, a fly ball is hit to center field. DiMaggio catches it easily, puts his head down, and begins trotting toward the infield. He thinks it's the third out and the end of the inning. The runner on second has tagged up, feigns a run to third just to draw a throw, when he sees DiMaggio, still head down, loping in, and he takes off. He rounds third base and heads for home. By the time DiMaggio realizes what is happening, it's too late. The runner scores, and Detroit is now ahead.

It was the sound following that I remember. No cheering, not even from Detroit fans, and no booing, not for DiMaggio, not in Yankee Stadium. But there is indeed a flood of sound. Not the white noise of unfocused sound, the sound of people voicing nothing but their indifferent presence. It is the sound of astonishment, disbelief, gathered into a single vocalization, growing louder and louder, the sound of celebrity vested in someone "more real than we" dissolving into ordinary humanness, unworded wonder as testament to the height from which it has fallen. The ball player stands absolutely still in the vast lighted expanse of Yankee Stadium centerfield, bent at the waist, hands on his knees, surrounded by still ascending sound that has already broken through the mental mistake that aroused it, with nowhere to go but an implicit celebration.

As Faulkner once wrote in a far removed context, "they are not to lose it."

Years later I met him, DiMaggio, in a New York hotel lobby. I remember that, too, probably the way Faulkner's Aunt Jenny remembers "dancing a valse in Baltimore in '58" with the cavalry commander Jeb Stuart. But that's another story.

And William Faulkner? Where is he in this culture of celebrity-making? We are talking about a writer fashioning an image, a public representation of himself in relationship to his condition as a writer and to the fiction he writes.

Faulkner's studied remoteness, amply verified, from what we think of as the literary world is now part of his celebrity, possibly its promotional center. He did not know well any writers or critics, his most sustained professional literary relationship, apart from that with his various publishers and editors, being the correspondence with Malcolm Cowley during the compilation of *The Portable Faulkner* in 1945–46. Except for a period of six months in New Orleans in 1925, when he associated with a number of writers, artists, and critics, he belonged to nothing like a coterie. From the age of five, he lived in the small town of Oxford, Mississippi, with various forays outward: Canada,

New Orleans, Europe, New York, Hollywood, Charlottesville, Japan. These are all pointed, purposeful expeditions: for experience, for bread, for service in the Canadian Royal Air Force, for two spring semesters at the University of Virginia, for several U.S. State Department tours. But home—his family, his society, the particular southern world where he did the bulk of his writing—is Oxford, Lafayette County, north Mississippi. While clearly one of the material sources of some of his greatest fiction, "the postage stamp of native soil" (*LIG* 255), it is far from any of the places and people where literary modernism was being written or read or talked about. Moreover, Faulkner seems to have been comfortable in inhabiting that isolation.

Nevertheless, despite this self-imposed remoteness, not only in terms of place but, even more important, in relation to the writers and critics with whom he shared a major literary movement, Faulkner did in fact participate in modernist celebrity, if largely in ways that were oddly consistent with the life he chose to live and the way in which he pursued his career as a writer. With his fourth novel, *The Sound and the Fury,* he created a distinctive literary style that clearly met one of the requirements of modernism and modernist celebrity, what Jaffe calls the modern "imprimatur"—the way in which "the modernist literary object bears the stylistic stamp of its producer prominently . . . turn[ing] the author into a formal artifact, fusing it to the text as a reified signature of value" (20).[9] He was familiar not only with the "upstream" work of the writers in the United States, England, Ireland, and France, but with the products of their "downstream" work as well: the critical essays, the manifestoes, the introductions and prefaces that were defining and sectioning off at least one version of the modernist revolution.

To be sure, much of what characterizes modernist celebrity-making Faulkner ignores. Once his career is in motion, and he is no longer writing regular reviews for the *Mississippian,* as he did while a special student at the university, or essays for the *Double Dealer* in 1925 while in New Orleans, he does not write critical or programmatic essays on contemporary writers, does not edit or collect, or join himself to any group, proclaims no manifestoes. His correspondence with other writers and critics, part of what constituted the "collaborative" work toward modernist celebrity, is minimal, except for the one with Cowley.[10]

What does he do then—and how does it compare with modernist celebrity-making going on elsewhere? There are two notable examples, both of which gained a fair amount of attention, although they were not always recognized as the self-promotional strategies they were intended to be. The first is the introduction, widely regarded as infamous, he wrote for the Modern Library edition of *Sanctuary*, published in 1932.

As Joseph Blotner puts it, the introduction did *Sanctuary* a "great disservice" (268), and that's putting it mildly. For him and other Faulkner readers, it amounted to an authorial blacklisting of the novel: an apology for the original version he was *not* publishing and condescension toward the revised version that was replacing it. Currently confined, in Noel Polk's Corrected Text edition, to the editorial apparatus at the back of the book—a historical footnote—the introduction no longer serves Faulkner's purpose in writing it. That purpose, I would argue, is not inconsistent with what had already become some of the tried and true strategies of literary celebratizing. It gives high praise to the writer and his earlier work and, through some tricky argument combining shame and pride, to the novel at hand, as well as making a critical statement that distinguishes serious "horrific" fiction from its purely commercial counterpart.

The introduction is actually less about *Sanctuary* than the two novels that surround it. After quickly announcing the purpose of "this" book "written three years ago"—"to make money"—Faulkner spends most of his time discussing *The Sound and the Fury* and *As I Lay Dying*. The first is one of the books that "got published and not bought," and Faulkner says nothing to indicate that he believes the second will have a different fate. Moreover, he does not care. The value of these novels has nothing to do with their sales nor, it seems, with any specifically literary qualities he can point to. It has to do solely with the spirit in which they are written. *The Sound and the Fury* is a triumph of endurance and sacrifice—"I had just written my guts" into it—unremarked until finished "because I had done it for pleasure." *As I Lay Dying* is a triumph of focus and discipline, written in the most uncongenial circumstances. Working a twelve-hour night shift as a coal passer in a boiler plant, Faulkner "invented a table out of a wheelbarrow." Between 12:00 midnight and 4:00 a.m., when the need for heat subsided, "I wrote *As I Lay Dying* in six weeks without changing a word," then sent it to his publisher, Hal Smith, saying: "by it I would stand or fall."

And what is the achievement of this writing, the sacrifice, the discipline, the long haul or the short visionary burst? Having not even considered the likelihood of profitable sales—thus adhering to one modernist celebrity credo—Faulkner aligns his work with another, more positive one: the autonomy of art, as measured by its utter indifference to anything but the integrity of its conception and execution. He makes no mention of the excellence of the product, no claim of the modernist triad: Originality, Mastery, Scarcity. There is only the psychic and emotional condition of creation, the absolute dedication of the artist: to make this thing.

In the midst of such self-celebration, Faulkner introduces the devil of lucre; made filthy it appears only when it becomes the purpose of art. What is wrong with the first version of *Sanctuary*? It is "the most horrific tale I could imagine and wrote it in about three weeks." The revised version is at least as horrific, and apparently the six weeks to write *As I Lay Dying* sounds like the testimony of a writer to whom a novel has miraculously descended intact—"I knew when I put down the first word what the last word of that would be"[11]—whereas three weeks on *Sanctuary* suggests the haste with which one handles, if he must, carrion.[12]

Surprisingly—we wonder just how surprisingly—the galleys of the novel that presumably would put Faulkner and Hal Smith in jail arrive. The return of *Sanctuary* comes across as an instance of psychoanalytic repression. Faulkner committed the heinous act, violating the high motives of modernist art, and then forgot he had committed it. The galleys return like a nightmare of guilt, but this time, as in classic psychoanalytic transference, he is going to replay that heinous act and, as Freud put it, "lead the revived conflict to a better outcome than that which ended in repression."[13]

The novel in galleys he says is "terrible." Given that he will carry its "horrific" nature fully into the revision, it is clear, as Noel Polk and Frederick Karl have persuasively demonstrated,[14] that Faulkner's decision to revise depends less on the work's perversity than on his concern with structure and focus: primarily to replace the centrality of Horace with that of Temple and Popeye. What Faulkner mentions in the introduction, however, is only the money—the novel's "immediate purpose"—which also reemerges, like a disease that still lives in the contaminated carcass: "It might sell; maybe 10,000 of them will buy it."

Faulkner is shuttling back and forth, like a man caught between good and bad angels. He confirms his integrity—"I had to pay for the privilege of rewriting it"—and then turns to the revision with an altered motive: not the 10,000 sales, but to produce "something which would not shame *The Sound and the Fury* and *As I Lay Dying* too much and I made a fair job." With *Sanctuary* Faulkner boasts of his talent, in addition to his commitment. Talent is what the writer needs when the purpose has been compromised.[15]

The three novels now have a curious coexistence, the works by which "I would stand or fall," primarily owing to the pain and pleasure of their creation, and the revised, horrific tale, still smelling of the hope for profit. Not only co-existing, however, but sharing to a "fair" degree whatever is the achievement of the first two. Faulkner seems to be working both sides of the "great divide" of the mass market and high modernism, but in fact he is simply walking back and forth on the same side, with an occasional glance across the street. His self-promotion in fact reaches a new height. It is one thing to extract pure gold from the ground; it is quite another to perform the alchemy of drawing it from base metal. He can even afford now to return, this master of comedy as well as horror, to the pitchman mode: "and I hope you will buy it and tell your friends and I hope they will buy it too." He has not only preserved his elitist status, but has demonstrated how the modernist can display both hands at the same time, indulge in what is normally regarded as a market-oriented genre, and still come out smelling like a genius.[16]

Faulkner's second most significant effort at self-promotion in the modernist vein comes not in a formal essay or preface, but in response to a question raised by a student in a class at the University of Mississippi in 1947. He repeated these remarks several times over the next ten years with greater elaboration, but essentially making the same point, which ultimately became as well known—and in some quarters as infamous—as his introduction to *Sanctuary*. Asked to rank his literary contemporaries, Faulkner initially named five, but ultimately focused only on three: Thomas Wolfe, whom he ranked first, Hemingway last, and Faulkner in between. Wolfe, whom, he later admitted, "I haven't read much of . . . one or two of his stories. I've opened his books and read pages or paragraphs" (*FIU* 206), is only a substitute for Faulkner. Essentially Faulkner is matching Hemingway against himself, and the criteria have to do solely with the ambition of the writer rather than the excellence of the work.

The criteria he brings to bear are comparable to those he uses in the introduction to *Sanctuary*. Instead of talking about having "written my guts" into one novel or completing another between shifts of shoveling coal, Faulkner, using Wolfe as his representative, speaks of trying to "do the greatest of the impossible . . . to reduce all human experience to literature" (*LIG* 81); "I think that the writer must want primarily perfection. . . . He can't do it in his life because he can't be as brave as he wishes he might, he can't always be as honest as he wishes he might, but here's the chance to hope that when he has pencil and paper he can make something as perfect as he dreamed it to be" (*LIG* 180).

For Faulkner, Hemingway is the lesser writer owing to a lack of ambition, of daring, of the desire for perfection: "Hemingway had sense enough to find a method which he could control and didn't need or didn't have to, wasn't driven enough by his private demon to waste himself in trying to do more than that. So, he has done consistently probably the most solid work of all of us. But it wasn't the splendid magnificent bust that Wolfe [i.e., Faulkner] made" (*FIU* 143–44).

Using what he once called "splendid failure" (*LIG* 238) to correspond with greatness, Faulkner is making the case for what he regards as the distinctive quality of modernism: to capture in literature the very essence of human experience, perhaps "the uncreated conscience of my race" (Joyce 253), to pursue in art a perfection lacking in life—ultimately to designate merely "solid work" as evidence of a writer content to "not make mistakes," to "not risk as we've risked," to "know his limitations and [have] enough sense to stay within them" (*LIG* 122, 225). Although Faulkner always insisted that "this judgment had nothing to do with the value of the work" (*LIG* 179), it had everything to do with the value of writing it.

The most unusual versions of Faulkner's celebrity-making are to be found in the self-representations he chose in his public behavior: his inclination to create masks for himself, ranging from performances acted out for the benefit of his hometown of Oxford, where he lived and wrote for nearly sixty years, to gross exaggeration or complete invention of his experience that he related in his frequent interviews, beginning as early as 1926 and extending to 1962, two months before his death. With the exception of the consistent distinction he drew in interviews between his writing and Hemingway's, in most of these public appearances he cultivates a celebrity of defense, a protection of himself and protection of his work.

The roles were multiple—wounded RAF pilot, English dandy, bohemian poet, town bum, bootlegger, gun-runner, aviation barnstormer, father of several illegitimate children, lastly the busy farmer who occasionally did some writing on the side—but the chief aim is surprisingly singular: to separate himself from his identity as a writer, and by extension from the fiction that bears his name. His form of public promotion, that is, is a ruse of presence, a presence-as-absence if you will, but unlike the absences of writers like Salinger and Pynchon, Faulkner's is in fact constantly present, "out there" as raconteur, as perfectly visible if not easily approached citizen of Oxford, and as participant in scores of published interviews and "conversations." This is not only Faulkner's version of modernist "impersonality," the absence of the merely human creator, but the representation of a self that virtually *has nothing to do with writing*—certainly nothing to do with writing the fiction of William Faulkner. In a word, he puts the "purloined letter" that is Faulkner in plain sight. The fix, however, is already in; the letter divulges nothing. Poe's Dupin is wasting his time, since "the honor of a personage of most exalted station" is perfectly safe.[17]

Among the roles, the most frequently presented and certainly the most widely known was that of an RAF fighter pilot who saw active duty in World War I. Testimony to the popularity of this particular mask is the fact that when Malcolm Cowley—who had never met the writer—was putting together *The Portable Faulkner* in 1945, he knew the story and fully expected to use it in his introduction.[18]

If, as I suggested previously, one intention of his masks was to protect his personal life from external probing, the larger purpose was to protect his work from any attempt to use that life as a point of entry into the meaning of that work. An interesting example of Faulkner's response when it appeared that the combat flier mask and the fiction might meet occurred during the making of *The Portable Faulkner.* Cowley wanted very much to include material on Faulkner's World War I combat experience. Faulkner requested that he not do so, but simply say that Faulkner "belonged to RAF 1918" (*FCF* 77), which, of course, given his membership as a cadet in the Canadian Royal Air Force, was true. Cowley thought the experience of combat was crucial, and had referred to it in the first paragraph of his introduction. As the correspondence continued, with Cowley urging Faulkner to allow him to use the material, Faulkner finally lost his temper: "Dear Cowley: Yours at hand. You're going to bugger up a fine dignified distinguished book with that war business" (*FCF* 82).

Why Faulkner's resistance? He had been telling the story for twenty-five years, and it had appeared in print several times, including a semi-fictional version in Sherwood Anderson's "A Meeting South" (1925) and a reference work of 1942: *Twentieth Century Authors* (*FCF* 71). Did he anticipate the wide readership the volume would eventually have? Was he worried about exposure? There was one major difference, however, between *The Portable* and all his tale-telling, and it may well have been what accounted for Faulkner's angry protest. Cowley's introduction would not simply state what had been stated many times. We know from the comments Cowley inserts between letters to and from Faulkner that he regarded Faulkner's combat as virtually a thematic template for his career: "I had come to think of Faulkner . . . as being among the 'wounded writers' of his generation, with Hemingway and others. It was hard for me to believe that his vivid stories about aviators in France . . . and his portraits of spiritually maimed veterans, living corpses, in *Soldier's Pay* and *Sartoris* were based on anything but direct experience" (*FCF* 72).

Assuming that this approach was apparent in the draft of Cowley's initial introduction (all we have is the opening paragraph) and that Faulkner read it, then perhaps he feared that the chief purpose of his masquerade would be subverted, which was to keep the author at a distance, irrelevant to the fiction. Rather than a barrier separating writer and work, the mask would become a bridge into the work—ironically, a bridge that was pure fabrication: not only an authorial identity on which to hang interpretation but a carefully constructed false one.

It is in the interviews that Faulkner's presentation of himself and his work are closest to the intentions (if not the specific means) of the high modernists: to separate himself as writer from the fiction and to provide instruction on how to appreciate it. His is not an easy fiction to read, Faulkner well knows—just as he knows, "modernistically," that his difficult style is his trademark, his signature, his imprimatur. But the correct approach to it, he constantly claims, is remarkably simple, and that simplicity is the core of what Faulkner has to say about his work. Like all his screens, it is a strategy of defense, a way of divorcing himself from the fiction by refusing to provide any stated intention that might be commensurate with its richness, that would constitute an identity that has written the fiction, or that, in the aftermath, has any special privilege in the interpretation of it.

Two aspects of the strategy are particularly prominent. One is his use of what Nancy Hale called "predictable" responses: "as if he had constructed a carapace for himself out of set phrases" (*LIG* 138). We are familiar with these, in some cases sufficiently to recite them ourselves: the fourfold failure of *The Sound and the Fury*—I tried with this brother, then that one, and that one, and tried myself and I failed but I couldn't throw it away etc. etc. (*FIU* 1); the fact that all his fiction has "failed" and will continue to fail—*The Sound and the Fury* being the "one that failed the most tragically and the most splendidly" (*FIU* 77); the tragedy of Joe Christmas, who didn't know what he was, and there was no way possible in life for him to find out (*FIU* 72); or Sutpen, the man "who wanted a son and got too many, so many that they destroyed him" (*FIU* 71).

Faulkner seizes every opportunity to recite these interpretations, like welcome pauses in the stream of questions when he is convinced that he has at hand a good enough answer—not necessarily the best answer, if there could be such a thing, but one that will do. These are more, however, than moments of welcome respite. In some cases, they are interpretations of a character or a work that Faulkner is not about to read again. Nor does he believe it's necessary to reread them, if all that's at stake is to offer another interpretation. Interpretation of character and theme, not to mention the symbols so attractive to readers in the 1940s and 1950s, are of course what students and interviewers are anxious for the writer to elucidate. Faulkner is prepared to oblige them, but this is not what he's really after, and so he merely repeats what he has said many times before. Moreover, he is quite genial about interpretations different from his own: "Q: Then you couldn't go so far as to say, for example, that Darl is the Quentin of the Bundrens and that Cash is the Jason of the Bundrens. A: Well, you could if that is any pleasure to you" (*FIU* 121).

Faulkner's repetitions are part of his general tendency to rid the fiction of "extractable meaning," something that can stand above the work, expressible independently of it, as if forcing its language into purposes that only dull its power as a fictional rendering of reality. On the one hand, he chooses the positive tactic of putting what seem to be tried and true interpretations into position, like a plug in the dike, momentarily finessing the flood of interpretation itself. On the other hand, he often chooses a more negative tactic of blocking the desire of readers to read too much into the work: too much of what Faulkner believes does not belong there, is not what the fiction is for. Faulkner's characteristic warnings against this approach to his fiction are his use of the adverbs "just" and "simply" and their equivalents. Especially notable are his references to the "tools," the "axes," the "background" that make up the "lumber room" from which he drew the imagery and to a large extent the material of his fiction, as if these too were not quite it, not the figure in the carpet he wants his readers to see and to feel.

Q. "Mr. Faulkner, would you care to say anything about the allegorical function of the horse in *A Fable*? He seems to have some very complex and interesting characteristics.
A. "Not to me, no. That was simply another struggle between man and his conscience and his environment. The horse was simply a tool—that is, that foul and filthy Cockney hostler was still capable of love for something." (*FIU* 63)

Q. What symbolic meaning did you give to the dates of *The Sound and the Fury*?
A. Now there's a matter of hunting around in the carpenter's shop to find a tool that will make a better chicken-house. And probably—I'm sure it was quite instinctive that I picked out Easter. (*FIU* 68)

Q. [On "The Bear"] Mr. Faulkner, you seem to put so much meaning in the hunt. Could you tell us just why you hunted when you were a little boy, or what meaning the hunt has to you?
A. The hunt was simply a symbol of pursuit. Most of anyone's life is a pursuit of something. . . . This was a symbolization of the pursuit which is a normal part of anyone's life, while he stays alive, told in terms which were familiar to me and dramatic to me. The protagonist could have been anything else besides that bear. (*FIU* 271)

Q. [The issue of Christian symbolism in *The Sound and the Fury* has come up. Faulkner denies he has consciously used it.] But Benjy, for example, is thirty-three years old, the traditional age of Christ at death.

A. Yes. That was a ready-made axe to use, but it was just one of several tools. (*FIU* 17)

Q. Mr. Faulkner, did you intend any Christ symbolism in *Light in August*?
A. No, that's a matter of reaching into the lumber room to get out something which seems to the writer the most effective way to tell what he is trying to tell. (*FIU* 117)

Q. In your Pulitzer prize–winning work *A Fable,* you wrote about the resurrection of a soldier. The Japanese writers consider that this is a new trend in your work. [Do you?]
A. No, I don't think so. I simply used a formula, a proven formula in our western culture to tell something which I wanted to tell, but that's no new trend. (*LIG* 99)

The lumber room, tools, axes, formulas. This is not facileness on Faulkner's part and not condescension either. Behind what might seem to be a certain glibness or even a willful, know-nothing refusal to acknowledge fully the imagery of his work, Faulkner is revealing a deep commitment to one of the chief qualities of modernist celebrity. The *material* of the fiction is not what is major. Material is what fictions are *made of;* it is the available language of an experience that is somehow more than its expression, a "more" that readers must attend to.

Q. [on the use of crucifixion in several novels]
A. Remember, the writer must write out of his background. He must write out of what he knows and the Christian legend is part of any Christian's background, especially the background of a country boy, a Southern country boy. . . . I grew up with that. I assimilated that, took that in without even knowing it. It's just there. It has nothing to do with how much of it I might believe or disbelieve—it's just there. (*FIU* 85–86)

It doesn't matter what I believe. It's "just" "simply" *there.* How far can Faulkner take this? At the moment he is talking about imagery, much of it Christian. But for Faulkner, what is *there* extends much further. At the United States Military Academy, 1962:

> **Q.** Sir, what is your opinion of the value of modern literature, of the writing about woman's suffrage and confusion of roles as present in modern literature?
> **A.** I look on them as the tools, the material of the trade; that is, they are the conditions which the writer can use in order to portray the human heart in some simple struggle with itself, with others, or with its environment. The sociological qualities are only, in my opinion, coincidental to the story. . . . Integration, segregation or the sociological conditions are simply tools which the writer uses in order to show the human heart in the struggle of that dilemma—in the battle which is any story.[19]

The material is tools, and includes social causes: integration, segregation, woman's suffrage, as well as conditions such as role confusion or religious traditions: they are what Faulkner calls "background"—and they're all in the lumber room. The important thing is not to attend exclusively to the material that is transferred into the fiction. *Watch the transferral itself. Watch the making into fiction.* It's not the material that matters, he is saying, any more than *I* do—at least the "I" as World War I fighter pilot, as resident of Oxford, or, for that matter, as the authorized interpreter of his work.

Does Faulkner lack what we think of as critical sense? Or even moral sense? Is he so much the pure novelist that he will not disturb the fiction with analysis? A better way of putting it is to say that he is practicing his version of modernist celebrity. He does not want to give you a "way in" because it will replace the work, the material supplant the making, the vehicle of entrance control the reading. There are no ways in, although there may be a *being* in. What he is saying with the "justs" and the "simplys," the references to axes and tools and lumber rooms, is this: *watch what the work is doing,* the work in which, as modern celebrity would have it, "I" exist, the "I," as Goldman writes, who is "created simultaneously with the text" (65). The author is as accessible, as worthy as the work, and as lasting: no more, no less.

It is not that the fiction lacks meaning or interpretation of the world in which it exists, but that its meanings must emerge out of some engagement between readers and a work that is coming into being with them—a work that is more and other than the "materials" of its making. That was the modernists' great gamble, the wager of all their strategies of making and celebrity, that the work must suffice: "The sum and history of my life . . . He made the books and he died."

* * *

Faulkner's status as a celebrity and his attitude toward it changed radically after he was awarded the Nobel Prize in 1950 (for the year 1949). This was an instance of celebrity bestowed on the writer, not sought after. Although he seems to have been aware that he was being considered for the prize, there is no evidence of Faulkner working the strategies of self-promotion other modernists writers had employed, or that the ones peculiarly his own—occasional oblique self-praise combined with a habit of conspicuously public absence—were generating fresh attention in literary circles. While there is little question but that *The Portable Faulkner* played an important role in enhancing Faulkner's reputation to the point where he would be considered for the Nobel Prize, it is also important to point out that the idea for *The Portable* was very much Cowley's, who had considered it soon after he had finished *The Portable Hemingway* in July 1945 (20).[20]

Although the matter of authorial agency in achieving celebrity is not relevant here, the story of Faulkner and celebrity bestowed is a fascinating coda as it relates to the last dozen years of his life. It is the story of how Faulkner responded to that celebrity, what he did with it, and how different that response was from the ways he had earlier treated any kind of public interest in him and his work. With the award of the Nobel Prize, Faulkner assumed a new responsibility—not simply the determination he had always felt to do his work as well as his talent and his drive for excellence would enable him, but a responsibility to *represent* communities and institutions that he had never considered before as part of his task as an artist. As a Nobel Prize laureate, Faulkner was no longer simply the individual tormented by demons, a "vessel" for "God or gods or whoever it was, selected me."[21] He had been recognized as a member of communities whom he felt obligated to represent: to speak *for* them and *to* them.

One was the community of the South, once more in the eye of a storm of racial conflict; another was the United States, embroiled in a Cold War that would last for decades; a third was the community of writers, with whom he may have felt the closest tie. In a series of trajectories that began with his Nobel Prize speech and continued for the rest of his life, Faulkner became a public person, not as the screen of his absence, but as a very particular presence: the American southern writer, the representative of specific constituencies that were collectively being honored by the prize and on whose behalf and for whose enlightenment he decided he must now speak.

Faulkner's efforts with regard to the South and the United States are well documented and have been discussed at length, especially the South. In a large number of public letters, speeches, and essays,[22] Faulkner held, for the most part with remarkable consistency, what he regarded as a moderate, middle-of-the road view, the essence of which was that integration in the South was morally right and necessary, but that southerners, rather than the federal government, must bring it about.[23] As middle-of-the-road stances often go, he managed to offend both northern liberals and southern conservatives, and by the end of his life he and his wife were planning to move permanently to Charlottesville, Virginia, where his daughter and her family lived.

Faulkner's multiple travels as a goodwill ambassador of the State Department were largely without controversy, once Faulkner learned to overcome his great shyness and the serious drinking to which it could lead. By most reports, he performed the task well, graciously and cooperatively, especially when it took the form of Q and A in formal settings rather than in social gatherings. His 1955 visit to Japan, still under U.S. occupation, during which Faulkner stressed the similarities he saw between the histories and cultures of the South and Japan, was regarded as exceptionally successful: "The U.S. Department of State concluded that the mission had done more to better Japanese-American cultural relations than any other single act of the department" (Blotner 608).

My chief concern is with Faulkner's Nobel Prize speech, which he directed primarily to the young writers of the world, and which reveals a conception of modernism and the modernist writer that, for Faulkner, was always at the core of their celebrity. He indicates this in the first line of his acceptance speech: "I hold the award was made, not to me, but to my work," continuing the modernist credo regarding the relation between writer and work. After drawing that distinction, and adding that he will "find a dedication for the money part of it commensurate with the purpose and significance of its origin," he turns to the "acclaim," the celebrity bestowed, which he will now use to speak for and to instruct the young writers of the world (*ESPL* 119–21).

The instruction is clear and candid. The writer must not yield to the fear that Faulkner believes has infected the world, the fear of worldwide disaster: "When will I be blown up?" The fear, we might infer, stems from the conflicts of nations, the current political order of the world, the external conditions that have come to rule our daily lives. Faulkner, however, does not identify the causes of the fear, nor does he consider how their power might be reduced. This is not his purview, nor is it the responsibility of the community he is addressing. The problems that bring nations to the brink of nuclear war are like the problems of integration, segregation, the sociological situation—they are the material, the tools of the writer.

So he does not call for peace, for diplomacy, for tolerance, for greater understanding. He instructs writers that they must go inward: "the problems of the human heart in conflict with itself which alone can make good writing because only that is worth writing about." The "universal physical fear" as well as its reversal, the realization that "the basest of all things is to be afraid"—they must be learned and then dispelled, "leaving no room in [the writer's] workshop for anything but the old verities and truths of the heart." The specific truths that writers must attend to have nothing to do with the fear of annihilation or with the way we might get rid of the conditions that have led to it.

Faulkner offers no program, no social or political agenda. The truths are "old" and "universal," "lacking which any story is ephemeral and doomed." They are, for Faulkner, the causes and consequences of the heart in conflict with itself: "love and honor and pity and pride and compassion and sacrifice": the great human emotions that have not healed the conflict but in fact have often sustained it, dignified, even glorified it, whatever the terrible costs. When love and honor and pride are at the core of the conflict, then pity and compassion must attend them, paid to the sacrifice that conflict demands. The outcomes of the heart in conflict with itself and the desires that have inspired it will always be "griefs" and "scars," redeemable only if they refuse to be "defeats in which nobody loses anything of value, [or] victories without hope, and, worst of all, without pity or compassion."

This human heart in internal conflict not only endures but prevails; it is immortal. It is a soul, "capable of compassion and sacrifice and endurance," and it is "the writer's duty . . . to write about" it, "reminding" readers of what exactly it is in human beings that must endure and prevail, always with the accompanying, confirming costs of grief, scars, victory, and defeat.

Was the speech a refutation of Faulkner's own work? There is no reason to think so. Is there a major Faulkner novel that does not overflow with what

Faulkner called the verities and truths of the human heart? We find ourselves astonished, even horrified, at the depth, the distortion, the madness, of love and honor and pride expended, at the pity and compassion we find echoing in ourselves, at how incredibly much his people are made to bear, are ready to bear. Faulkner's charge to writers is hardly to sweeten their work with false optimism, which can all too easily be "not of the heart but of the glands," but to write about what truly matters so that what is lost can be seen, must be seen to have had value, and that what is won, when it is won, leaves only the promise—it is enough—of hope.

While self-promotion is minimal here, the modernist credo of the work abides. What happens in the work is distinguishable from its matter, its tools, as it is from the identity and experience of the carpenter prior to entry into the workshop. What the work celebrates is its capacity to put everything aside in order to descend to the human heart, to encounter again the grandly human emotions that await their latest literary evocation—the testimony not only of their survival, but their triumph.

But to return once more to what Faulkner's sense of his relationship to the writer of his work generally was, when he did not need to exploit the writer's acclaim as a "pinnacle" from which to fulfill the responsibilities his celebrity had acquired. For reasons that I suspect we will never learn, he felt it necessary to erect a barrier between "himself" and the "writer"—a separation that was something other than the modernist desire to isolate the work from its mundane origin, to endow it with a mystery commensurate with its distinctive order of expression. For Faulkner, the man and the writer were virtually different species, and their separateness was necessary so that in each of these identities, however he had happened upon them, he could be what he needed to be.

Robert Linscott, one of Faulkner's editors at Random House, describes a scene on Fifth Avenue in New York in the early 1950s, as he and Faulkner were window shopping. A woman recognized Faulkner and rushed up to him: "Oh, I know who you are. You're William Faulkner. You look just like your pictures." Faulkner replied, "coolly but courteously, 'Madame, you're mistaken. I am not William Faulkner. But I have been told before that I look like him'" (*Conversations* 98).

NOTES

Epigraph: William Faulkner to Malcolm Cowley, February 11, 1949, in *The Faulkner-Cowley File: Letters and Memories, 1944–1962* (New York: Viking, 1966), 126. Hereafter cited parenthetically as *FCF*.

1. James Joyce, *A Portrait of the Artist as a Young Man: The Definitive Text Corrected from the Dublin Holograph* (New York: Viking, 1964), 215. Hereafter cited parenthetically.

2. For a thorough analysis of this perspective, see Pierre Bourdieu, "The Author's Point of View," in *The Rules of Art: Genesis and Structure of the Literary Field*, trans. Susan Emanuel (Stanford, CA: Stanford University Press, 1995), 214–82.

3. Pierre Bourdieu, *The Field of Cultural Production: Essays on Art and Literature*, ed. Randal Johnson (New York: Columbia University Press, 1993), 37.

4. Aaron Jaffe, *Modernism and the Culture of Celebrity* (Cambridge: Cambridge University Press, 2005), 69. Hereafter cited parenthetically.

5. Jonathan Goldman, *Modernism Is the Literature of Celebrity* (Austin: University of Texas Press, 2011), 65. Hereafter cited parenthetically.

6. William Faulkner, *Lion in the Garden: Interviews with William Faulkner 1926–1962*, ed. James B. Meriwether and Michael Millgate (New York: Random House, 1968), 250. Hereafter cited parenthetically as *LIG*.

7. For analysis of the differences in degree if not in kind between the world of U.S. literary celebrity from the 1980s on and that of modern celebrity in the first half of the century, see Joe Moran, *Star Authors: Literary Celebrity in America* (London: Pluto, 2000), particularly the chapter "The Reign of Hype: The Contemporary Star System," and his delineation of the extension of "promotion" to "publicity."

8. Leo Braudy, *The Frenzy of Renown: Fame and Its History* (New York: Oxford University Press, 1986), 6.

9. James F. English and John Frow expand what Jaffe calls the imprimatur into its more vulgar yet complementary offshoot, the "brand": "Rather than forming contrasting regimes of value, the aesthetics of the signature and of the brand are successive but complementary orders, where the latter is at once more explicitly commercial in its orientation and yet more openly concerned with the value of the signature (that is, of authorial presence). This is the source of the paradox that informs it: that it constitutes a (further, enhanced) commercialization of something that is, in principle, beyond considerations of commercial value. The authorial brand name, the name as a mark of trade and of quality control, undermines its own first premise" (James F. English and John Frow, "Literary Authorship and Celebrity Culture," in *A Concise Companion to Contemporary British Fiction*, ed. James F. English [Malden, MA: Blackwell, 2006], 52).

10. Promotion of the early Faulkner was primarily in the hands of his fellow Oxonian Phil Stone. Except for the poems themselves, *The Marble Faun* was Stone's project: its typing, publishing, and selling, as well as its promotion (for details, see Joseph Blotner, *Faulkner: A Biography* [Jackson: University Press of Mississippi, 2005], 116–25; hereafter cited parenthetically).

11. William Faulkner, *Faulkner in the University: Class Conferences at the University of Virginia 1957–1958*, ed. Frederick L. Gwynn and Joseph L. Blotner (New York: Vintage, 1965), 207. Hereafter cited parenthetically as *FIU*.

12. As Philip Cohen points out, the original *Sanctuary* took at least four months, not three weeks, to write (Philip Cohen, "'A Cheap Idea . . . Deliberately Conceived to Make Money': The Biographical Context of William Faulkner's Introduction to *Sanctuary*," *Faulkner Journal* 3 [Spring 1988]: 55).

13. Sigmund Freud, *Introductory Lectures on Psychoanalysis*, vol. 16 of *The Standard Edition of the Complete Psychological Works of Sigmund Freud*, ed. and trans. James Strachey (London: Hogarth, 1963), 438.

14. Noel Polk, afterword to *Sanctuary: The Original Text*, by William Faulkner, ed. Polk. (New York: Random House, 1981), 293–306; Frederick R. Karl, *William Faulkner: American Writer* (New York: Ballantine, 1989), 351–75.

15. It is well to keep in mind that "a fair job" for Faulkner is high praise. His most commonly used expression of approval was the low-key "it's all right," as in his late review of Hemingway's *The Old Man and the Sea:* "His best. Time may show it to be the best single piece of any of us. . . . It's all right" (Faulkner, *Essays, Speeches, and Public Letters, Updated, with Material Never Before Collected in One Volume* [New York: Modern Library, 2004], 193; hereafter cited parenthetically as *ESPL*).

16. For an important and different account of the introduction, see Cohen, "A Cheap Idea," who argues that Faulkner is contemptuous of the novel and the readers and reviewers who praised it because they often did so at the expense of *The Sound and the Fury* and *As I Lay Dying*, owing to their much greater difficulty.

17. Noel Polk cites a particularly ironic instance of Faulkner seen and not seen, or rather a being-seen erased in its staging, in the 1952 *Omnibus* TV program: Faulkner is "looking into the TV camera that stands on the other side of that living room bastion, sitting comfortably in an easy chair throne, and saying: 'No pictures' to the tens of thousands of people watching that very picture" (Noel Polk, *Children of the Dark House: Text and Context in Faulkner* [Jackson: University Press of Mississippi, 1996], 243).

18. Why Faulkner clung to this particular mask for so long remains a mystery. To be sure, his fascination with his great-grandfather, William C. Falkner, who had served as an officer in the Civil War, may account for his need to go to war as a commissioned officer, and the Lost Cause era in which he grew up explains something of his longing for combat experience. But Faulkner's willingness to maintain the deception for most of his writing career, when he had significant attention and respect, if not compensation, as a writer, is puzzling. In a 1944 interview (not published until 1965) with Stephen Longstreet, whom he knew in Hollywood, he admitted he had not been a fighter pilot during World War I and expressed shame at his dishonesty. His explanation as to why he did it: "It seemed to me then the thing to do" (William Faulkner, *Conversations with William Faulkner*, ed. M. Thomas Inge [Jackson: University Press of Mississippi, 1999], 55; hereafter cited parenthetically as *Conversations*). For further discussion of Faulkner's imagined military experiences, see Donald Kartiganer, "'So I, Who Never Had

a War': William Faulkner, War, and the Modern Imagination," *Modern Fiction Studies* 44, no. 3 (1998): 619–45.

19. William Faulkner, *Faulkner at West Point*, ed. Joseph L. Fant III and Robert Ashley (Jackson: University Press of Mississippi, 2002), 49.

20. It should be noted, however, that Faulkner's response to Cowley's original idea of a long essay on his work and *The Portable* was enthusiastic, in both cases reflecting a sense that he might be coming to the end of his best writing and that his future reputation might be precarious. With regard to the essay: "I would like very much to have the piece done. I think (at 46) that I have worked too hard at my (elected or doomed, I don't know which) trade . . . to leave no better mark on this our pointless chronicle than I seem to be about to leave" (*FCF* 7). As for *The Portable*: "The idea is very fine. . . . By all means let us make a Golden Book of my apocryphal county. I have thought of spending my old age doing something of that nature: an alphabetical, rambling genealogy of the people, father to son to son" (*FCF* 24–25). Faulkner also cooperated fully with Cowley in making selections and in responding to his queries regarding interpretation. The one exception, as I discussed earlier—that had very much to do with one dimension of the celebrity he had created for himself—was his insistence that Cowley not include any reference to his combat experience in World War I.

21. Faulkner to Joan Williams, Spring 1954, in *Selected Letters of William Faulkner*, ed. Joseph Blotner (New York: Random House, 1977), 348.

22. See Faulkner, *Essays, Speeches, and Public Letters*, for a full collection.

23. The great exception to Faulkner's position was, of course, the 1956 interview with Russell Howe, in which, along with his standard position of "take off the pressure" from southern whites, he added that, "if it came to fighting I'd fight for Mississippi against the United States even if it meant going out into the street and shooting Negroes" (*LIG* 259, 261). When the interview appeared in print, Faulkner denied that he had taken such an extreme position (see *LIG* 257, 265).

II

Sound and Vision

The Unsynchable William Faulkner

Faulknerian Voice and Early Sound Film

JAY WATSON

There is a seemingly irresistible temptation in Faulkner studies to hunt for the turning point, the elusive experience or insight, that transformed Faulkner into "Faulkner," propelling him into the front ranks of modern writers. Bruce Kawin has wondered in print whether the breakthrough might be Faulkner's discovery of montage in art films he may have viewed during his residence in Paris in 1925.[1] The slightly different thought experiment I have in mind for this essay is to propose an authorial ontogenesis for Faulkner catalyzed more specifically by sound film—by the *techno*-genesis and contested infancy of a new media and popular culture phenomenon whose emergence was exactly contemporaneous with the development in the Faulkner oeuvre of a set of new approaches to the literary representation of sound and especially the speaking voice. In this line of development, *The Sound and the Fury* is the pivotal novel, the imaginative breakthrough. Even its title announces a new focus on aurality, in comparison with the admittedly cinematic but also silent image evoked by the title of its immediate precursor, *Flags in the Dust*. I want to suggest, then, that Faulkner was entering his own "sound era" as a writer at the same moment as the motion picture industry. I will pursue this thought experiment by focusing on two areas in which early sound film offered new aesthetic possibilities to period writers, possibilities that Faulkner seems to have intuited and embraced: (1) the spatial and temporal alignment of acoustic phenomena, especially voices, with their visible sources, or *synchronization*, and (2) the use of *silence* as a creative effect in its own right.

Synchronization and Its Discontents

It might seem counterintuitive to link the coming of film sound with a new commitment to artistic experimentation on Faulkner's part, since so many period commentators and film studies scholars have characterized sound's impact on cinema in wary or even deleterious terms, as inhibiting rather than fostering artistic creativity and innovation in the medium. Sergei Eisenstein and his collaborators on the 1928 "Statement on Sound" worried that the new technology would reorient the art form around people talking, thus threatening to reexcavate cinema's disavowed and also delimiting historical links to bourgeois theater and its aesthetic of realism.[2] The following year, John Gould Fletcher predicted that "the talking film . . . will merely confuse the already badly muddled problem of the relation of the pictures to their musical accompaniment still further . . . and will only serve to remove the film one step further from anything that can be remotely called fine art."[3] Though generally optimistic about the radical potential of cinema and other new media formations of the modern era, Walter Benjamin came to conclude by 1938 that "the launching of the sound film must be regarded as an operation of the cinema industry designed to break the revolutionary primacy of the silent film, which generated reactions that were hard to control and hence politically dangerous."[4] Here Benjamin was in a rare moment of agreement on the subject of film with his friend and fellow Frankfurt school thinker Theodor Adorno, who singled out sound film as "the most characteristic product" of the culture industry and its stultifying authoritarian agenda.[5]

The coming of sound, however, was a more complex affair than these scenarios of corruption, conformity, and decline suggest. Even Eisenstein recognized the new technology as "a double-edged invention."[6] As Peter Wollen has observed, sound introduced new possibilities that in turn brought "a chain of bizarre secondary problems and solutions" to the production and reception of cinema;[7] but by the same token these new problems represented potential opportunities for those working in the medium. A quick tour through some of the technical challenges and implications of sound film will help reveal how this might be so.

Jean-Louis Baudry's work on the cinematographic apparatus has revealed that the film medium performs masking functions that operate in service of a bourgeois ideology stressing representational verisimilitude and possessive individualism, the subject's self-presence and self-ownership.[8] Though actually consisting of a sequence of discontinuous photographic images—film's fundamental contradiction or "cut"—the medium could nonetheless capitalize on the perceptual response to camera cranking speeds above a certain threshold to produce the visual effect of continuous motion, as if the apparatus were simply reproducing or transmitting phenomenal reality (or, as it is sometimes called, "pro-filmic" reality, the world "before the camera") in its givenness, naturalness, and fullness. Other elements of the film recording and editing process worked to obscure the fact that the viewer's experience and pleasure were products of a technological apparatus and a labor- as well as capital-intensive industrial process, mediated by machines and workers rather than emerging spontaneously and unproblematically from the pro-filmic world.

According to Mary Ann Doane, Rick Altman, John Belton, Alan Williams, and other theorists of film sound, the coming of the new technology brought with it the potential to assist in this suturing work. To begin with, sound took the two-dimensional space of the filmic event, visually confined to the rectangular screen, and three-dimensionalized it, giving cinema a new sense of fullness and depth that enhanced its reality-effect.[9] In so doing, it also helped to cover up the noise of the projector, furthering the illusion of a direct encounter with pro-filmic reality. The ability to orchestrate a visual link between a discrete sound and its specific source—to "explain" the sound of ringing, for instance, by aiming the camera at a telephone, in what Altman says is "the most characteristic practice of classical film narrative"[10]—subtly reinforced an ideology of private property and possessive individualism that associates every aspect of the phenomenal world—even acoustic data—with the notion of legitimate origins and rightful ownership. And the editing technique of "staggering" cuts between the image track and the sound track enlisted aural continuity to smooth over breaks in the flow of visual images and vice versa.[11] Indeed, sound helped stabilize the image track in at least two additional ways as well: by forcing the standardization of cranking speeds and by incentivizing directors to fix film tempo to the pace of speech.[12]

Sound film could not reap these ideological rewards, however, without assuming some significant ideological risks. If the defining contradiction or "lie" of silent-era film lay in the visual cut, the fundamental discontinuity of the image track, the practice of staggered editing points to the defining "scandal" of sound film, which lies in the separability of sound and image as results of different mechanical processes. The actual source of a film sound, after all, is not the filmed image but an acoustic recording and playback technology. Sound film is not, properly speaking, "a" medium at all but rather what Friedrich Kittler calls a media link, yoking together two information-storage technologies, one for optical and one for acoustic data flows. As such, sound film is attended at every moment by a pair of related hazards: first, that the seemingly organic unity of the on-screen sound-image continuum will disaggregate into discrete, even incoherent, aural and visual phenomena; and second, that what Sara Danius calls the "compartmentalization" of the senses that results will split the cinema-going subject herself and even fragment her *body* into discontinuous viewing and listening faculties.[13]

Filmmakers responded to this second-order scandal or gap—what we could call the audio-visual cut—with a second-order suturing effort, a set of recording, mixing, and editing strategies designed to mystify the independent mechanical origins of image track and sound track. Foremost among these techniques were the hierarchical differentiation of the sound field to privilege the speaking voice as what Doane calls "the dominant form of sonorous expression in the cinema,"[14] and the synchronization of spoken dialogue to the image of the speaking body, the coordinated movements of lips, teeth, tongue, facial expressions, and other physical gestures. Assigning each voice to a clearly delineated source, an individual owner, shored up the ideology of self-presence, self-possession, and subjective interiority and depth that the technological basis of sound cinema threatened to expose as a fiction.

It is a commonplace of film history that *The Jazz Singer* was the first feature-length film to synchronize spoken dialogue, which, according to Michel Chion, took up about one-quarter of the total running time.[15] The pivotal year was 1927, the month October—mere days after Faulkner had completed *Flags in the Dust*, his first novel set in and around the fictional community of Jefferson, Mississippi. We should not, however, think of synchronized sound as arriving on the scene full-blown and seamlessly realized at this time. Rather, the period from 1927 to 1930 in particular was characterized by growing pains for the new technology, including competition between disc-based and optically based recording and playback systems, experimentation with the placement of loudspeakers in the cinema space, and an elaborate trial-and-error process in the realms of miking, mixing, and editing. Many of these developments elicited specific commentary in the technical publications of the film industry and from period artists and intellectuals. What seems clear in retrospect from their remarks is that *near*-synchrony pretty much boiled down in practice to *a*synchrony, eliciting a variety of anxious responses from contemporary audiences ranging from amusement to distraction to irritation to something approaching vertigo.

Synchronization, as it turned out, could stumble in several different ways. First, temporally—the sound could run out ahead of the film image, its ostensible source, or drag along behind it. The effect was especially conspicuous in the case of on-screen dialogue, as anyone will recall who has ever rolled her eyes at a poorly dubbed foreign film. But there was also a spatial dimension to the synchronization process that brought its own complications. Because the loudspeaker was most often located behind the screen and near its center, the placement of the human face within the rectangular screen image was crucial to sustaining the illusion that assigned each cinematic voice to a rightful owner. If the face of the speaker strayed too far from the center of the screen, her voice could appear to issue from slightly to one side of her, from above, below, or even behind her. Fitzhugh Green, author of the 1929 study *The Film Finds Its Tongue*, noted that in such cases "the movie voice seemed to wander away from its owner and the listener no longer connected it with him; it might have been anybody's voice."[16] Later innovations like the use of multiple loudspeakers or the development of stereo sound tracks would attempt to compensate for these difficulties. But period moviegoers noticed, and often complained. They also noted incongruities between what we might call the "depth" or z-dimension of the visual and sound fields, as when, in an example cited by Doane, the footsteps of a character appeared to grow louder as the character moved *away* from the camera eye,[17] or when a figure filmed from a great distance could nonetheless be overheard speaking in the hushed tones that suggest intimate proximity. In such moments, when the camera eye and, as it were, the camera "ear" fail to mesh properly, the cinematic illusion slips—the suture tears—and the moviegoer is split into potentially antagonistic viewing and listening faculties. The effect could be unnerving, spectral, even repulsive; one early commentator described "disembodied entertainers gesturing flatly on the screen and making gramophone-like noises."[18] An industry insider cited by Doane observed of an especially egregious combination of miking and mixing procedures that the resulting sound track failed to "represent any given point of audition" but instead evoked "the sound which would be heard by a man with five or six very long ears, said ears extending in various directions."[19] The grotesque materialization of the listening body in this remark clearly signals unease at the splitting of the senses by the dual apparatus of sound cinema.

In contemplating the gaffes and glitches that plagued sound film in its infancy, however, we would do well to remember Adorno's claim that "works which have not completely mastered their technique, conveying as a result something . . . uncontrolled and accidental, have a liberating quality."[20] If so, the ostensible problem of asynchrony also meant opportunities for the new art form, for those imaginative enough to identify and embrace them. A number of radical artists and intellectuals rose to the challenge. In 1928, Eisenstein's group heard in the coming of sound an opportunity to extend dialectical montage effects from the image track into the auditory realm, via "contrapuntal" methods pursuing "a sharp discord with the visual images."[21] The following year, Vsevolod Pudovkin, another of the collaborators on the "Statement on Sound," expounded on these possibilities in "Asynchronism as a Principle of Sound Film," a chapter of his book *Film Technique,* and René Clair championed asynchronous techniques at roughly the same time.[22] Béla Balázs sounded a similar note in 1930, inveighing against conventional synchronization for leading sound cinema back down the slippery slope toward theater.

To this list of asynchrony's proponents as an aesthetic technique (rather than a technological error), we might add William Faulkner. Imagine, if you will, the artist late in 1927, a thirty-year-old author of three novels, taking his exquisitely attuned sensibilities to the cinema to sample the novelty and multisensory sweep of the talkies. Imagine him witnessing the minor asynchronies and other unintentionally estranging effects produced by the not-yet-perfected technology. Or, if you will, imagine him hearing about such experiences and effects from relatives or acquaintances who took in a talkie, or reading about the technical challenges of the new medium in the newspapers or magazines. Now picture him, after this impromptu introduction to the radical potential of the emergent technology, turning, in his next work of literary fiction—and in the single most avant-garde move of his entire career—to create a character whose interior life, whose consciousness and perceptual apparatus, mimics sound-film technology to an uncanny degree. Where the Soviet director Dziga Vertov at almost precisely this time was busy immortalizing the man *with* the movie camera, here Faulkner, in the figure of *The Sound and the Fury*'s Benjamin Compson, gives us a man *as* a movie camera, a living media linkage for the recording and playback of sensory data flows, and a powerful literary vehicle for the exploration of the sensory faculties.

A word is in order here about media's enabling role in such explorations. Kittler is probably the best known of a group of theorists and critics who have drawn on insights from media studies in order to resituate literary modernism.[23] He has famously characterized literature "around 1900" as an expressive response to the late-century emergence of new media devices that mimicked and extended the work of the human senses by capturing optical and acoustic information directly. These devices, including Kittler's immortal trio of gramophone, film, and typewriter, represented what the critic Douglas Kahn calls a "machine critique" of the liberal subject, in ways that directly contributed to the critical project of literary modernism.[24] Kittler's modern machines, however, were themselves products, practical applications, of mid-nineteenth-century scientific research into the neurophysiology of human sense perception: the cognitive processes, neural circuits, and sensory pathways that governed the perceptual faculties. That research also left its mark on modern literature, as period authors turned to imaginative writing to conduct their own investigations into the nature of perception.

The Sound and the Fury's debts to the montage techniques of silent cinema have been well known among Faulkner scholars at least since the publication of Bruce Kawin's *Faulkner and Film* in 1977 and are evident from the first jump-cut scene shifts of section 1. An equally innovative engagement with sound-film conventions, however, is underway even sooner, with the evocations of spoken dialogue on the novel's opening page:

> *"Listen at you now." Luster said.* "Aint you something, thirty three years old, going on that way. After I done went all the way to town to buy you that cake. Hush up that moaning. Aint you going to help me find that quarter so I can go to the show tonight."
>
> They were hitting little, across the pasture. I went back along the fence to where the flag was. It flapped on the bright grass and the trees.
>
> *"Come on." Luster said.* (italics added)[25]

Or, a few pages farther along:

> Mother came out, pulling her veil down. She had some flowers.
>
> *"Where's Roskus." she said.*
>
> *"Roskus cant lift his arms today." Dilsey said.* "T.P. can drive all right."
>
> *"I'm afraid to." Mother said.* (9; italics added)

Now everyone knows what these passages are *supposed* to look like, grammatically and orthographically. Standard written English has developed conventions for the representation of speech that anticipate the suturing strategies of early sound film. Quotation marks, for instance, distinguish spoken utterance from other aural events, hierarchizing the sound field to privilege speech in much the same way as the recording and mixing practices of the early talkies. In addition, the use of the comma at the end of a quotation creates a sense of continuity and flow between the sound event and the objectified presence of a speaker, "synching" the written sound track and image track while assigning spoken sounds to a discrete, knowable source. In reproducing Benjy's severely attenuated thought process, Faulkner here follows convention in using quotation marks to indicate speech. But in replacing the comma that ordinarily links utterance and speaker with a period, a full stop, that interrupts that transition, Faulkner is conspicuously deviating from grammatical and ideological business as usual. When teaching *The Sound and the Fury,* I often invite students to think of Benjy, at least in his role of focalizer in section 1, as something like a human movie camera—or, to pursue a more contemporary analogy, a video recorder.[26] I mean this as a way of stressing Benjy's basic trustworthiness as a narrator, of calling attention to his perceptual apparatus as so largely unfiltered and concrete that if he says something happened we can be relatively confident that it did in fact happen, and happened more or less the way he says it did, since he offers so little interpretive processing (not quite to say *none*) that might color his account of an event or experience. Benjy's sheer strangeness as a narrator, then, is arguably an index of his reliability.

But if Benjy is a movie camera, section 1's unorthodox punctuation and formatting techniques, what Stephen M. Ross has called its "unique but formally consistent representation" of utterance, suggest that the talkie he produces remains imperfectly synchronized.[27] The full stop that separates quoted material from the assertion that someone spoke introduces a temporal displacement that dooms the spoken utterance to run forever just ahead of, or in other cases just behind, the speaking body. It also visually underscores the spatial gap between one discrete sentence reproducing a sound event and another depicting a sound source.[28] As a subject, then, Benjy is split into discontinuous sensory faculties whose technological equivalents would be a phonograph and a movie camera that don't quite mesh. The reader of section one is split in a similar way: while the eye registers the work of the period in distancing utterance and utterer, the unorthodox punctuation makes no difference in how the passage "sounds" to a reader either reciting the text aloud or voicing it internally through so-called "silent" reading.[29] This is the same "compartmentalization" of the senses that confronts the subject of sound cinema when the suturing or "gluing" function of synchronization breaks down—whether accidentally or as a deliberate effect pursued by filmmakers.[30] Even on those rare moments in section 1 where commas materialize to bolster the effect of continuity between speaker and utterance, Faulkner's use of line breaks still manages to frustrate expectations, assigning spoken words and their human source to different *paragraphs*, different spatial zones on the page:

> Uncle Maury was putting the bottle back in the sideboard. He called Caddy. *Caddy said,*
>
> *"Take him in to the fire, Versh.* Go with Versh." she said. "I'll come in a minute."
>
> We went to the fire. *Mother said,*
>
> *"Is he cold, Versh."* (7; italics added)

It is as if, throughout section 1, audible voices and visible bodies go about their own separate agendas, aligning every now and then but more often remaining at an insistent spatial and temporal remove from one another. If *The Jazz Singer* was synching dialogue by late 1927, then, Faulkner was already at work *de*-synchronizing it only months later, joining the European experimentalists cited earlier in an emerging "asynchronist" aesthetic.

Faulkner's unusual technique moreover suggests that in Benjy's mental activity we are witnessing a far more radical form of fragmentation and estrangement than that usually associated with section 1, making Benjy at once a test case and a limit case in human perception.[31] Faulkner scholars are accustomed to confronting fragmentation in *The Sound and the Fury* at the narrative level, in the montage-like juxtapositions or outright collisions of discrete episodes—as when Benjy gets his clothes snagged on a fence in 1928 and is abruptly hurled in his own awareness back to a similar event from his early childhood—and to some extent at the cognitive level, where Benjy's inability to make the conceptual leap from temporal seriality to the *post hoc propter hoc* logic of causality dooms potentially coherent event ensembles such as "burning one's hand on the stove" to scatter into their disjointed components. But the discontinuities between voice and speaking subject, sound track and image track, signaled by Faulkner's punctuation choices are of another order altogether. So granular are the disturbances they register within the perceptual apparatus, within the sensory linkages responsible for the experience of phenomena discrete and coherent enough to be arrangable as elements of narrative montage in the first place, as to suggest that Benjy simply doesn't benefit from the "persistence of vision" still understood by many film theorists of Faulkner's era to be the neural basis for cinema's illusion of continuous movement. For Benjy, consciousness may not, after all, be calibrated on the molar scale of the event or the "time-level," as the narrative organization of section 1 would appear to indicate, but instead on a molecular scale: frame by frame, as it were, rather than scene by scene—where the "flicker" between frames is capable of disrupting even the seemingly organic nexus of speaker and voice. If so, the effect is to place Benjy on the frontier, or perhaps the vanguard, of human perceptual activity.

This in turn might help account for the nearly unrelieved *distress* that is the hallmark of Benjy's affective life. Perhaps we should see his chronic misery less as grief for a lost sister or as a pathological aversion to change than as the product of a perceptual acuity so fine—a sampling rate so high—as to be utterly debilitating, as if Benjy were the human equivalent of those insects that can actually see the strobe effects produced by electric light bulbs on alternating current, the discrete pulsations whose nightmarish intensities happily lie beyond our sensory threshold. Significantly, this perceptual crisis is at its most acute around the phenomenon of the speaking voice, much like Benjy's own emotional agony, which crests whenever someone utters the word "Caddy" (or its homophone, "caddie").

Once initiated in section 1, this crisis of voice persists for the remainder of the novel. By section 2, Quentin's monologue, voices are wandering a thousand miles and many months away from the human circumstances of their production, acquiring uncanny new overtones and properties, even morphing into instruments of violence: "*Quentin has shot Herbert he shot his voice through the floor of Caddy's room*" (105). Here asynchronies on the perceptual level yield to a deeper psychopathology, the discorporated interior voices that are the phonic hallmark of psychosis.[32] Section 3, by contrast, is a shrill, unconvincing attack on asynchrony, a strained attempt to reestablish a sense of normalcy by resuturing the voice to the speaking subject by any means necessary, as Jason Compson doles out ascriptive tags ("I says," "he says," "she says," "what I say") right and left, to virtually any utterance that sounds halfway credible as spoken dialogue, including numerous remarks that he doubtless does *not* actually "say" to his mother or anyone else, however much he might wish to. Even when the narrative emerges from interior monologue in section 4, Reverend Shegog falls prey to an asynchronous effect resembling bad dubbing, the lack of a plausible fit between the speaking body and the texture or inflection of the voice issuing from it.[33] At first, the minister's voice is not only physically incongruous with his "undersized" (293) frame but *racially* incongruous with his "wizened black face": "When the visitor rose to speak he sounded like a white man. His voice was level and cold. It sounded too big to have come from him and they listened at first through curiosity, as they would have to a monkey talking." Indeed, the preacher's voice goes through multiple avatars, as if an entire gallery of voiceover specialists had been "goat-glanded"[34] one after another into the image track of the pulpit performance: one taking on "a sad, timbrous quality like an alto horn" (294), another "flesh[ing] its teeth in" Shegog, "succubus-like," before yet another finally "bec[omes] negroid" as the sermon hits its vernacular stride (295).[35] We might even think of the elements of cross-racial ventriloquism at work in Shegog's performance as a response to *The Jazz Singer*, whose own scenes of blackface minstrelsy offered a self-reflexive commentary on the *technological* ventriloquism that grafted Al Jolson's voice onto his visual image to earn the film its place in movie history.

We get glimpses of an asynchronous aesthetic in other Faulkner narratives from the late 1920s and early 1930s. There are, for example, the unique acoustic properties of the Bundren house in *As I Lay Dying*. As Darl explains:

> Tilting a little down the hill, as our house does, a breeze draws through the hall all the time, upslanting. A feather dropped near the front door will rise and brush along the ceiling, slanting backward, until it reaches the down-turning

> current at the back door: so with voices. As you enter the hall, they sound as though they were speaking out of the air about your head. (19–20)

Tull notes the same phenomenon: "We can hear the talking, coming out over the draft. Cash too, knocking and hammering at the boards. 'There's company in there,' he says" (31). And again, at Addie's funeral:

> The women sing again. In the thick air it's like the voices come out of the air, flowing together and on in the sad, comforting tunes. When they cease it's like they hadn't gone away. It's like they had just disappeared into the air and when we moved we would loose them again out of the air around us, sad and comforting. (91–92)

John T. Matthews has linked these discorporated vocal effects with a modern(ist) imaginary registering the impact on consciousness and the senses of new media devices and consumer items such as the graphophone so eagerly coveted by Cash,[36] but it is possible to detect the informing presence of another machine-age technology at work in these scenes. In each case, after all, the sound track is accompanied by an image track that either explicitly or implicitly portrays the voices as "live," produced in real time by speakers or singers present in the Bundren home. The text suggests, then, that, unlike the sounds of phonography, these voices are temporally "synched" to their sources. But they are *spatially* out of sync with them, subject to lateral or vertical displacements, wandering away from the speaking body or hovering above it like the uncanny voices of sound cinema described by Fitzhugh Green. In *Light in August,* Faulkner even experiments with such aural displacements along the z-axis: as Lena Grove imaginatively scripts, blocks, and directs a long-awaited reunion scene with Lucas Burch in Jefferson, the sound track again gets loose from the image track, running far out ahead of it in time and in the depth dimension of space. Noting that the sound of an approaching wagon reaches her well before a clear view of its occupants, "as though it were a ghost traveling half a mile ahead of its own shape" (8), Lena muses, "And if [the driver] is going all the way to Jefferson, I will be riding within the hearing of Lucas Burch before his seeing. He will hear the wagon, but he wont know it. So there will be one within his hearing before his seeing" (8–9). As her fantasy unfolds, Lena imagines her lover as a modern subject split into discontinuous viewing and listening faculties: the emergent subject of sound cinema.

The Sound of Silence

Asynchrony was not the only artistic technique available to period writers seeking to glean new ideas and strategies from sound film. The coming of sound also helped cultivate a new awareness of silence as an active, dynamic element of the soundscape. For the first thirty years of the new medium, silence was an imposed condition rather than an artistic choice for film directors; while the typical movie theater of the era was far from silent, the film itself was, as "a photographic spectacle" in which "humans laughed and babies cried without auditory traces" and "trains and motorcars sped across the screen in utter silence."[37] According to Chion, film before 1925 was not so much "mute" as "deaf," unable to *hear* the rich variety of sounds so obviously present in the pro-filmic scene: "there was no true silence within the fiction itself, but only a silence imposed on the filmgoer by the deaf cinema."[38] Ironically, then, the coming of sound brought Chion's "true silence" into play as an aesthetic strategy in cinematic storytelling. As Chion writes, "the talkies allowed us not only to *hear silence* . . . but also to have truly silent, mute characters," to "*make their silence heard.*"[39] As such, sound film "authorized silence as a new creative element."[40]

Over the years of the early sound era we can see—or rather, hear—Faulkner growing into a fuller understanding of and command over precisely this creative potential: not so much the silence of the unnarrated as the narration of silence itself as a tangible sensory presence exerting pressure on awareness in its own right. In a series of vivid passages that have compelled the attention of generations of critics, he perfects the technique of torquing up the tension of a scene—sometimes thrillingly, sometimes unbearably—by dialing *down* the volume, often all the way down. Significantly, what we could call the Faulknerian phenomenon of "terrific silence" does *not* appear in *Flags in the Dust,* the manuscript Faulkner completed on September 29, 1927, exactly one week prior to the premiere of *The Jazz Singer.* Though the novel opens provocatively with a pair of deaf men shouting at each other, allowing us to imagine how the enframing of dramatic events within old Bayard Sartoris's deafness might have produced the effect of terrific silence, this remains a road not taken in the novel. Instead, silence is associated throughout the text with a pastoral or domestic "quietude" sought unsuccessfully by disillusioned World War I veterans like Horace Benbow and young Bayard Sartoris.[41] Silence, in other words, has not yet become a dynamic aspect of the sound field for Faulkner. That quality is reserved for noise, the sounds that attend explosive movement: the "clamor" of dogs on the hunt (354–55), the "thunder" of a runaway horse's hooves (140–41), the roar of a wide-open car engine (351). Silence, by contrast, remains static, passive. The one near-exception to this rule occurs in a brief, "vacuum-like interval" during an automobile accident, "[a]n interval utterly without sound and in which all sensation of motion was lost" (352). Even here, however, the emphasis is not on the presence of silence so much as on the absence of sound.

That begins to change in *The Sound and the Fury,* where, during Quentin Compson's long monologue on June 2, 1910, a monologue punctuated by hundreds of individualized acts of hearing and listening, silence starts to acquire more substantive properties. It exhibits mobility and palpable borders, as when Quentin remembers running on a summer night through a "vacuum of crickets" "sawing away in the grass pacing me with a small travelling island of silence" (149). It is capable of rising—turning up its own volume, as it were—to eclipse sound, as Quentin notes upon attending to the humming of bees in the spring air, a sound that "diminishe[s], sustained yet, as though instead of sinking into silence, silence merely increased between us, as water rises" (123). It exhibits the characteristics of a discrete reserve or fund drawn on to balance against sound or cancel it out altogether: a bakery bell tinkles with "a single clear small sound so as not . . . to require the expenditure of too much silence in restoring it" (125). And for perhaps the first time in Faulkner, silence vibrates with tension, impinges on awareness with palpable force, when Quentin recalls a scene from his grade-school days:

> I wouldn't begin counting until the clock struck three. Then I would begin, counting sixty or folding down one finger and thinking of the other fourteen fingers waiting to be folded down, or thirteen or twelve or eight or seven, until all of a sudden *I'd realise silence* and the unwinking minds, and I'd say "Ma'am?" "Your name is Quentin, isn't it?" Miss Laura would say. *Then more silence* and the cruel unwinking minds and hands jerking into the silence.

> "Tell Quentin who discovered the Mississippi River, Henry." "DeSoto." (88; italics added)

In each case, silence emerges as an aural presence enlisted to limn Quentin's stubborn, doomed resistance to a "loud world" of modern mobility and social transformation (177).[42]

In Faulkner's next novel project, the original version of *Sanctuary* composed between January and May 1929, the technique reaches maturity. Silence becomes dynamic, providing the acoustic scaffolding for scenes of dramatic intensity and immediacy. At one point during Temple Drake's first harrowing night as a captive in a Memphis brothel, two dogs cower beneath her bed, "the dry complaint of mattress and springs [dying] into the terrific silence in which they crouched."[43] At a pivotal juncture in Lee Goodwin's sensational murder trial, a thick, "musty silence" envelops the courtroom to absorb the sighs and hisses of the scandalized gallery (276). The novel's most striking and extended aesthetic deployment of silence, however, is reserved for its most infamous scene, that of Temple's brutal corncob rape at the hands of the Memphis gangster, Popeye. Commencing sonically with a silenced pistol shot "no louder than the striking of a match, a short, minor sound shutting down upon the scene . . . with a profound finality, completely isolating it" (140), Faulkner proceeds to escalate the scene's tension to terrifying heights by dialing down its sound—or more precisely, by paradoxically pumping *up* the volume of its silence, turning the acoustics of the episode inside out to accentuate its dramatic power and, as Chion might put it, to make Popeye's menacing silence *heard.* As the gunman stalks down Temple in the corncrib, "he made no sound at all; the released door yawned and clapped against the jamb, but it made no sound either; it was as though sound and silence had become inverted. She could hear silence in a thick rustling as he moved toward her, thrusting it aside" (140). Even when Temple screams, the words are "void[ed] . . . like hot silent bubbles into the bright silence about them" (140). The simultaneous crescendo of violence and silence—violence *as* silence—is Faulkner's innovative attempt to evoke a trauma sensorium, a perceptual overload so severe as to obliterate perceptual acuity itself, an effect perhaps reinforced by the literal deafness and blindness of the scene's other significant "witness," the decrepit old man, Pap. The passage is a tour de force in the aesthetic possibilities of silence as a *form* (and not just a lack) of sound.

When Faulkner revised the *Sanctuary* galleys for publication in 1931, he added a new episode that is the equal of the rape scene in its deployment of terrific silence. After Lee Goodwin is convicted for the murder (and accused of the rape) committed by Popeye, the townspeople of Jefferson proceed to lynch him in spectacular fashion, raping and mutilating him before setting him on fire with coal oil. Goodwin's attorney, Horace Benbow, is present at the lynching, and as it unfolds, the "panting shouts" of the mob and the "furious sound of gasoline" give way to a mounting silence, as Horace's overtaxed faculties threaten to shut down.[44] "[F]rom the central mass of fire," the focus and apex of the scene's horror, "there came no sound at all. . . . He couldn't hear the fire, though it still swirled upward unabated, as though it were living upon itself, and soundless: a voice of fury like in a dream, roaring silently out of a peaceful void" (296). Once again, sound and silence switch roles in the pursuit of maximum narrative tension.

Thus established in Faulkner's technical repertoire, terrific silence becomes a go-to strategy for leveraging the dramatic energy of key scenes. In *As I Lay Dying*, the novel written and published between the two iterations of *Sanctuary*, the Bundren family's funeral journey to Jefferson is threatened by a pair of elemental catastrophes, the flooding of the Yoknapatawpha River and the burning of the Gillespies' barn, in which extremes of sound and silence again collide and blur. As described by Darl Bundren, the "thick dark current" of the swollen river "talks up to us in a murmur become ceaseless and myriad" (141), yet at the same time "silent, impermanent, and profoundly significant." Similarly, in Darl's account of the barn fire, the thunder of flames, screams of livestock, and shouts of men and women are juxtaposed against "an abrupt and soundless explosion" as the structure becomes fully involved (218). At the moment of greatest danger, as Jewel rushes into the collapsing building to try to rescue his mother's coffin singlehandedly from the flames, the aural mix mimics that of the river scene, as Darl explicitly notes: "The sound of it has become quite peaceful now, like the sound of the river did" (221). *Light in August* (1932) features the "soundless yelling" of Gail Hightower's phantom cavalry squad as it "crashe[s] silently" into the twilight, evoking at once the intensity and illusoriness of the minister's Lost Cause fantasizing.[45] Even more unforgettable is the way Faulkner punctuates Percy Grimm's dogged pursuit and cold-blooded slaughter of the fugitive Joe Christmas with the "slow and sustained scream" of a fire siren that weaves its "soundless vibration" in and out of "the realm of hearing" (460; cf. 461, 465). Again and again, during the early years of the sound era, Faulknerian prose marks the presence of physical force—and especially destructive power—by plunging the reader into a sonic vacuum, a silence that forcibly occupies, then swells to dominate, the auditory field. It was a lesson learned in part from the new creative emphasis placed by the talkies on the strategic withdrawal of sound.

Talkies and Typies

As Tim Armstrong points out, the so-called "sound panic" of 1928 created an unprecedented demand for film dialogue that meant lucrative new opportunities for writers through screenwriting assignments or the sale of film rights to their works.[46] By the early 1930s, Faulkner was cashing in on both sorts of opportunities, but well before that, the talkies were already making important contributions to his artistic sensibility. Though Faulkner's restless experimentation with the sound field, his insistence on surveying the contours of voice, body, and subjectivity for fault lines and contradictions, and his desire to conduct his own iconoclastic researches into the physiology and phenomenology of perception should doubtless be credited to the *total* media ecology of his era—including radio, phonography, PA technology, the telephone, and eventually television—it is important to give sound film its due in catalyzing a more complex awareness on the artist's part of the technical possibilities of his work.

In fact, if I may be allowed a closing digression, we should probably pause to give the typewriter *its* due in this ecology as well. Returning to section 1 of *The Sound and the Fury*, if we shift our focus from Benjy Compson himself to the narrator responsible for transcribing the contents of his consciousness, we are left with a renewed appreciation for the way this narrator relies on unusual orthographic techniques that are more precisely typographic effects. The role of this narrating figure, in other words, is to convert the sensory data streams that comprise Benjy's awareness into typing, as if in accordance with Mallarmé's "instant insight" that in the era of the typewriter literature consists "of no more and no less than [the] twenty-six letters" of the alphabet[47]—graphic matter, to which we could add periods, commas, typefaces, and areas of white space on the page, all to be employed in the construction of printed artifacts. The illustration *Dictating to the Phonograph* offers a suggestive if

Dictating to the Phonograph. Harper's Weekly, June 6, 1888. Reproduced by permission of HarpWeek, http://businessmachines.harpweek.com.

still incomplete way to begin visualizing the narrator of section 1, or rather the narrative apparatus responsible for section 1, with its constitutive media linkages and human figure at their interface.

I am tempted to dub this image "*Her* Master's Voice" for the revealing glimpse it offers into the gendered media imaginary of modernism. As Kittler reminds us, around the turn of the nineteenth century, not only the machine on the right but also its human operator would have been called a "typewriter."[48] In the business world, such typewriters served as relays in media linkages such as the one pictured here, in which the operator is listening to a dictaphone as she types, no doubt transcribing the dictated words of her boss into a letter or memo. But if we imagine that what this early dictaphone pours into her ear is not her master's voice but instead Luster Gibson's voice, and a golfer's voice, and a series of moans and bellows, and Dilsey's voice, and the buzzing sounds of insects in the trees and grass; and if we moreover imagine this busy typist looking not down at her keyboard but ahead, past her desk to a screen mounted on the wall beyond where filmed images flicker—curling honeysuckle blossoms, a flag waving in the breeze, a girl splashing in a creek or climbing a pear tree, the play of flames in a stove grate—then we will have taken an important step toward conceptualizing the techno-narrative apparatus for Benjy's interior monologue, and it would not be unreasonable to suppose that the typing that would emerge from this apparatus would look a good bit like section 1 of *The Sound and the Fury.* For me, part of the heuristic value of the slightly altered version of the illustration I have described—gramophone to the side of the operator, movie screen in front of her, volleying and thundering—is the way it assigns the acoustic and optical contents of Benjy's awareness to discrete sources, thereby illustrating the potential for the asynchronous effects that do in fact emerge in the narrative. I am suggesting—not altogether fancifully, I hope—that the Benjy narrator finds its—or *her*?—media equivalent in a modern assemblage of Kittler's holy trinity of gramophone, film, and typewriter: a talkie integrated into the production of a "typie." All we lack is a fourth, as yet nonexistent machine capable of storing, reproducing, and projecting olfactory data streams, wafting before the operator's nostrils the evocative scents of leaves, trees, rain, and cold, and the Benjy effect would be nearly complete. And if at this point my thought experiment seems to be getting away from me entirely, I would only point out that the motion picture industry briefly dabbled in precisely such olfactory technology a half century ago, in efforts to enhance sound film with "Smell-O-Vision" and "Aroma-Rama."

In conclusion, the troubled infancy of the talkies invited Faulkner to cultivate a healthy skepticism toward a bourgeois ideology of voice, opening up a new and productive distance between the maturing writer and the realist aesthetic that to a considerable extent had shaped his early novels. It also helped give him license to explore and reconceptualize the interplay of the sensory faculties at work behind human cognition, as well as the interplay of the new machines that mimicked and extended those faculties. And it introduced him to the thematic and affective potential of silence as a dynamic form of sound irreducible to mere "quietude." In all of these ways, the coming of the sound era played an important supporting role in the making of one of modern literature's most "unsynchable" figures.

NOTES

1. Bruce F. Kawin, *Faulkner and Film* (New York: Ungar, 1977), 10–11.

2. Sergei Eisenstein, Vsevolod Pudovkin, and Grigori Alexandrov, "Statement on Sound" (1928), in *Film Theory and Criticism*, 6th ed., ed. Leo Braudy and Marshall Cohen (New York: Oxford University Press, 2004), 371. As Rick Altman and others have noted, theater functions throughout the silent era as cinema's "repressed" (Rick Altman, introduction to "Cinema/Sound," special issue, *Yale French Studies* 60 [1980]: 13).

3. John Gould Fletcher, *The Crisis of the Film* (Seattle: University of Washington Book Store, 1929), 27–28.

4. Walter Benjamin to Adorno, "Reply," December 9, 1938, trans. Harry Zohn, in *Aesthetics and Politics* (New York: Verso, 2007), 140.

5. Theodor Adorno and Max Horkheimer, "The Culture Industry: Enlightenment as Mass Deception," in *Dialectic of Enlightenment: Philosophical Fragments*, ed. Gunzelin Schmid Noerr, trans. Edmund Jephcott (Stanford, CA: Stanford University Press, 2002), 100.

6. Eisenstein, Pudovkin, and Alexandrov, "Statement on Sound," 371.

7. Peter Wollen, "Cinema and Technology: A Historical Overview," in *The Cinematic Apparatus*, ed. Teresa de Lauretis and Stephen Heath (New York: St. Martin's, 1980), 17.

8. See Jean-Louis Baudry, "Ideological Effects of the Basic Cinematographic Apparatus" (1970), trans. Alan Williams, *Film Quarterly* 28, no. 2 (Winter 1974–75): 39–47.

9. Daniel Percheron, "Sound in Cinema and Its Relationship to Image and Diegesis," trans. Marcia Butzel, *Yale French Studies* 60 (1980): 18.

10. Altman, introduction to "Cinema/Sound," 15.

11. Mary Ann Doane, "Ideology and the Practice of Sound Editing and Mixing," in *The Cinematic Apparatus*, ed. Teresa de Lauretis and Stephen Heath (New York: St. Martin's, 1980), 51.

12. See Tim Armstrong, *Modernism, Technology, and the Body: A Cultural Study* (New York: Cambridge University Press, 1998), 223; Wollen, "Cinema and Technology," 17; and Douglas Kahn, *Noise, Water, Meat: A History of Sound in the Arts* (Cambridge: MIT Press, 1999), 146.

13. Friedrich A. Kittler, *Gramophone, Film, Typewriter* (1986), trans. Geoffrey Winthrop-York and Michael Wutz (Stanford: Stanford University Press, 1999), 170; Sara Danius, *The Senses of Modernism: Technology, Perception, and Aesthetics* (Ithaca, NY: Cornell University Press, 2002), 147.

14. Mary Ann Doane, "The Voice in the Cinema: The Articulation of Body and Space" (1980), in *Film Theory and Criticism*, 6th ed., ed. Leo Braudy and Marshall Cohen (New York: Oxford University Press, 2004), 374.

15. Michel Chion, *The Voice in Cinema*, trans. Claudia Gorbman (New York: Columbia University Press, 1999), 156–57.

16. Quoted in Armstrong, *Modernism*, 224. See also Chion, *Voice in Cinema*, 11.

17. Doane, "Ideology," 55.

18. Quoted in Armstrong, *Modernism*, 229–30.

19. Quoted in Doane, "Ideology," 54.

20. Theodor Adorno, "Transparencies on Film," trans. Thomas Y. Levin, in *The Culture Industry: Selected Essays on Mass Culture*, ed. J. M. Bernstein (New York: Routledge, 1991), 179.

21. Eisenstein, Pudovkin, and Alexandrov, "Statement on Sound," 371.

22. Altman, introduction to "Cinema/Sound," 12.

23. Other members of this group include Tim Armstrong, Sara Danius, Lisa Gitelman, Douglas Kahn, Jeffrey Sconce, and Juan A. Suárez.

24. Kahn, *Noise, Water, Meat*, 8.

25. William Faulkner, *The Sound and the Fury: The Corrected Text* (New York: Vintage International, 1990), 3. Hereafter cited parenthetically.

26. Ross has also noted this "recording" capacity on Benjy's part, though without really developing its media context or implications (see Stephen M. Ross, *Fiction's Inexhaustible Voice: Speech and Writing in Faulkner* [Athens: University of Georgia Press, 1989], 178–79).

27. Ibid., 178.

28. Compare Ross's account of such scenes: "A gap opens between the voice and its sound, for the one begins and ends before the other starts and stops" (ibid., 38).

29. Garrett Stewart's account of "the conjoint cerebral activity and suppressed muscular action of a simultaneously summoned and silenced enunciation" (1) that he terms "evocalization" (2), "a stratum of response located between a merely evoked aurality and an oral vocalizing," should be enough to lay to rest once and for all the stubborn mischaracterization of the practice of reading-to-ourselves as "silent" (see, more generally, Garrett Stewart, *Reading Voices: Literature and the Phonotext* [Berkeley: University of California Press, 1990], 1–3, 28–29).

30. Danius, *Senses of Modernism*, 147. See also Michel Chion citing Alexandre Arnoux, *Voice in Cinema*, 11.

31. Noting that "Faulkner's discourse habitually disengages voice from person," Ross suggests that the effect of such moments is to "implant" the individual subject "in a broader communal nexus" (*Fiction's Inexhaustible Voice*, 26), rather than, as I argue here, to dissolve or decenter individual subjectivity more radically. For Ross, in other words, the technique "shifts the perceived origin of meaning away from individual consciousness into a disseminated 'consciousness'" that pervades "the novel's overall texture" rather than challenging the notion of originary meaning or consciousness more fundamentally (ibid., 28).

32. Though Ross observes that "fill[ing] the psyches of his characters with voices of many and varied kinds" is a hallmark of Faulkner's fiction (*Fiction's Inexhaustible Voice*, 134), he recognizes that Quentin Compson represents a special case: "So much do voices dominate Quentin's consciousness that psychic voice in his section is a chorus. . . . The major portion of Quentin's memories are either quotations or paraphrases of spoken words" (179–80).

33. This is a problem Shegog has in common with Reverend Whitfield of *As I Lay Dying*. At Addie Bundren's funeral, Vernon Tull observes that Whitfield's "voice is bigger than him. It's like they are not the same. It's like he is one, and his voice is one, swimming on two horses side by side across the ford and coming into the house, the mud-splashed one and the one that never even got wet, triumphant and sad" (William Faulkner, *As I Lay Dying: The Corrected Text* [New York: Vintage International, 1990], 91; hereafter cited parenthetically).

34. As Armstrong explains, "goat-glanding" was a period term for "the adding of sound to Silents" (Armstrong, *Modernism*, 226).

35. For a fuller account of Shegog's vocal performance see Ross, *Fiction's Inexhaustible Voice*, 36–45, esp. 41.

36. John T. Matthews, "*As I Lay Dying* in the Machine Age," *boundary 2* 19, no. 1 (Spring 1992): 76, 86.

37. Danius, *Senses of Modernism*, 149.

38. Chion, *Voice in Cinema*, 95.

39. Ibid.

40. Ibid., 10.

41. William Faulkner, *Flags in the Dust* (New York: Vintage, 1974), 191, 282. Hereafter cited parenthetically. As such, this early work bears out, more credibly than the ones that will follow it, Zender's assertion that silence expresses an authorial "yearning for reconciliation with the world" (Karl F. Zender, *The Crossing of the Ways: William Faulkner, the South, and the Modern World* [New Brunswick, NJ: Rutgers University Press, 1989], 30). For Zender, this fulsome silence "is always liable in Faulkner's fiction to invasion by noise." Yet as I hope to demonstrate, silence is also capable, in the novels immediately following *Flags*, of exhibiting an invasive dimension in its own right, exerting a force approaching that of noise.

42. A project that arguably culminates in Quentin's suicide, in which, as Ross notes, he "find[s] a soundless void away from his loud world of voices" (*Fiction's Inexhaustible Voice*, 183).

43. William Faulkner, *Sanctuary: The Original Text*, ed. Noel Polk (New York: Random House), 179–80. Hereafter cited parenthetically.

44. William Faulkner, *Sanctuary: The Corrected Text* (New York: Vintage International, 1993), 296, 295. Hereafter cited parenthetically.

45. William Faulkner, *Light in August: The Corrected Text* (New York: Vintage International, 1990), 493, 75.

46. Armstrong, *Modernism*, 234. Hereafter cited parenthetically.

47. Kittler, *Gramophone, Film, Typewriter*, 14.

48. Ibid., 183

Faulkner, Adorno, and "the Radio Phenomenon," 1935

MICHAEL ZEITLIN

This study of what Adorno has called "the radio phenomenon" emerges from an encounter with Faulkner's airplane narratives, which range across a broad scene of world history and politics: the Great War; the rise of European fascism in the 1920s and 1930s; the Second World War; and the aviation arms race as it extends from the Wright Flyer in 1903 into the Cold War era. This material would include (merely an essential sampling) "Landing in Luck" (1919), "Love" (1921), *Soldiers' Pay* (1926), *Flags in the Dust* (1928), "All the Dead Pilots" (1931), "Turnabout" (1932), "With Caution and Dispatch" (1932), "Death Drag" (1932), *Pylon* (1935), "The Life and Death of a Bomber" (Faulkner's film treatment from 1943), *A Fable* (1954), and the letters he wrote to the *New York Times* about the crash of the Italian airliner in 1954 and the downing of the U-2 pilot Francis Gary Powers in 1960. These narratives take us inside aviation's terminal logic as expressed in Faulkner's *A Fable:* "to be tough and to endure until the flash, crash, whatever it will be, when he will no longer be anything and none of it will matter anymore, even the fact that he was tough and, until then, did endure."[1] Nastier, more sarcastic versions of this *dromology*[2] are hiding in plain sight on the airmeet's mimeographed program of events in *Pylon*—an uncanny oracle:

> Thursday (Dedication Day) [. . .]
> 3:30 P.M. Aerial Acrobatics. Jules Despleins,
> France. Lieut. Frank Burnham, United States
> 4:30 P.M. Scull Dash. [. . .]
> 8:00 P.M. Special Mardi Gras Evening Event.
> Rocket Plane. Lieut. Frank Burnham[3]

"Say, what do you suppose happened?"

"Blinded, probably."

"Yair. Blinded."

"Yair. Probably couldn't read his altimeter at all. Or maybe forgot to watch it. Flew it right into the ground."

"Yair. Jesus, I remember one time I was . . . (152)

In such moments Faulkner imagines—or gives us a screen for imagining—the scene in the spiraling cockpit along with (in necessary dialectic) "the gaped and upturned faces" (*Pylon* 236) of the death witnesses on the ground.

Faulkner had imagined himself into the pilot's seat from an early age, at least from his attempt with his brothers to launch a homemade airplane in the year 1909 (six years post–Kitty Hawk, when Faulkner was twelve years old). Drawing on the memoirs of Faulkner's younger brothers, Murry and John, Joseph Blotner describes the scene: "With a last lunge they launched it. It pitched as the tail rose and then swung through an arc and thumped upside down into the bottom of the ditch in a flutter of paper and beanpoles. Billy silently picked his way out of the shattered fuselage as Jack, Johncy, and Sallie Murry looked on, dumb with disappointment."[4] The episode contains the major elements to be amplified in Faulkner's subsequent representations of "the furious, still, and legendary tale of what man has come to call his conquering of the infinite and impervious air" (*Pylon* 35) (the tonal blending of plain admiration and withering irony is symptomatic): the brave testing of limits; the inevitable failure of the machine; the humiliating loss of control; the dumb gaze of the witnesses.

In exhibiting the essentially oneiric quality of Faulkner's myriad representations, across his work, of the experience of lifting off, soaring, cruising, looping, diving, spiraling down, or crashing, "Landing in Luck" (1919), Faulkner's first published prose story, is his archetypal representation of aviation modernity as the "mysterious unity of ego and actuality, destiny and character, doing and happening . . . the mystery of reality as an operation of the psyche."[5] Cadet Thompson is about to embark on his first solo flight:

> He had been angry enough to kill his officer for the better part of a week. . . . He was a strange mixture of fear and pride as he opened the throttle wide and pushed the stick forward—fear that he would wreck the machine landing,

> and pride that he was on his own at last. He was no physical coward, his fear was that he would show himself up before his less fortunate friends to whom he had talked largely of spins and side slips and gliding angles. . . . His subconscious mind had registered a cable across the end of the field, and he had flown enough to know that it was touch and go as to whether he would clear it. [. . .] A shock; he closed his eyes. [. . .] So the cable had broken! [. . .] Below at the edge of the aerodrome stood the ambulance, its crew gaping foolishly at him. [. . .] He had stripped a wheel on that cable, then.[6]

There follows the inevitable crash landing, and the resolution of the turbulent scene in a characteristic tableau (Faulkner would assume a version of this story as his own in countless retellings throughout his life):

> Hanging face downward from the cockpit, Cadet Thompson looked at [his officer]. [. . .] [H]is eyes filled with utter adoration. Then he became violently ill.[7]

With Freud we should say that "the insistence with which this dream exhibits its absurdities could only be taken as indicating the presence in the dream-thoughts of a particularly embittered and passionate polemic."[8]

The symbolic aviation scene in Faulkner is structured by what Georg Simmel in 1903 called the new "sensory foundations of mental life," to be grasped in "deep contrast with the slower, more habitual, more smoothly flowing rhythm of the sensory-mental phase of small town and rural existence":[9]

> Queenie moved again, her feet began to clop-clop steadily again, and at once Ben hushed. Luster looked quickly back over his shoulder, then he drove on. The broken flower drooped over Ben's fist and his eyes were empty and blue and serene again as cornice and façade flowed smoothly once more from left to right, post and tree, window and doorway and signboard each in its ordered place.[10]

In his aviation fiction Faulkner occupies the space of this "deep contrast" as he confronts the twentieth century's new mental velocity, its "increase in technological artifacts, in power sources, in tempo."[11]

Faulkner's primary analysis of the new psychic velocity in relation to machine flight takes place in *Pylon* (1935). As I read the novel in the global context of its time, two events—Charles Lindbergh's New York–to-Paris solo flight in 1927, and Italo Balbo's Rome to Chicago squadron flight in 1933—trace out the main lines of modernism's transatlantic media ecology in the period marked by the rise of European fascism and the technological steeplechase toward total war—"the disaster, toward which without yet being conscious of it apparently, they moved" (*Pylon* 174). A key scene of the novel in this respect involves the successful attempt of the reporter and pilot Roger Shumann to legally hijack the lethal aeroplane (Faulkner's spelling) that Matt Ord (famous, record-breaking speed flyer) refused to let them have in the first instance. This machine is

> a lowwing monoplane with a big nose and a tubular fuselage ending in a curiously flattened tailgroup which gave it the appearance of having been drawn lightly and steadily through a huge lightlyclosed gloved fist. "There it is," the reporter said. "Yair," Shumann said. "I see.—Yes," he thought, looking quietly at the queer empennage, the blunt short cylindrical body. (219)

After a test flight, with the reporter serving as dead weight to help their flying coffin "ride on a balance,"[12] Shumann pilots the notorious aeroplane the forty miles over to Feinman Airport (Ord's record-breaking machine can make the trip in ten minutes). But the word has somehow gotten out—transmitted mysteriously across the ether apparently—and a large crowd has assembled for Shumann's arrival at the field. "[A]nd by the time he landed you would have thought he was Lindbergh," as Jiggs tells it later (224).[13]

At an earlier point in the novel, after their meeting with the Aeronautical Committee in the superintendent's office, Shumann and the parachute jumper, Jack,

> went out and around toward the hangar, walking now in a thin deep drone from somewhere up in the sun, though presently they could see them—a flight of army pursuit singleseaters circling the field in formation to land and then coming in, fast, bluntnosed, fiercelyraked, viciously powerful. "They're over souped," Shumann said. "They will kill you if you don't watch them. I wouldn't want to do that for two-fifty-six a month." (156)

As the American aviation arms race in response to the threat of European fascism revs up its powerful engines, Roger Schumann's hesitation marks a radical change. The solo aviation exploit (and whatever fragile expression of individual freedom and heroic mortality inheres in it) is being driven into obsolescence by the military squadron and the formation flight of its lethal supermachines.[14]

If the "viciously powerful" machines are there, ostensibly, to defend the nation, in the first instance they menace their own pilots while signaling the presence of an international system organizing itself for an apocalypse. Recall that Japan invaded Manchuria in 1931. Hitler took dictatorial power on January 30, 1933. The American mass media—newsprint, magazines, photography, newsreels, radio—is covering the rising global terror with massive daily exposure as the borders of the republic (real, symbolic, imaginary) become ever more permeable and porous. It is within the context of this media environment that we might imagine the visual and sonic effects of the Italian air force's spectacular American appearance in July 1933. Italo Balbo, Italian Blackshirt leader and secretary of state for air in Mussolini's Fascist Italy, led a squadron of twenty-four seaplanes from Rome across the Atlantic to Chicago, site of the World's Fair in celebration of "A Century of Progress"—a flight of 6,100 miles (undertaken in seven stages). Newspapers describe "the ecstatic welcome they encountered in Chicago when the squadrons put down on Lake Michigan on 15 July before a cheering crowd of a hundred thousand onlookers."[15] Motorcades, parades, banquets, receptions, and honorary degrees followed. "Saluted by nineteen cannon shots fired from the warship *Wilmette* and escorted by thirty-six American fighters, the Italians took off for New York on the morning of the 19th."[16] Then "Balbo and twenty of his pilots were flown to Washington, D.C., where the most senior of them were invited to a luncheon at the White House hosted by President Roosevelt."[17] Although Balbo boasted in response to the crowd's feverish welcome that "Anti-Fascism Here a Myth" (*New York Times*), "heavy security forces had been mobilized in Chicago and New York to forestall the possibility of embarrassing anti-Fascist demonstrations."[18]

Given the levels of European armaments in this period and the escalating displays of aviation rhetoric and technology on both sides of the Atlantic—and in Russia and Japan—it was impossible not to have somewhere in mind "at least some conception of the next war" (as Walter Benjamin put it in 1930, while reviewing a book by Ernst Jünger in which Jünger and his fellow Freikorps members are already referring to the Great War as merely the *first* world war).[19] Indeed, the coming war promised to offer the ultimate "artistic gratification of a sense perception altered by technology, [. . .] [humankind's] self-alienation [having] reached the point where it can experience its own annihilation as a supreme aesthetic pleasure."[20] In exploring Faulkner's representation of his own alienated fascination with the scene of militarized aviation in the 1930s—its machines, systems, people; its sonic, visual, and phenomenological effects—I turn to the sound of the amplified voice in *Pylon,* and hence to what Adorno has called "radio physiognomics."

Adorno had left Germany a year after Hitler came to power in January 1933, arriving in New York (after a sojourn in England) in February 1938. His first appointment in America was with the Princeton Radio Research Project, for which he wrote a series of studies, compiled posthumously as *Current of Music: Elements of a Radio Theory* (2008).[21] In his chapter titled "Radio Physiognomics," Adorno makes the following observation:

> A person who enters a room where a radio is turned on may be momentarily struck by the sound before being able fully to realize what the content of the broadcast is. In this study our attitude is largely like that of this man, confronted by a radio phenomenon without understanding the meaning of its material, but only the fact that "radio is speaking to him."[22]

Faulkner anticipates this exemplary moment at a number of points in *Pylon*:

> And here the voice met them again—or rather it had never ceased; they had merely walked in it without hearing or feeling it like in the sunshine; the voice too almost as sourceless as light. . . . (26)

> Now suddenly he heard the amplifyer too in the rotundra; it had been speaking for some time but he had just noticed it:
>
> "—— second day of the Feinman Airport dedication invitation meet [. . .]" (142)

> He could hear the voice again now from the amplifyer above the entrance:
>
> "—— wish to announce [. . .]" (145)

> . . . he did not walk back into the voice, he had never walked out of it:

"... an in-ver-ted spin, folks; he's going into it still upside down—oh oh oh oh [...]" (236)

If the medium is the message, the message, the medium, is electricity, the current of energy that produces the spectrum of amplified echo-effects at the brand-new airport, whose architecture renders sound as a kind of echoey suspension liquid: "the rotundra was full of people and with a cavernous murmuring sound which seemed to linger not about the mouths which uttered it but to float somewhere about the high serene shadowy dome overhead" (245). As it gathers itself within the focalized alcoholic interiority of the reporter, the primacy of mediation produces a kind of "circumambient" narcissism, the medium of reality itself bringing about an "implacable infiltration" of the human cells via all the organs and orifices of apperception: "for a while he could not see at all; he just stood there in some ultimate distillation of the savage bright neartropical day, not knowing now whether he was still blinking or not, in an implacable infiltration which not even walls could stop, from the circumambient breathing of fish and coffee and sugar and fruit and hemp and swampland" (269).

New Valois (New Orleans) is the permeable domain par excellence, site of the most fundamental and uncanny of animistic "confusions": "the glare of neon, the pulse and glitter of electrics [...] bathed the idle slow Sunday pavementthrong as it drifted from window to window beyond which the immaculate, the unbelievable wax men and women gazed back at them with expressions inscrutable and Delphic" (287). "As soon as he closed them he would find himself, out of some attenuation of weariness, sleeplessness, confusing both the living and the dead" (268). It is as if the radial currents of electricity have stopped up the ears, transforming from within the very quality of general acoustics even when there are no microphones or amplifiers present, as when the reporter leads his group across Lethe into the New Valois nighttown of Grandlieu Street: "The reporter was still talking but they did not appear to hear him, as though they had arrived too recently to have yet unclogged their ears of human speech in order to even hear the tongue in which the guide spoke" (79–80). Later, in the editor Hagood's office, the supremacy of mediation is evident as the reporter "spoke quietly, apparently into the green lampshade like it was a microphone" (181).

Adorno places mediation or amplification (whether through radios, phonographs, or loudspeakers) under the sign of "the radio phenomenon" (RP 113)—the word "radio" to be understood in relation to "radiation" or "radial" bands or waves of projected sound. Whatever issues from the wired speaker is the uncanny, witchy "radio voice" itself. Its essence is to be grasped in relation to this observation: "Even if the set is functioning properly, the electric current can be heard when it is tuned in" (RP 114). This is the so-called "hear-stripe" (RP 114), a slightly crackling, continual noise beneath or behind or onto which is projected the musical or human language streaming forth from the electrical speaker. Observes Adorno, as "an objective characteristic of the phenomenon it certainly plays a role in the apperception of the whole, and will be effective unconsciously" (RP 114). When the editor Hagood hangs up on the reporter, Faulkner renders *Pylon*'s "hear-stripe" as a kind of umbilicus linking us, via "the whole apparatus of assimilation,"[23] to the cosmic death drive:[24]

> Now he too heard only dead wirehum, as if the other end of it extended beyond atmosphere, into cold space; as though he listened now to the profound sound of infinity, of void itself filled with the cold unceasing murmur of aeonweary and unflagging stars. (*Pylon* 74)

What is the "dead wirehum" *saying* in what it is saying? For Adorno, this is a matter of "physiognomics," the relation of electric sound to "expressive movements of the human face" (RP 43). "Now it is obvious," he observes, "that this concept of physiognomics is obsolete" (RP 43) in a posthuman age. Yet he must deploy it in accordance with these observations: "The absence of visible persons makes the 'radio voice' appear more objective and infallible than a live voice; and the mystery of a machine which can speak may be felt in atavistic layers of our psychical life" (RP 47)—as he puts it in the language of the Freudian period. *A machine which can speak*: "In form the older loudspeakers resemble the mouth" (RP 48). In other words, "the radio phenomenon" has a physiognomy because we have one (even as our human physiognomy becomes metallic, standardized, robotic). (Consider Faulkner's description of the crowd in *Pylon*.) The original speaker or source behind the microphone may be invisible, yet we feel the pressure of "the will and the power behind the instrument" (RP 77) as it projects itself "virtually everywhere in space" (RP 76). If "the listener assumes an attitude to radio which is not fully rational" (RP

84), this is because the radio voice issues from a "loud speaker" (literally). The listener always responds *as if* "to an authoritarian voice even if the content of that voice or the speaker to whom the individual is listening has no authoritarian features whatsoever" (RP 70). Think, here, in this connection, of the faux-folksiness of the announcer's voice in *Pylon*. He speaks mainly about the prize money and the technical specifications of the machines, but there is also a kind of leering, voyeuristic quality in his attention to Laverne, and in the imperative to "WATCH" (*Pylon* 28–29). Even at its most bland and innocuous, the voice, in Adorno's words, "is spread unconsciously among the masses of listeners" and so acquires thereby a kind of "mystical social power" (RP 51).

Though we catch two glimpses of the human announcer in *Pylon*, the essential "loud speaker" of the novel (anticipating Orwell) is a metallic orifice, unmistakably a face, skull, mouth, or eye, replicated and interspaced in accordance with the proscriptive logic of the age of mechanical reproduction:

> Then he was interrupted; it was the amplifyer; all the amplifyers up and down the apron began to call his name, telling the stands, the field, the land and lake and air, that he was wanted in the superintendent's office at once. . . . (226)

> The amplifyer began to repeat itself. It faced him; it seemed to stare straight at him while it roared his name deliberately as though he had to be summoned not out of the living world of population but evoked peremptory and repetitive out of the air itself; the one in the rotundra was just beginning again when he entered; the sound followed him through the door and across the anteroom. [. . .] (226–27)

We are dwelling on the radio phenomenon, writes Adorno, "*because it is actually the phenomenon which determines the reaction of the listeners, and it is our ultimate aim to study the listener*" (RP 65; Adorno's emphasis). In this study of the listener, the category of what has so far "escaped the attention of researchers" (RP 45) is paramount. *Pylon* is all about what has heretofore escaped the attention of researchers in the study of the listener. The novel is dominated by the shocked sensibility of the reporter, whose obsessive notation of all that is capable of inscribing a mark on the human sensorium renders visible, and audible, what is being seen or heard for the first time (by anybody):

> The amplified voice still spoke, profound and effortless, as though it were the voice of the steel-and-chromium mausoleum itself. . . . (25)

> The amplifyers at regular intervals along the apronedge erupted snatched blares of ghostlike and ubiquitous sound. (26)

> The voice of the amplifyer, apocryphal, sourceless, inhuman, ubiquitous and beyond weariness or fatigue. . . . (36)

Indeed, "it is difficult to describe in exact terms acoustic phenomena so new and unusual" (RP 53):

> and now the band had begun to play, heard twice: once the faint light almost airy thump-thump-thump from where the sun glinted on the actual horn-mouths on the platform facing the reserved section of the stands, and once where the disembodied noise blared brazen, metallic, and loud from the amplifyer which faced the barrier. (20)

The sound color here is silvery metallic, grey, "canned." (Observes Adorno: "In every-day experience the term 'canned,' applied to radio and phonograph music, expresses this image-character. The difference between the image sound and the real sound can very well be compared with the difference between fresh and canned food" [RP 118].) Inherent in every element of its architectural design and material substance, the new airport is an echo space wired for sound, a space in which sound always bears the innate character of canned reproduction:

> Now the first starting bomb went—a jarring thud followed by a vicious light repercussion as if the bomb had set off another smaller one in the now empty hangar and in the rotundra too. Within the domed steel vacuum the single report became myriad, high and everywhere about the concave ceiling like invisible unearthly winged creatures of that yet unvisioned tomorrow, mechanical instead of blood bone and meat, speaking to one another in vicious highpitched ejaculations as though concerting an attack on something below. There was an amplifyer in the rotundra too and through it the sound of the

> aeroplanes turning the field pylon on each lap filled the rotundra and the restaurant. (22)

"Physiognomically," the "starting bomb" and its "steelfiltered" reverberations are ceaselessly image-generating, producing an unmistakably martial premonition (as if out of Marinetti's thirty-year string of futurist manifestoes): the dome above the metropolis—above the "painwebbed globe itself"—is soon to be darkened by the formation flights of the robot bombers. (Faulkner's imagery here extends to his review of Jimmy Collins's *Test Pilot* and to the general's speech in *A Fable,* among other places).

If amplified or echoey sound "possesses something of the vagueness and lack of clarity of bad photographic enlargments" (RP 53), we are nonetheless certainly justified in attributing "an aggressive character to the radio voice" (RP 66) and to describe its essential physiognomic "expression" as "barking and bellowing." The loudspeaker's voice always "resembles somewhat a political harangue, hostile and threatening to the listener" (*Pylon* 53). When the sound carries inside, "the disproportion between the power of the 'radio voice' and the power of the individual endangers the latter: it sounds as if the sound could blow up the room" (RP 53). Or, as the great art historian E. H. Gombrich puts it in his pamphlet *Myth and Reality in German War-Time Broadcasts* (1970):

> People [in Germany, during the war and leading up to it] were encouraged to listen in groups, in factories and barracks, for the idea of the hearer alone in the privacy of his room and capable even to switch off was anathema [to Goebbels]. It has often been remarked how diametrically opposed to this fiction of an extended super rally was Roosevelt's conception of what he called a "fireside chat." Here the speaker pretended to visit the home, there the home was swept into the Sportspalast.[25]

Pylon is a sounding of this explicitly post-1933 fascist media ecology and the so-called "ether war"[26] that is gaining in intensity during this period.

With Adorno, and with respect to Faulkner, that is, I mean to invoke "the other extreme of the same theater,"[27] the torrent of words pouring forth at this time from the German loudspeakers in Munich, Dresden, Berlin. All of Adorno's writing has been conditioned by his post-1933 German experience.

This is what gives it its edge, and we cannot have it, and would not want it, without this edge. "The author knows of the following fact from his own German experience" (RP 74) is a characteristic sentence in *Current of Music*. Or: "Totalitarian governments have not overlooked the loophole of turning off the radio. During the Czechoslovakian crisis the German authorities unambiguously expressed their expectation that every inhabitant in Germany listen to Hitler's speech. In other words, anyone who might try to escape the voice of his Führer was virtually threatened" (RP 113).

Victor Klemperer's diary of the Nazi years is an incomparable account of the listener's alienated fascination as he is forced to listen.

> March 10, 1933:
>
> the never ending propaganda in the street, on the radio, etc. On Saturday, the fourth, I heard a part of Hitler's speech from Königsberg. The front of a hotel at the railway station, illuminated, a torchlight procession in front of it, torchbearers and swastika flag bearers on the balconies and loudspeakers. I understood only occasional words. But the tone! The unctuous bawling, truly bawling, of a priest.[28]

> November 11, 1933:
>
> Demonstrations and chanting into the night, loudspeakers on the streets, vehicles (with wireless apparatus playing music mounted on top), both cars and trams. . . . A mostly hoarse, strained, agitated voice, long passages in the whining tone of the sectarian preacher. Content: I know no intellectuals, bourgeois, proletarians—only the people. (41)

> September 14, 1934:
>
> Everything is aimed at deafening the individual in collectivism.—In general pay attention to the role of *radio!* (87)

> October 31, 1935:
>
> Hitler undoubtedly has cancer of the larynx, he can only whisper, the thunder of his speeches is produced by the loudspeakers. (138)

> March 8, 1936:
>
> Yesterday on Bismarckplatz I ran into the middle of Hitler's Reichstag

speech. . . . I could not get away from it for an hour. First from an open shop, then in the bank, then from a shop again. He spoke in a completely healthy voice, most of it was well formulated, read, not overladen with pathos. (155)

Already in 1933 Klemperer declares in his diary, "If I have no choice but to read and hear something everywhere, it is forced upon me" (42). Adorno speaks in this connection of the "*Volksempfänger* (radio sets for the masses) . . . built to allow the listener to tune in only government-controlled German stations" (RP 96). Indeed, the essential pattern of intense circulation around a close circuit is central to the case of *Pylon*, which is dominated by ubiquitous radial patterns of all kinds. As one walks around the airport listening to the same sound pouring out of countless different speakers, "there is no escape from the field of the radio mechanism" (RP 61). Adorno's key question is, therefore, "how far the radio's ear and the radio's voice replace the listener's own ear and voice" (RP 48). Here is the reporter:

> He had to walk through the voice again to pass through the rotundra, and again it met him outside though for the moment he did not listen to it for listening to himself: "It's all the same! I did the same thing myself! I dont intend to pay Hagood either! I lied to him about money too!" and the answer, loud too: "You lie, you bastard. You're lying, you son of a bitch." So he was hearing the amplifyer before he knew that he was listening. (164)

Adorno and Klemperer, too, are fascinated by the phenomenon of what we might call "tuning out" as a prelude to bringing up the volume of one's own voice:

> September 11, 1938:
>
> Village just before Oschatz, "Long Distance Lorry Drivers' Restaurant." The huge vehicles outside, the huge portions inside. The Party Rally was coming over the loudspeaker. Announcement, the arrival of Field Marshal Goering. Introductory march, roars of triumph, then Goering's speech, about the tremendous rise, affluence, peace and workers' good fortune in Germany, about the absurd lies and hopes of its enemies, constantly interrupted by well-drilled roars of applause. But the most interesting thing about it all was the behavior of the customers, who all came and went, greeting and taking their leave with "Heil Hitler." But no one was listening. I could barely understand

> the broadcast because a couple of people were playing cards, striking the table with loud thumps, talking very loudly. It was quieter at other tables. One man was writing a postcard, one was writing in his order book, one was reading the newspaper. And landlady and waitress were talking to each other or to the cardplayers. Truly: Not one of a dozen people paid attention to the radio for even a single second, it could just as well have been transmitting silence or a foxtrot from Leipzig. (267)

Contrapuntally, in *Pylon,*

> the voice of the announcer reverberant and sonorous within the domed shell of glass and steel in a running commentation to which apparently none listened, as if the voice were merely some unavoidable and inexplicable phenomenon of nature like the sound of wind or of erosion. Then the band would begin to play again, though faint and almost trivial behind and below the voice, as if the voice actually were that natural phenomenon against which all manmade sounds and noises blew and vanished like leaves. (23)

Adorno warns that there is no refuge from

> the threatening sea of mechanization and reification. We want to face the danger of this sea, not for the sake of fleeing to cultural islands, but for better navigation. Any investigator who does not see the dangers of that sea and who simply allows himself to be drugged by its grandeur, and who sees its waves as waves of unbroken progress, is very likely to be drowned. (RP 62)

Better navigation: let the reporter, then, Ulysses-like, be "the guide" (*Pylon* 80) as he inscribes his voice "savagely in pencil" (324) across the novel's final "sheet of copy" (324), the newsprint meant for mass circulation, "the dead instant's fruit of forty tons of machinery" (110–11). The human voice should be sounded aloud, though without amplification: "*I guess this is what you mean you bastard and now I am going down to Amboise st. and get drunk a while and if you dont know where Amboise st. is ask your son to tell you and if you dont know what drunk is come down there and look at me and when you come bring some jack because I am on a credit*" (324).

NOTES

1. William Faulkner, *A Fable*, in *Novels, 1942–1954: Go Down, Moses, Intruder in the Dust, Requiem for a Nun, A Fable*, ed. Noel Polk and Joseph Blotner (New York: Library of America, 1994), 854.

2. Paul Virilio, *Speed and Politics: An Essay on Dromology*, trans. Mark Polizzotti (Los Angeles: Semiotext[e], 2006).

3. Faulkner, *Pylon* (New York: Vintage, 1987), 24. Hereafter cited parenthetically.

4. Joseph Blotner, *Faulkner: A Biography*, one-volume ed. (New York: Vintage, 1991), 35.

5. Thomas Mann, "Freud and the Future," in *Thomas Mann: Essays of Three Decades*, trans. H. T. Lowe-Porter (New York: Knopf, 1968), 412.

6. Faulkner, "Landing in Luck," in *William Faulkner: Early Prose and Poetry*, ed. Carvel Collins (Boston: Atlantic Monthly Press, 1962), 43–36.

7. Ibid., 49.

8. Sigmund Freud, *The Interpretation of Dreams*, in *The Standard Edition of the Complete Psychological Works of Sigmund Freud*, vols. 4 and 5, trans. and ed. James Strachey (London: Hogarth, 1953), 5:436.

9. Georg Simmel, "The Metropolis and Mental Life" [1903], in *German History in Documents and Images*, n.p., http://germanhistorydocs.ghi-dc.org/sub_document.cfm?document_id=747.

10. Faulkner, *The Sound and the Fury* (New York: Vintage, 1990), 320–21.

11. Walter Benjamin, "Theories of German Fascism: On the Collection of Essays *War and Warriors*, edited by Ernst Jünger," trans. Jerolf Wikoff, in *Walter Benjamin: Selected Writings*, vol. 2, pt. 1, *1927–1930*, trans. Rodney Livingstone et al., ed. Michael W. Jennings, Howard Eiland, and Gary Smith (Cambridge: Belknap Press of Harvard University Press, 2005), 312.

12. Faulkner, *As I Lay Dying* (New York: Vintage, 1985), 96.

13. Lindbergh landed at Le Bourget on Saturday, May 21, 1927, before an estimated crowd of 150,000 spectators. They stormed the airplane, pulled the pilot out of the cockpit, and carried him aloft. Eventually he was rescued by the French military police. See Robert Wohl's account of the event's mediated repercussions: "Lindbergh's flight was a dazzling demonstration of the magical powers of the new technologies of communication. News of this progress was circulated instantaneously by cable and wireless, then flashed on electric bulletin boards, broadcast over the radio, and diffused in special editions of newspapers whose headlines raised the hopes and anxieties of their readers to fever pitch. Motion pictures of his takeoff in New York and reception in Paris were seen in newsreels throughout the world. His image quickly became as familiar as Charlie Chaplin's." "The crowds along the route he traversed in an open car down the Champs-Elysées and along the Rue de Rivoli were estimated at between five hundred thousand and a million people." "On 13 June, four million people jammed the streets of New York to hurl eighteen tons of paper and confetti on Lindbergh's caravan." "Lindbergh addressed the crowd and an estimated radio audience of 30,000,000 people after having been decorated by Coolidge in June 1927" (Robert Wohl, *The Spectacle of Flight: Aviation and the Western Imagination, 1920–1950* [New Haven: Yale University Press, 2005], 44, 23, 29, 34).

14. See Jimmy Collin's *Test Pilot* for an insider's report on the formidable power of the American military aviation industry. Faulkner reviewed the book in 1935 (William Faulkner, Review of *Test Pilot*, by Jimmy Collins [1935], in *William Faulkner: Essays, Speeches and Public Letters*, ed. James B. Meriwether [New York: Modern Library, 2004], 188–92).

15. Wohl, *The Spectacle of Flight*, 93–94.

16. Ibid., 95.

17. Ibid., 96.

18. Ibid., 101–2.

19. Benjamin, "Theories of German Fascism," 313.

20. Benjamin, "The Work of Art in the Age of Its Technological Reproducibility," second version, in *Walter Benjamin: Selected Writings*, vol. 3, *1935–1938*, trans. Edmund Jephcott, Howard Eiland, et al., ed. Eiland and Michael W. Jennings (Cambridge: Belknap Press of Harvard University Press, 2002), 122.

21. My thanks to Adam Frank for alerting me to the presence of this book.

22. Theodor W. Adorno, "Radio Physiognomics," in *Current of Music: Elements of a Radio Theory*, trans. Robert Hullot-Kentor (Cambridge: Polity, 2008), 45. Hereafter cited parenthetically as "RP."

23. Don DeLillo interviewed by Adam Begley in "Don DeLillo: The Art of Fiction, 135," *Paris Review* 135 (Fall 1993).

24. "Once Bill said to me, a few years before his death, that perhaps each of us will become a sort of radio wave in the hereafter" (Murry C. Falkner, *The Falkners of Mississippi: A Memoir* [Baton Rouge: Louisiana State University Press, 1967], 24).

25. E. H. Gombrich, *Myth and Reality in German War-Time Broadcasts* (London: Athlone, 1970), 4–5.

26. Ibid., 2.

27. Michael Herr, *Dispatches* (New York: Vintage, 1991), 6.

28. Victor Klemperer, *I Will Bear Witness: A Diary of the Nazi Years, 1933–1941*, trans. Martin Chalmers (New York: Random House, 1998), 5. Hereafter cited parenthetically.

Auditory Exposures

Faulkner, Eisenstein, and Film Sound

SARAH GLEESON-WHITE

Writing to his wife, Estelle, from Santa Monica on 20 July 1934, William Faulkner announces that he has "finished the final treatment of SUTTER" and adds, in an offhanded post-script, that he has "[d]one a little on the novel from time to time" ("To Mrs. William Faulkner"). It would be easy to think no more of these passing allusions to two seemingly disparate projects—a film treatment and a novel—one of which is unnamed. Finding this casual contiguity tantalizing, however, I unravel in this essay as yet unacknowledged affinities between "Sutter's Gold" and *Absalom, Absalom!*—the two texts in question—that reveal their soundscapes and what I claim is Faulkner's auditory experimentalism. Scholarship on literary sound is rare. Douglas Kahn has observed that modernism, for example, "has been read and looked at but barely heard" (*Noise* 4).[1] Only Stephen M. Ross and John T. Matthews have broached the topic of sound in Faulkner's fiction. In a compelling account of the creation and use of voices in Faulkner's stories and novels, Ross focuses on the southern oratorical influences on speech in *Absalom, Absalom!* Matthews argues that the incorporation of a graphophone in *As I Lay Dying* enabled Faulkner to "consider . . . the effects of the novel's existence in print—the writer's instrument of mechanical reproduction" (67). Faulkner's career coincided with the advent of new sound technologies and the increasing popularity of associated entertainments in the late 1920s and the 1930s: radio, the tape recorder, ventriloquist performances, and, of course, documentary and narrative sound film.[2] Just as significant, Faulkner first arrived in Hollywood to write for the talkies in May 1932, when the most important developments in film sound were occurring.[3]

Faulkner wrote the 108-page "Sutter's Gold" treatment for Howard Hawks at Universal Studios in July 1934, nearly twelve months before "he settled down to rewrite . . . *Absalom, Absalom!*," which he completed in January 1936.[4] What is particularly striking about the treatment is Faulkner's almost palpable struggle with the problem of ideographically representing sounds, not only dialogue but music and sound effects too. The Soviet filmmaker Sergei Eisenstein also wrote a "Sutter's Gold" scenario, in 1930, which Faulkner read carefully. There is clearly much at stake, then, in Faulkner's overlooked film treatment. The all-too-common assumption that his so-called real work—the fiction—"was slowed by his having to serve some time in Hollywood" should be put to rest (Meriwether 693). Faulkner's screen writing, influenced by Eisenstein's cinematic aesthetic, transformed his literary practice in terms of an evident emerging interest in and grappling with the ideographic representation of sound.[5]

Faulkner's "Sutter's Gold" is an adaptation of Blaise Cendrars's 1926 best-selling novel of the same name.[6] Cendrars's novel tells of the transnational and then continental travels of a nineteenth-century pioneering colonel—Swiss-born Johannes Sutter—who, in his fanatical drive to execute his design, establishes an ill-fated empire, New Helvetia, with the use of foreign labor (indigenous Hawaiians) on the Californian frontier. Eventually, his empire is destroyed by a fire that also consumes his son. This skeletal outline of Cendrars's novel resonates with the plot of *Absalom, Absalom!* and that novel's characterization of Thomas Sutpen.[7] Jay Bochner, in an important yet neglected essay about the influence of Cendrars on American literary modernism, is the only scholar who has brought *Sutter's Gold* to bear on Faulkner's novel. Although Bochner can only speculate on its relation to *Absalom, Absalom!*, believing that Faulkner's "Sutter's Gold" treatment is lost (50),[8] his essay is indicative of the work still to be done "en confrontant, dans le cas des adaptations de livres, l'imaginaire faulknérian, avec celui de leurs sources" 'in confronting, in the case of the adaptation, the Faulknerian imaginary with that of their sources' (Liénard-Yeterian 12; my trans.).

Eisenstein wrote his treatment of *Sutter's Gold* for Paramount Studios.[9] Although I have not been able to establish how Faulkner, under contract to Universal at the time, obtained Eisenstein's Paramount scenario, it is nonetheless clear that he read Eisenstein's treatment with great care, as evidenced by the many similarities between the two treatments, including a two-page montage sequence that Faulkner repeats almost verbatim from Eisenstein's treatment (Faulkner 66–67; Eisenstein 174–75).[10]

Additional features shared by both treatments and related obliquely to Cendrars's novel confirm that Faulkner acquainted himself with Eisenstein's redaction of "Sutter's Gold" to write his own. Both Eisenstein's and Faulkner's Sutter dresses as a "fakir" at a circus (Faulkner 25–26; Eisenstein 157–58). (In Cendrars's novel, Sutter appears as a "ringmaster in a circus" [18].) Cendrars's *Sutter's Gold* briefly—and tantalizingly for the Faulkner reader—alludes to Sutter's boxing "a giant negro" (18). Eisenstein (159–60) and Faulkner (28) enlarge on Cendrars's hurried detail, although in Faulkner's treatment the boxing contest is transformed into a slave whipping. (Cendrars's and Eisenstein's pugilist slave will appear in *Absalom, Absalom!*)

On arrival in New York, Sutter works as an assistant shoe salesman (Eisenstein 158; Faulkner 24) and then as an animal dentist (Eisenstein 158; Faulkner 25). While Cendrars's Sutter interrupts his continental journey to settle in Missouri for some time (20–26), Eisenstein's and Faulkner's Sutter passes quickly through Missouri (Eisenstein 161; Faulkner 29). Indians attack Sutter and his party on the journey westward in both treatments (Eisenstein 162–63; Faulkner 51), but there is no such attack in Cendrars's *Sutter's Gold*. Eisenstein's and Faulkner's Sutter writes a letter from California to his wife in Switzerland, a detail not found in Cendrars. Finally, Faulkner's description of the elderly, worn-out Sutter toward the end of the narrative resonates more closely with Eisenstein's characterization than with Cendrars's. Eisenstein (198–99) and Faulkner (90) dress Sutter in a glittering gold uniform, and in both treatments Sutter is mistrustful of the cheering crowd as he is paraded before them. In Cendrars's novel, he is merely incredulous (141–42).

Such striking resonances between the two "Sutter's Gold" treatments prove that Faulkner was familiar with Eisenstein's film praxis—even if on the page alone—defined largely by its montage, visual and sonic. While Faulkner names Eisenstein in *If I Forget Thee, Jerusalem* (*Wild Palms* 157) and while first J. R. Raper and then Bruce Kawin draw on Eisensteinian montage to describe a comparable dynamic in Faulkner's fiction, there has been no conclusive evidence that Faulkner was aware of Eisenstein's films, scenarios, or film theory. At best, Kawin wonders whether Faulkner encountered Eisensteinian montage—or ideas about it—on his 1925–26 European travels.[11] Clearly, as early as mid-1934 Faulkner was familiar with Eisenstein's cinematic aesthetic. More surprising, perhaps, the Eisenstein-Faulkner nexus reveals auditory—not merely visual—qualities that inform and characterize Faulkner's industrial and literary writings.

Examples of visual montage pepper Eisenstein's and Faulkner's treatments of *Sutter's Gold.* While some elementary form of montage had been used in Hollywood since the teens, as David Bordwell notes, by the late 1920s it had become safely installed in the classical paradigm, employed to indicate the passing of time in the most seamless and thus least disruptive way and to offer insights into a character's psychology (Bordwell, Staiger, and Thompson 29). In the 1944 essay "Dickens, Griffith, and the Film Today," comparing Hollywood and Soviet montage practices, Eisenstein contends that Griffith's "montage concept," while technically revolutionary, is in the end constrained by a liberal outlook: "as primarily parallel montage, [it] appears to be a copy of [Griffith's] dualistic picture of the world, running into two parallel lines of poor and rich towards some hypothetical 'reconciliation'" (235). By contrast, Soviet filmmakers "find in the *juxtaposition of shots an arrangement of a new qualitative element*, a new *image*, a new *understanding*" (245). Instead of smoothing over cuts or resolving the "dualistic picture of the world," Eisensteinian montage disrupts temporal and spatial continuities to underscore "a worldview both monistic and dialectic" (235–36). In sum, Eisensteinian montage is an art of "unresolution" (Kawin, *Faulkner and Film* 8–9).

In Eisenstein's "Sutter's Gold" the most striking examples of montage are found in accompanying sketches—for example, a forest of "big trees (about 15–20 feet high)" placed directly above a couple of "artificial cactuses" (167). Eisenstein also evokes visual montage in the scenario itself. The layering of images of a Swiss village—a fountain, and then a police station, a church, the Sutter house, and finally a mountain landscape (154–55)—is used not to indicate the lapse of time but to present a multifaceted thick scene of largely metaphoric significance: the encounter of two conflicting forms of justice, evoked by the police station and the church, that underpin the entire narrative and lead to Sutter's downfall.

Faulkner, in his treatment of *Sutter's Gold,* takes pains to specify the relation between scenes with intricate technical directions indicating fades, pans and trucks. He also calls for dissolves and resolves, elements of montage frequently used in classical cinema to soften the transitions between sequences and images rather than to foreground conflict. However, Faulkner's use of dissolve—for example, from Washington's face to Rousseau's and then to Sutter's (20)—does not affect the passing of time or smooth over cuts. It is the (heavily ironic) relation between these images that matters, something that is crucial to Eisensteinian montage. Sometimes Faulkner imagines an even harsher cut, more typical of Eisenstein's practice: double exposure, whereby one image is superimposed onto another before the fade-out. The first instance of double exposure in Faulkner's "Sutter's Gold" appears when Sutter, on arrival in New York, is thrown down the gangplank, clutching the dog he has befriended:

> DOG is flung back.
> DOUBLE EXPOSURE to:
>
> SUTTER being dragged aft along deck.
> DOUBLE EXPOSURE TO: SUTTER being flung down companionway.
>
> DOUBLE EXPOSURE to: SUTTER facing CAPTAIN, prisoner. RESOLVE SUPERPOSE: title
> (17–18)

The work of the double exposure is clear in the (not too subtle) correlation of Sutter and the dog and is characteristic of Faulkner's imagined use of editing and camera work throughout this treatment, revealing a knowledge of the technical aspects of moviemaking whose profundity is remarkable considering that he had had only four months' screen writing experience, at MGM, before writing this treatment. We can to some degree attribute his familiarity and willingness to experiment with cinema's technical possibilities to his awareness of Eisenstein's "Sutter's Gold" scenario.

Double exposure, of which Faulkner is so fond throughout "Sutter's Gold," is the term Marina Burke uses to describe Eisenstein's conceptualization of the cinematic relation between sound and image: "Music, sound effects and visuals would be sensed as a composite, with what he theorized as the gestural elements of both music and visuals creating an effect of 'double exposure.'" Sound, not just the image, is crucial to Eisenstein's theory and practice of montage. Eisenstein, with V. I. Pudomn and G. V. Alexandrov, produced a statement on film sound as early as August 1928. Here he denounces Hollywood for taking this new technology, with its seemingly endless possibilities, "in an incorrect direction . . . in which sound recording will proceed on a naturalistic level, exactly corresponding with the movement on the screen, and providing a certain 'illusion' of talking people, audible objects, etc," thus ensuring that cinema becomes nothing more than the "photographing of plays." Eisenstein instead calls for a radical disjuncture of sound and image—sound's "DISTINCT NONSYNCHRONIZATION WITH THE VISUAL IMAGES"—to create "an ORCHESTRAL COUNTERPOINT of visual and aural images."[12]

Stalin sent Eisenstein to Hollywood in 1929, instructing him (with Eduard Tisse and Alexandrov, who were to accompany him) to "[s]tudy the sound film in detail. This is very important for us. When our heroes discover speech, the influential power of films will increase enormously" (qtd. In Kahn, *Noise* 146). The possibilities of sound that Eisenstein imagined are everywhere inscribed in his "Sutter's Gold" scenario, which one scholar has called an "experiment with sound" (Frayling 18). This experiment's most notable components include the frequent counterpoint of sound and image as well as its purely sonic montage sequences. As Sutter gallops toward his burning house, the "tinkle" of "the trappings of the horse . . . the sound of the hooves, and the sound of the pantings of the belly of the horse" soon "mingle . . . [with] the sound of the burning . . . [t]he crackling of burning wood" until we are directed to see a horse and hear burning wood simultaneously in a fine example of sound-image double exposure (203), the counterpoint Eisenstein describes as "orchestral." A scene in "Sutter's Gold," which narrates the lust and greed of the forty-niners who destroy Sutter's land, records the sounds of the gold rush in the form of a "symphony" for over two pages:

> The sound of the sand moving in the wooden working pans, the dashing of water, begins to creep over the forests and fields.
> The sound of the picks, and the sounds of the stones that are discarded from the working pans grows louder and louder . . .
> The sounds pervade the whole land. . . .
> Sutter, deserted by his people, wanders through this wasted desolation, hearkening to the symphony of the working of the mines . . .
> And then, from the depths of these canyons, arrives a symphony of new sounds.

> These sounds are the sounds of thousands of feet tramping upon the stones. . . .
> Sutter is maddened by these sounds. . . .
> [T]his terrible symphony of sounds. (181–82)

Immediately, we cut to "[t]he gentle, melancholy bell of a Swiss church tower tolling its song" (183), one of many examples of sound montage employed throughout the scenario not to soften sonic and visual cuts but to render them more jarring.

One of the most distinctive of Eisenstein's experimental uses of sound in "Sutter's Gold" is its choric voice. The chorus appears in different forms throughout the treatment: the singers of "a song of California"; the "chorus of girls and vigorous young men . . . singing Swiss songs" (151); the crowd whose "chatter, singing, clamor, whistling" define the fair scene (157); and the chant of "Gold," when James Marshall discovers gold on Sutter's land, that "rings through the forest" (181), side by side with "the murmur of endless mobs" (182) that becomes the gossip accompanying Mrs. Sutter on her travels from Switzerland to California: "Sutter . . . Sutter . . . Sutter . . . Sutter" (184–86), looking forward to Faulkner's choric "Sutter Sutter" (101) and further to Yoknapatawpha's "steady strophe and antistrophe: *Sutpen. Sutpen. Sutpen. Sutpen*" (*Absalom* 32).

In his "Sutter's Gold" treatment, Faulkner takes as much care with the annotation of sound directions as he does with camera directions. The sound directions appear in typescript in the left-hand margins on 61 of the treatment's 108 pages; on average, that means one on every one-and-a-half pages. Such close attention to sound (including painstaking instructions on the sounds of snow, gurgling water, and tramping feet and on diegetic and nondiegetic music) was unusual for a screenwriter and particularly noteworthy in one who had so recently come to Hollywood to work in a medium and genre that only two years earlier were unfamiliar to him. Although Kawin identifies an example of sound montage in an earlier MGM screenplay—"War Birds: A Ghost Story"—nowhere in his previous screen writings does Faulkner include the comprehensive sound directives of the particular format found in "Sutter's Gold" (*Faulkner's MGM Screenplays* 264). Faulkner pays similarly scant attention to sound in his post–"Sutter's Gold," Twentieth Century-Fox screen writings. Whether Hawks instructed Faulkner to include those directions in the "Sutter's Gold" treatment does not especially matter. What matters is that

Faulkner was poised to transform "The Dark House" into *Absalom, Absalom!* at the moment of Hollywood's most significant developments in sound technology, roughly 1932–35 (Bordwell, Staiger, and Thompson 300–01), and sound was clearly on his mind. Eisenstein's experiments in sound in "Sutter's Gold" must have prompted Faulkner's similar preoccupation at this critical creative juncture.

Faulkner's sonic experimentalism in the "Sutter's Gold" treatment includes the counterpoint of sound and image that Eisenstein advocates. This feature is more starkly realized in Faulkner's than in Eisenstein's treatment because Faulkner's use of marginal instructions means that the reader can *see* the relation. The opening of the treatment is exemplary in this. We hear first the sound of wheels, then the sound of feet as a title appears—"(Town), Switzerland. January 1830"—before a pan takes us to "brass plate beside door: German letters: Rittsmueller Brothers. Enter MAN's shadow" (1). The sound of footsteps continues for two pages, and yet we do not see the feet's owner throughout this entire sequence; we see a shadow and then a "grilled window with a clerk behind it. Enter HAND showing paper to clerk. . . . Shadow moves as clerk pointed; . . . DISSOLVE through to: Countingroom, PAN to vacant desk" where sits another clerk (2). In the margins of these first three pages are directions concerning the sound of the feet: "One pair of feet approaching, "feet cease, feet begin," "feet stop," "feet begin, grow fainter," and so on, until the final "Angry feet begin, die away. Hushed feet of clerks" (1–3). Then, in a new scene, the camera finally pans to Sutter "playing flute" (3), our first sighting of the owner of the feet and hand. This opening scene—which would have lasted for about three on-screen minutes—illustrates the disembodied or detached way of employing sound that Eisenstein favoured; there is no real correlation between what we hear (the sound of footsteps) and what we see (clerks writing at desks).[13] In a further move away from classical Hollywood's preferred naturalistic use of sound, Faulkner uses, like Eisenstein, another form of frequently unattributed voice: the chorus, which is heard sometimes as voice-over and usually evokes a scene's tone or its arguments by laughter, murmurs, shouts, or the chants "Gold! Gold!" (88) and "Sutter Sutter" (101)—seeming to replicate Eisenstein's chanting chorus—and by gossip and rumor (e.g., "it is said of him that he is now the richest man in the world" [72]).

The experiments in film sound that I have identified in Eisenstein's "Sutter's Gold" and then traced through Faulkner's own treatment of Cendrars's novel reverberate throughout that quintessential novel of American modernism *Absalom, Absalom!* But the cinematic qualities that scholars have noticed in the novel, such as montage and tableaux, are exclusively visual. To read Faulkner's novel alongside his and Eisenstein's film-sound experiments recovers the sound track of this cinematic Faulkner.

Absalom, Absalom!'s preoccupation with sounds is striking from its first to its last pages. The opening "dry vivid dusty sound" of sparrows and Rosa's "grim haggard amazed voice" (7) are compact synesthesic sound-image montages ("vivid . . . sound," "haggard . . . voice"), or what Eisenstein calls "vertical montage," which involves the abolition of "dualist contradictions and mechanical parallelism between the realms of sight and sound." He adds, "[P]roblems of the unity of audio-visual synthesis . . . are not even on the agenda of American researchers" ("Dickens" 254). Faulkner's vertical montage, predating Eisenstein's observation by at least eight years, straightaway flags *Absalom, Absalom!*'s interest in sound, which is sustained right up to the closing "sound of the idiot negro," Jim Bond, who is all that remains of the burning House of Sutpen (376), and Quentin's final "I don't hate it [the South]" (378). *Absalom, Absalom!* defies the strategies and effects of realism (what Eisenstein terms the "photographing of plays") as it draws attention to voices and other sounds as sounds: the "rasp, rasp, rasp" of a saw (151);[14] the townsfolk's "*Sutpen. Sutpen. Sutpen. Sutpen*" (32); and the oxymoronic "quiet thunderclap" (8), "thunderous silence" (136), and description of Wash Jones as one who "could . . . bellow placidly" (135). *Absalom, Absalom!* is also a loquacious novel, with its conglomeration of "garrulous outraged baffled ghosts, listening, having to listen" and to vie across time for their listeners attention, including our own (9): Quentin Compson listening (or trying to listen) to Rosa Coldfield; Mr Compson listening to General Compson; General Compson listening to Colonel Sutpen; and Quentin and Shreve McCannon listening to each other. One of the conceptual problems at the heart of the novel, then, concerns the inscription, audibility, and transmission of ideographic sound, and this, I suggest, arises in the wake of Faulkner's Hollywood experiments in writing film sound and his awareness—indeed, his appreciation—of Eisenstein's theories and praxis thereof. It is thus difficult to accept wholesale Peter Lurie's observation that, although Faulkner's novels "engaged with filmic practices at the same time as they invent new versions of the novel form," the "scripts he wrote show Faulkner . . . willing to subordinate his experimental tendencies to the need for accessibility or narrative coherence" (21). Not only is "Sutter's Gold" typical of Faulkner's cinematic experimentalism; it also informed the most formally groundbreaking of his novels.

Indeed, *Absalom, Absalom!* marks a shift in Faulkner's creative practice, as several scholars have noted. While Lurie links this shift to "an ever stronger emphasis on vision" in the novels of the 1930s (170), for Joseph Urgo the shift concerns *speaking*. In both *The Sound and Fury* and *As I Lay Dying*, Faulkner's

> use of multiple narration is characterized by the individual narrators' lack of dialogic interaction with one another. Benjy, Quentin, and Jason may each have a say in representing the Compson story, but they do not say it to each other, only to the reader. Narrator interaction in *As I Lay Dying* is similarly low, with the Bundren family members talking into a kind of narrative "space." . . . In *Sanctuary* and *Light in August*, perspectives on events clash and collide with greater violence but still without significant or productive interaction. . . .
>
> In *Absalom, Absalom!* however, the various narrators are not talking into space but directly *at* each other. (58–59)

Carolyn Porter makes a similar observation about the discernible shift from the earlier novels to *Absalom, Absalom!*: "Although dialogues [in *As I Lay Dying*] are represented within some of the monologues, the novel itself exists exclusively in monologue form, a form that is private by nature" (68). The recognition that what distinguishes *Absalom, Absalom!* from the earlier fiction might reside in its auditory qualities remains overlooked in Faulkner scholarship. Connecting the two observations I make here—that film sound informs *Absalom, Absalom!* and that the novel's audibility makes it distinctive—I want to suggest that where *The Sound and the Fury* and *As I Lay Dying* might be silent (there is no real "dialogic interaction"), *Absalom, Absalom!* is a talkie.

One of the ways in which sound is amplified in *Absalom, Absalom!* is in its use of what Ross calls "'textual voice' through which physical features of print articulate visual differences that signify just as the speaking voice can articulate meaningful aural differences" (145).[15] Ross cites as examples the colored inks that Faulkner famously requested *The Sound and the Fury* be printed in;[16] the graphics in that novel and in *As I Lay Dying* and *Go Down, Moses;* and the uses of italics in *Absalom, Absalom!* Textual voice in *Absalom, Absalom!* is also indicated by parentheses, the presence or absence of quotation marks, dashes of varying lengths, phonetic spellings (to record Wash Jones's dialect, for example), and the absence of apostrophes in contractions: all the typographic elements that ignore conventional roman type, spellings and so forth.[17] The novel's textual voice attests to Faulkner's continued preoccupation with the ideographic representation of sound.

Many "garrulous" voices constitute the novel: the four character-narrators—Rosa, Mr Compson, Quentin, and Shreve—whose voices seem recorded directly (sometimes with and sometimes without quotation marks; sometimes in italics); the voices of the dead that are transmitted second- and sometimes thirdhand (Sutpen and Ellen, Charles, Henry and Judith, Wash Jones, and others); and finally the narrator, who opens the novel and intervenes throughout. There are such inconsistencies and ambiguities regarding the inscription and attribution of these voices—sometimes they are indistinguishable from others, sometimes sourceless, and sometimes unheard—that it becomes difficult and frequently impossible to align speakers with their speech. The disruption of the verisimilitudinous transmission and reception of sound of course concerned Faulkner in *As I Lay Dying*, in the evident incommensurability of that novel's poor whites and their at times sophisticated patterns of speech and thought. In *Absalom, Absalom!*, however, this disruption becomes a complete rupture: who exactly is speaking?

The way that sound breaks up in Faulkner's novel contrasts with the norms of classical Hollywood film, whereby sound and image were considered analogous. Like Faulkner's "Sutter's Gold," *Absalom, Absalom!* bears out Michel Chion's insights about sound film more generally: sound film "doesn't hang together; it's decidedly not a seamless match" between voices and bodies, although "it does its best to restitch the two together at the seam" (125). This seemingly inherent quality of sound film characterizes Eisenstein's theoretical pronouncements and film praxis, in particular his resistance to the alignment of sound and its source and thus to the "illusion of talking people, audible objects." *Absalom, Absalom!*'s comparable sonic indecipherability is an effect of several different strategies of the entextualization of speaking voices. These include the mismatch between speaker and speech,[18] disembodied voices, and the fusion of—and even confusion over—speakers.

Rosa Coldfield's italicized chapter 5 sounds suspiciously Faulknerian, as do several of the monologues—supposedly the inner speech of poor whites—in *As I Lay Dying.* The italics in this chapter only amplify Rosa's rhetorical flourishes as she tells Quentin about the South, denaturalizing her voice to create rupture and more, a gap, between speaker and words spoken. The following passage is characteristic of Rosa's rhetoric throughout the chapter:

> *[T]hat brute progenitor [Walsh Jones] of brutes whose granddaughter was to supplant me, if not in my sister's house at least in my sister's bed to which (so they will tell you) I aspired—that brute who (brute instrument of that justice which presides over human events which, incept in the individual, runs smooth, less claw than velvet: but which, by man or woman flouted, drives on like fiery steel and overrides both weakly just and unjust strong, both vanquisher and innocent victimized, ruthless for appointed right and truth) brute who was not only to preside upon the various shapes and avatars of Thomas Sutpen's devil's fate but was to provide at the last the female flesh in which his name and lineage should be sepulchered. . . .* (134)

And so on, to such extent that, with Urgo and Noel Polk, we have to wonder, surely "to what extent is any of Rosa's 'monologue' a transcription of what she actually has said" (56).[19]

Rosa's—if we can attribute any of this to Rosa—parenthetical "*so they will tell you*" introduces another element of the novel's soundscape, and this is the disembodied voice-over style of 1930s classic documentary and the disembodied voices of its antecedents—radio, telephone, and gramophone—this choric voice is also familiar from Eisenstein's and Faulkner's "Sutter's Gold" treatments.[20] The unseen chorus, whose function is largely rumor and gossip, forms the novel's white noise that travels "back and forth among the places of business and of idleness and among the residences" (32). In another passage, again from chapter 5, Rosa seems to ventriloquize this chorus, as signalled in the shift from her narrating first person to the choric third person:

> *[T]hey will have told you: daughter of an embusque who had to turn to a demon, a villain: and therefore she had been right in hating her father since if he had not died in that attic she would not have had to go out there to find food and protection and shelter. . . . Yes, Rosa Coldfield, lose him, weep him; caught*

> *a beau but couldn't keep him; (oh yes, they will tell you) found a beau and was insulted, something heard and not forgiven. . . . But I forgave him.* (169–71)

Rosa becomes a kind of sound-recording machine as she reproduces the voice of the chorus, effectively fusing it with her own. Speaking voices fuse and so become confused throughout the novel, making it all the more difficult to determine who speaks.[21]

Right toward the end of *Absalom, Absalom!*, as if in some last-ditch attempt to solve once and for all the problem of the ideographic representation of sound, Faulkner embeds the screenplay format to figure imagined conversations between, first, Sutpen and Henry and then Henry and Charles.[22] The screenplay genre here is characterized by present-tense scene setting and pared-back dialogue, which continue for seven pages:

> Shreve ceased again. It was just as well, since he had no listener. Perhaps he was aware of it. Then suddenly he had no talker either, though possibly he was not aware of this. Because now neither of them were there. They were both in Carolina and the time was some forty-six years ago, and it was not even four now but compounded still further, since now both of them were Henry Sutpen and both of them were Bon, compounded each of both yet either neither, smelling the very smoke which had blown and faded away forty-six years ago from the *bivouac fires burning in a pine grove, the gaunt and ragged men sitting or lying about them, talking not about the war . . . the two picket lines so close that each could hear the challenge of the other's officers passing from post to post and dying away: and when gone, the voice, invisible, cautious, not loud yet carrying:*
>
> *—Hey, Reb.*
>
> *—Yah.*
>
> *—Where you fellers going?*
>
> *—Richmond.*
>
> *—So are we. Why not wait for us?*
>
> *—We air.* (351)

This passage opens with one of the several accounts in the novel of the merging not only of Quentin and Shreve with each other but also, frequently, of each of them with Henry and Charles. It becomes impossible to determine the vocal frame that attends the italicized dialogue in this passage. Whose words are recorded here? Those of Quentin, Shreve, or both, "compounded each of both yet either neither"? Those of Henry, Charles, or both as Quentin, Shreve, or both? Or is this entire passage an act of ventriloquism by the narrator who introduces this scene? *Absalom, Absalom!* refuses to "show lips moving in time with the sound track," to use Rick Altman's conceptualization of film sound ("Moving Lips" 69). Lips and sound track are frequently out of sync or their connection ruptured throughout the novel. The illusion of "talking people," for which Eisenstein harshly criticized Hollywood, is shattered in *Absalom, Absalom!* at that moment in Hollywood when "nearly every important technological innovation can be traced back to the desire to produce a persuasive illusion of real people speaking real words" (Altman, Introd. 7).

One of the major epistemological upsets of *Absalom, Absalom!*, then, occurs on the auditory plane. Sound is a force of destabilization in the novel; it cannot be relied on to convey the information needed to confirm one's place in the world. Sound, as Altman observes, "will always carry with it the tension of the unknown until it is anchored by sight"; every sound seems to ask, "[W]here did that sound come from?" ("Moving Lips" 74). The use of nonsynchronous sound in *Absalom, Absalom!*, possibly informed by Eisenstein's practice, means that we are frequently unable to answer this question definitively, an experience that is disconcerting or disorientating not only for readers. For disembodied sounds, especially voices, have the effect in *Absalom, Absalom!* of creating, or transforming men and women into, shadows and "outraged baffled ghosts" whose speech is heard secondhand at best: according to Rosa, Sutpen is "a walking shadow" (171); Charles remains "*shadowy*" as if he had "*never been*" (153); and Ellen is "unreal and weightless" (106). As Mr Compson declares, "We have a few old mouth-to-mouth tales; . . . men and women who once lived and breathed are now merely initial or nicknames out of some now incomprehensible affection which sound to us like Sanskrit or Choctaw." "[S]omething is missing," he continues (100–01). Without the simultaneous projection of moving lips, to paraphrase Altman, the transmission of sound, and thus meaningful communication, is compromised, or worse, fails altogether.

Something that contributes to the unstable relations between the projected image and the recorded voice operating throughout the novel is the ability or inability of the spoken word to conjure the image. For Ross *Absalom,*

Absalom's "representation depends upon the power of voice to evoke a world—the world of past events and people for the narrating characters, the fictional world for the reader" (218). This means that as Quentin and Shreve appear to sit by the bivouac fire among the rebel soldiers in the passage quoted earlier, Quentin can announce, "*If I had been there I could not have seen it this plain*" (190), such is the power of the spoken word to evoke image. Indeed, it is possible to conceive of the bulk of the final chapter of the novel as a sustained evocation; there is nothing in the punctuation of typography to indicate that Quentin is speaking to Shreve here. At first Shreve hears Quentin's narrating voice but then he sees, rather uncannily, what Quentin too can see "though he [Quentin] had not been there" (374). There are significant moments in the novel, however, where this dynamic of evocation fails, and its failure arguably drives the narrative. Mr Compson learns that as a child in backwoods Virginia, Sutpen "didn't listen to the vague and cloudy tales of Tidewater splendour . . . because there was nothing in sight to compare and gauge the tales by and so give the words life and meaning" (222). Here the novel seems to foreshadow what film-sound scholars have learned: "Sound achieves authenticity only as a consequence of its submission to tests imposed upon it . . . primarily by sight" (Belton 64). In this instance, the failure of evocation equates to the failure of socialization; Sutpen is unable to insert himself successfully into the southern class hierarchy, and this sets him on his demonic (according to Rosa) path to execute his design.

Speech can either fail to evoke, as it does here, or vanish altogether to make way for the image. The dialogic situation of Quentin and Rosa in chapters 1, 2, and 5 pivots on this very tension between sound (of the speaking voice) and image (ideally, evoked for the listener) and a related tension between speaking and hearing, not always a "marriage" in this novel. Rosa's voice cannot hold Quentin's attention—far from it. Indeed, on several occasions he appears not to be listening at all; or listening would "renege" (7). In the place of listening, an image (of Sutpen) forms: "the long-dead object of her impotent yet indomitable frustration would appear" or "abrupt" "out of the biding and dreamy and victorious dust," so that Quentin seems "to watch" the scene before him (7–8). It is only when Rosa's voice vanishes that the image might be evoked (13). On another occasion, Quentin ceases to listen to Rosa "because there was . . . something which he . . . could not pass—that door, the running feet on the stairs beyond it almost a continuation of the faint shot, the two women, the negress and the white girl in her underthings" (172). The transmission of sound is intercepted and displaced by the image that captivates, preventing further listening and so disrupting the "happy marriage of speaking and hearing" (316).

It is no coincidence that Faulkner's preoccupation with sounds and with the "unrational hearing-sense" (145) in *Absalom, Absalom!* came about at the same time he was immersed in the new medium of the talkies and discovered Eisensteinian cinematic practice, one of the most pressing concerns of which is sound and the seemingly endless possibilities of the new film-sound technology. The auditory affinities between Eisenstein's and Faulkner's "Sutter's Gold" treatments and *Absalom, Absalom!* coalesce around Eisensteinian double exposure—that is, the nonsynchronous relation of sound and image, voice and its source. *Absalom, Absalom!* proves a troubling and thus productive intervention into the examination of the auditory culture of modernism, bearing as it does traces of the screen writing and film-sound technology that, I argue, contributed to it. While the idea of film might have reanimated discussions around literary modernism, surprisingly little scholarly work has been undertaken on the screen writings of the many key modernist writers who worked in the motion picture industry and have become the focus of these revisionary accounts, writers such as F. Scott Fitzgerald, Nathanael West, Erskine Caldwell, and of course Faulkner. Listening closely to the sounds of Yoknapatawpha within their specific moment of technical production dislodges the visual from its dominant position in the project of rethinking literary modernism. Kahn foresaw that "because of the visualist presumptions underscoring theories of modernity and representation, questions of the auditory have the potential to reconfigure time-honored accounts and ask formerly unconsidered sets of question" (Rev.). Film sound—including Eisensteinian theory and praxis—needs to be included in the compelling scholarship currently investigating the intersection of twentieth-century literature and the new sound technologies of broadcasting and communications.[23]

NOTES

I am particularly grateful for the generosity of Paul Giles and Robert Jackson, who provided invaluable feedback on an earlier version of this essay. I would also like to thank Universal Studios for allowing me to reproduce excerpts from Faulkner's unpublished "Sutter's Gold" treatment.

1. It is not surprising that literary sound has been somewhat neglected when film sound has attracted little critical attention: "The dominance of the image in cinema studies [has prevented] sound from being recognized as more than simple 'add-on' to the image" (Beck and Grajeda 2). Similarly, dialogue "in film has received very little attention in comparison to the technical and theoretical sophistication of image-based studies of cinema" (Price 135). Mary Ann Doane reminds us that the cinematic experience is not limited to images but includes sounds and text. The scholarly neglect of film sound means that this "heterogeneous" medium has not always been comprehensively understood (163). Studies of sound in literary texts are even less common. Exceptions include recent scholarship by Tim Armstrong, Angela Frattarola, Sarah Wilson, Philipp Schweighauser, and Kata Gellen. However, nowhere do scholars examine the literary engagement with film sound, which is this essay's project. This is no doubt also an effect of film's frequent conceptualization as an exclusively visual medium. Michel Chion, one of the first and most important film-sound scholars, has argued that even silent film was never really silent: it "was always accompanied by music from the outset . . . not to mention the sound effects created live in some movie houses. . . . There were also the commentators, who freely interpreted the intertitles that the audience could not read" (8).

2. Susan Douglas argues that radio "introduced a new orality into American culture" (12). For a contemporary engagement with radio's possibilities, see Brecht, *Brecht*. On documentary film sound, see Kahana. On the significance of the invention of the tape recorder in the 1930s, see Cox and Warner xiii–xiv; Schaeffer 81. Ventriloquist performances, such as Edgar Bergen and Charlie McCarthy's, became increasingly popular on radio and stage during this era.

3. Although 1927 has gained almost mythic significance in film-sound historiography because of the release of *The Jazz Singer* that year, it was in 1932–35 that film sound became widespread and that the most important advances took place (Bordwell, Staiger, and Thompson 300–301.)

4. Meriwether 693. Although Faulkner started to write "The Dark House," which became *Absalom, Absalom!*, in January 1934, he acknowledged in a letter to his publisher, Hal Smith, that "when I took it up again [in March 1935] I almost rewrote the whole thing" (qtd. in Blotner 346–47).

5. My project here is consonant with recent examinations of the intersection of high and low cultural forms. Thomas Strychacz, for example, argues that "this move toward seeing the modernist text as irrevocably linked to and penetrated by the dense, complex social formations of a burgeoning mass culture is a crucial one, for it denies the common view of modernism as being merely antagonistic to the cultural formations it defines itself against" (6). This turn has been predominantly visual. Michael North's exploration of the roles that movies played "in the aesthetic transformation of modern literature and art" characterizes film as a purely visual medium (206). This visual turn also typifies recent scholarship on Faulkner and film (e.g., Kawin, *Faulkner and Film;* Lurie). While, as I mention above in note 1, scholarship in the field of literary modernism and auditory culture is emerging, I have encountered no examination of literary modernism's specific engagement with film sound, besides Frattarola's comment that "one could argue that the advent of the talkie made [Dorothy] Richardson keenly aware of the significance of accurately rendered voice in narrative" (141).

6. Titled *L'or* in the original 1925 French publication, the novel was translated into English as *Sutter's Gold* in 1926. All three narratives—Cendrars's, Eisenstein's, and Faulkner's—are indicative of an international fascination with the Sutter story during the 1930s. Universal's *Sutter's Gold* appeared in 1936 and was directed by James Cruze; Hawks and Faulkner had been taken off the project. The film became the studio's flop of the year. Luis Trenker's "Nazi Western" *Der Kaiser von Kalifornien* (Koepnick 100), which tells the same story, was released in Germany several months later (1937 in the US). Trenker's handling of the Sutter material differs from Eisenstein's and Faulkner's. The synchronization of sound was, according to Koepnick, central to Nazi cinema—"The sensitive execution of film dialogue . . . was to play an essential role in [the] nationalization of mass culture" (112)—and *Der Kaiser*'s score, for example, "synthesizes sounds and sights into one overwhelming experience" (121).

7. See Gleeson-White for a detailed account of the striking similarities between Cendrars's Sutter and Faulkner's Sutpen narratives.

8. Similarly, Kawin, not having read Faulkner's "Sutter's Gold" treatment, can only speculate that Faulkner's writing of it "may well have influenced [his] plans for *Absalom, Absalom!* since both are stories of drifters who 'strike it rich' and whose love-lives reflect their ambitions" (*Faulkner and Film* 88).

9. Montagu recounts Eisenstein's Hollywood experiences. Eisenstein's "Sutter's Gold" and "American Tragedy" treatments are reproduced in Montagu's volume and include several of his scene sketches. For further commentary on Eisenstein's "Sutter's Gold," see Frayling; Richardson.

10. Bordwell indicates one way Faulkner could have received Eisenstein's treatment: "If a studio purchased a 'property,' the other studios kept track of it in case they decided to buy it later" (Bordwell, Staiger, and Thompson 322). Universal may have "kept track" of the original Paramount project. Paramount produced *The Story of Temple Drake* (an adaptation of Faulkner's novel *Sanctuary*) in 1933, three years after Eisenstein worked at the same studio. Perhaps this enabled Faulkner's entrée to the studio. One of Faulkner's letters, postmarked 12 July 1934, is written on Paramount letterhead, which might indicate that he had access to the studio ("To Mrs. William Faulkner"). However, he could have obtained the stationery at any time and by other means. The most appealing explanation is the possible existence of alternative routes of textual circulation beyond the oversight of the film studios.

11. Faulkner scholars have long identified certain visual qualities and strategies in Faulkner's fiction—e.g., "montage, freeze-frame, slow motion, and visual metaphor" (Kawin, *Faulkner and Film* 55)—informed by what Lurie terms "the film idea": "the manner of impression and visual activity [Faulkner's] novels emulate from the cinema" (6). Kawin's examples of Eisensteinian (visual) montage in Faulkner's fiction include the radical intercutting between scenes in *The Sound and the Fury* (19) and the "breaking into fragments (words and scenes)" of the central Sutpen story in *Absalom, Absalom!* (130). That Eisenstein was interested in the work of another southerner in Hollywood, D. W. Griffith—in particular, Griffith's revolutionary editing techniques—adds yet another layer to our thinking about visual montage across different media and national cultures.

12. Brecht's 1930 notes on *The Flight of the Lindberghs*, his *Lehrstück* first performed in

1929, describe a comparable counterpoint between the sounds transmitted by a radio and the listener-speakers on stage: " a collaboration develops between apparatus [radio] and participant" ("Explanations" 39).

13. Chion designates disembodied voices in cinema "acousmatic." Taking his term from Schaeffer, he defines the "acousmatic" as a sound whose source cannot be seen (18).

14. Surely an echo of the "Chuck. Chuck. Chuck" of Cash Bundren's adze in *As I Lay Dying* (4).

15. The graphic nature of "textual voice" only highlights the inherent difficulty—and paradox—in literary representations of sound. Ross also observes that anaphora in *Absalom, Absalom!* has the effect of amplification (199). He cites, by way of example, Rosa's repetition of "that brute" (*Absalom* 134–35).

16. Noel Polk and Stephen Ross have produced a color edition of *The Sound and the Fury,* published by the Folio Society (2012).

17. There is really no identifiable pattern in Faulkner's use of italics, parentheses, quotation marks, and dashes. I agree with Ross; the most we can say about the typographic variations is that they indicate some shift: a temporal shift or a shift in voice, discourse, or levels of consciousness (Ross 145–46).

18. One of the most cited examples of the mismatch between Hollywood sound and image in scholarship is *Singin' in the Rain* (1952), where Kathy Selden (Debbie Reynolds) is hired to dub the voice of the nasally intoning Lina Lamont (Jean Hagen) on the arrival of the talkies (e.g., Chion 133; Silverman 45–47).

19. Silverman's psychoanalytic reading of the female voice in Hollywood's cinema provides another possible way to account for Rosa's arguably near hysterical volubility throughout the novel.

20. On the introduction in the 1930s of voice-over to documentary film, see Kahana: "By contrast with the feature-film industry, where recorded sound tended to be used to shore up the illusion of realism . . . the independence of sound from image opened documentary film-making to entirely new possibilities of assemblage" (105). According to Chion, another antecedent of feature film voice-over is the commentary of magic lantern shows (4).

21. There are countless examples of the fusion and subsequent confusion of the speaking voice throughout *Absalom, Absalom!* (e.g., 174–76, 181–87, 212–15, 293, 303, and 333–34).

22. Urgo makes a similar observation about the screenplay format (64). See also Urgo and Polk 188. Citing another section from this screenplay format, Urgo observes that "Judith and Henry . . . are 'speaking to one another in short brief staccato sentences like slaps' [*Absalom* 172]. . . . The 'staccato' sentences, of course, were popular in the movies of the 1930s, and Faulkner had written some of his own in the film version of 'Turn About' (called *Today We Live* [1932]) on which he worked for Hawks" (64–65).

23. A handful of scholars have explored the place of Eisenstein's visual practice in modernist writing in the United States. See, e.g., Edward's examination of "Eisenstein's theory of juxtapositional imaging" and of John Dos Passos's *The Big Money* (249) and Kadlec's account of "the influence upon [Louis Zukofsky and William Carlos Williams] of Soviet newsreels and newsreel-style films" (301).

WORKS CITED

Altman, Rick. Introduction. *Cinema/Sound.* Spec. issue of *Yale French Studies* 60 (1980): 3–15. Print.

——. "Moving Lips: Cinema as Ventriloquism." *Cinema/Sound.* Spec issue of *Yale French Studies* 60 (1980): 67–69. Print.

Armstrong, Tim. "Player Piano: Poetry and Sonic Modernity." *Modernism/Modernity* 14.1 (2007): 1–19. Print.

Beck, Jay, and Tony Grajeda. "The Future of Film Sound Studies." Introduction. *Lowering the Boom: Critical Studies in Film Sound.* Ed. Beck and Grajeda. Carbondale: U of Illinois P, 2008. 1–20. Print.

Belton, John. "Technology and Aesthetics of Film Sound." *Film sound: Theory and Practice.* Ed. Elisabeth Weis and Belton. New York: Columbia UP, 1985. 63–72. Print.

Blotner, Joseph. *Faulkner: A Biography.* 1984. Jackson: UP of Mississippi, 1991. Print.

Bochner, Jay. "La fortune de *L'or en Amèrique.*" *Cendrars aujourd'hui: Prèsence d'un romancier.* Ed. Michel Decaudin. Paris: Minard, 1977. 35–61. Print.

Bordwell, David, Janet Staiger, and Kristin Thompson. *The Classical Hollywood Cinema: Film Style and Mode of Production to 1960.* New York: Columbia UP, 1985. Print.

Brecht, Bertolt. *Brecht on Film and Radio.* Trans. and ed. Marc Silberman. London: Methuen, 2000. Print.

——. "Explanations [about *The Flight of the Lindberghs*]." Brecht, *Brecht* 38–41.

Burke, Marina. "Eisenstein and the Challenge of Sound." *Kinema: A Journal for Film and Audiovisual Media* (Fall 2007) n.p. Web. 10 Jan. 2011.

Cendrars, Blaise. *Sutter's Gold.* New York: Harper, 1926. Print.

Chion, Michel. *The Voice in Cinema.* Ed. and trans. Claudia Gorbman. New York: Columbia UP, 1999. Print.

Cox, Christoph, and Daniel Warner. "Music and the New Audio Culture." Introduction. *Audio Culture: Readings in Modern Music.* Ed. Cox and Warner. New York: Continuum, 2004. xiii–xvii. Print.

Doane, Mary Ann. "The Voice in the Cinema. The Articulation of Body and Space." *Film Sound: Theory and Practice.* Ed. Elisabeth Weis and John Belton. New York: Columbia UP, 1985. 162–76. Print.

Douglas, Susan. *Listening In: Radio and the American Imagination.* Minneapolis: U of Minnesota P, 2004. Print.

Edwards, Justin. "The Man with a Camera Eye: Cinematic Form and Hollywood Malediction in John Dos Passos's *The Big Money.*" *Literature Film Quarterly* 27.4 (1999): 245–54. Print.

Eisenstein, Sergei. "Dickens, Griffith, and the Film Today." *Film Form: Essays in Film Theory.* By Eisenstein. Ed. and trans. Jay Leyda. London: Dobson, 1951. 195–255. Print.

——. "Sutter's Gold." Montagu 151–206.

Eisenstein, S. M., V. I. Pudomn, and G. V. Alexandrov. "A Statement." [1928]. Web. 10 Jan. 2011.

Faulkner, William. *Absalom, Absalom!* London: Vintage, 1995. Print.

——. *As I Lay Dying.* New York: Norton, 2010. Print.

——. "Sutter's Gold." July 1934, MSS 1404. Howard Hawks Collection, 1925–1970. Arts and Communications Archives, L. Tom Perry Spec. Collections, Harold B. Lee Lib., Brigham Young U.

——. "To Mrs. William Faulkner." 12 July 1934. *Selected Letters.* Ed. Joseph Blotner. New York: Random, 1977. 82–83. Print.

——. *The Wild Palms [If I Forget Thee, Jerusalem].* New York: Vintage, 1995. Print.

Frattarola, Angela. "Developing an Ear for the Modernist Novel: Virginia Woolf, Dorothy Richardson and James Joyce." *Journal of Modern Literature* 33.1 (2009): 132–53. Print.

Frayling, Christopher. *Spaghetti Westerns: Cowboys and Europeans from Karl May to Sergio Leone.* London: Tauris, 1998. Print.

Gellen, Kata. "Hearing Spaces: Architecture and Acoustic Experience in Modernist German Literature." *Modernism/Modernity* 17.4 (2011): 799–818. Print.

Gleeson-White, Sarah. "William Faulkner, Screenwriter: 'Sutter's Gold' and 'Drums along the Mohawk.'" *Mississippi Quarterly* 62.3–4 (2009): 427–42. Print.

Kadlec, David. "Early Soviet Cinema and American Poetry." *Modernism/Modernity* 11.2 (2004): 299–331. Print.

Kahana, Jonathan. *Intelligence Work: The Politics of American Documentary.* New York: Columbia UP, 2008. Print.

Kahn, Douglas. *Noise, Water, Meat: A History of the Arts.* Cambridge: MIT P, 1999. Print.

——. Rev of *Sound Technology and the American Cinema,* by James Lastra. *Modernism/Modernity* 8.2 (2001): 337–38. Print.

Kawin, Bruce. *Faulkner and Film.* New York: Ungar, 1977. Print.

——. *Faulkner's MGM Screenplays.* Knoxville: U of Tennessee P, 1982. Print.

Koepnick, Lutz. *The Dark Mirror: German Cinema between Hitler and Hollywood.* Berkeley: U of California P, 2002. Print.

Liénard-Yeterian, Marie. *Faulkner et le cinéma.* Paris: Houdiard, 2010. Print.

Lurie, Peter. *Vision's Immanence: Faulkner, Film, and the Popular Imagination.* Baltimore: Johns Hopkins UP, 2004. Print.

Matthews, John T. "Faulkner and the Reproduction of History." *Faulkner and History.*

Ed. Michel Gresset and Javier Coy. Salamanca: U of Salamanca P, 1985. 63–76. Print.

Meriwether, James B. Rev of *Faulkner's Revision of* Absalom, Absalom!: *A Collection of the Manuscript and the Published Book*, by Gerald Langford. *American Literature* 44.4 (1973): 693–95. Print.

Montagu, Ivor. *With Eisenstein in Hollywood: A Chapter of Autobiography*. New York: International, 1969. Print.

North, Michael. "Words in Motion: The Movies, the Readies, and the 'Revolution of the Word.'" *Modernism/Modernity* 9.2 (2002): 205–23. Print.

Porter, Carolyn. *William Faulkner*. New York: Oxford UP, 2007. Print.

Price, Steven. *The Screenplay: Authorship, Theory and Criticism*. London: Palgrave, 210. Print.

Raper, J. R. "Meaning Called to Life: Structure in *Absalom, Absalom!*" *Southern Humanities Review* 5 (1971). 9–23. Print.

Richardson, William. "Eisenstein and California: The 'Sutter's Gold' Episode." *California History* 59.3 (1980): 194–203. Print.

Ross, Stephen M. *Fiction's Inexhaustible Voice: Speech and Writing in Faulkner*. Athens: U of Georgia P, 1989. Print.

Schaeffer, Pierre. "Acousmatics." *Audio Culture: Readings in Modern Music*. Ed. Christoph Cox and Daniel Warner. New York: Continuum, 2004. 76–81. Print.

Schweighauser, Philipp. *The Noises of American Literature, 1890–1985: Toward a History of Literary Acoustics*. Gainesville: UP of Florida, 2006. Print.

Silverman, Kaja. *The Acoustic Mirror: The Female Voice in Psychoanalysis and Cinema*. Bloomington: Indiana UP, 1988. Print.

Strychacz, Thomas. *Modernism, Mass Culture, and Professionalism*. New York: Cambridge UP, 1993. Print.

Urgo, Joseph R., and Noel Polk. *Reading Faulkner:* Absalom, Absalom! Jackson: UP of Mississippi, 2010. Print.

Wilson, Sarah. "Gertrude Stein and the Radio." *Modernism/Modernity* 11.2 (2004): 261–78. Print.

Skin and Structure
William Faulkner's Media Surfaces

ROBERT JACKSON

> About the biography. Dont tell the bastards anything. It cant matter to them. Tell them I was born of an alligator and a nigger slave at the Geneva peace conference two years ago. Or whatever you want to tell them.
> —WILLIAM FAULKNER to Ben Wasson, 1930

> Yes, he will be remembered. The pyramid will keep his memory alive. In that he built better than he knew.
> —*Land of the Pharaohs* (1955)

William Faulkner cherished a vision of privacy that shaped his sense of media in modern American society. He expressed this ideal, and its threat of extinction in the postwar era during which he was most well known, in architectural terms:

> The American sky which was once the topless empyrean of freedom, the American air which was once the living breath of liberty, are now become one vast down-crowding pressure to abolish them both, by destroying man's individuality as a man by (in that turn) destroying the last vestige of privacy without which man cannot be an individual. Our very architecture itself has warned us. Time was when you could see neither from inside nor from outside through the walls of our houses. Time is when you can see from inside out though still not from outside in through the walls. Time will be when you can do both. Then privacy will indeed be gone; he who is individual enough to want it even to change his shirt or bathe in, will be cursed by one universal American voice as subversive to the American way of life and the American flag.[1]

These lines come from an essay entitled "On Privacy," which carried the ominous subtitle "The American Dream: What Happened to It?" and was published in *Harper's* magazine in July 1955. The occasion for complaint, he noted, was the publication of an article about Faulkner "as a private citizen, an individual," by what he called "a wealthy widely-circulated weekly pictorial magazine" without his consent or participation—a very thinly veiled reference to the two-part *Life* magazine profile by Robert Coughlan appearing in the fall of 1953 (66). Privacy, Faulkner argued, was the basis of individuality, and without individuality the very idea of America was impossible. Privacy, in this formulation, was necessary for art as well as democracy, since both were impossible without the maturation of individualism. Faulkner's simmering resentment at the current media landscape is evident a few pages later in the same piece, as he speaks to the inordinate influence of celebrity in contemporary consumer culture:

> America has not yet found any place for him who deals only in things of the human spirit except to use his notoriety to sell soap or cigarettes or fountain pens or to advertise automobiles and cruises and resort hotels, or (if he can be taught to contort fast enough to meet the standards) in radio or moving pictures where he can produce enough income tax to be worth attention. (75)

This is an interesting claim not least because Faulkner seems to be lamenting the lack of a *public* identity and role for the artist, an idea not so strange in itself but rather paradoxical in the context of an essay insisting on the necessity for the artist's privacy and, indeed, anonymity. As I will discuss in more detail in what follows here, throughout his career Faulkner staged a series of performances in which the problematically public construction of his own sense of privacy had recourse to a consistent set of terms—national, regional, local, and racial, as well as architectural, sartorial, and epidermal—in order to reach ever-broadening audiences from whom he begged, with all apparent exasperation, to be left alone. Faulkner found himself in a predicament perhaps best summarized by a newsreel epitaph for Charles Foster Kane early in Orson Welles's *Citizen Kane* (1941), one of the central narratives of empire-building celebrity and publicity culture in modern American mass-media history: "Few private lives were more public." In Faulkner's case, the mediatory power of race itself would take on added importance in this paradox, revealing itself in his fiction and nonfiction as well as his often-agonized self-presentation.

In our 2007 essay "'We're Trying Hard as Hell to Free Ourselves': Southern History and Race in the Making of William Faulkner's Literary Terrain," Grace Hale and I argued that Faulkner was left placeless during the mid-1950s, those years after *Brown v. Board of Education* (1954) in which the moderate white southern liberalism that had been possible twenty years earlier was no longer tenable, and the luxury of deferring action on civil rights no longer available.[2] "But the time Faulkner asks for does not exist," a forward-looking James Baldwin more accurately observed, "and he is not the only southerner who knows it."[3] Faulkner's more notorious writings on race during this period invite a contextualization of "On Privacy" that emphasizes the latter's production in the same historical moment that saw Faulkner publish "A Letter to the North" (1956), which called for a regional equivalent to this ideal of privacy, so that white and black southerners could work out their differences on their own, without the invasive legal mandates, media coverage, and moralism that certain other parts of the country were all too eager to export. To my knowledge, Faulkner never used the phrase "outside agitators," as many white segregationists and massive-resisters did, to demonize nonsoutherners who came to the South to participate in the civil rights movement, but Faulkner's intense sense of privacy anticipates and evokes that stock phrase all the same. Indeed, Faulkner's choice of words was sometimes far more explicit, as in 1956 when he told a London *Sunday Times* journalist that, if the South were overrun (whether by federally mandated racial segregation or some other force, he did not specify), he would "fight for Mississippi against the United States even if it meant going out into the street and shooting Negroes."[4] An important aspect of Faulkner's formulation of privacy arises from the fact that it is implicitly racialized, not merely because of its proximity to such inflammatory statements on race in the 1950s, but also, and in a more general sense, because his model of individualism was grounded in the culture of whiteness in which he had lived all his life and beyond which he never quite traveled—except, perhaps, fictionally.

Faulkner misrepresented his military service for many years, beginning as soon as the train brought him back to Oxford in December 1918. Rather than wearing his coarse wool Royal Air Force cadet's uniform, Faulkner spent some of his discharge pay of $73.69 on an officer's uniform, and there-

William Faulkner in RAF uniform, 1918. Courtesy of Cofield Collection, Southern Media Archive, Special Collections (B1F38), University of Mississippi Libraries.

after presented himself as a lieutenant of the older and more famous Royal Flying Corps.

In the mid-1940s, when World War I veteran Malcolm Cowley was writing a biographical essay for inclusion in *The Viking Portable Faulkner* (1946), Faulkner would struggle to disassociate himself, or at least his work, from his own elaborate fabrications. Of course, many more recent biographers have exposed Faulkner's fraudulent claims of aerial combat, severe war wounds including broken legs and head injuries, and the more general experience of a romantic sense of doom surrounding the daily life of a war pilot.[5] Joseph Blotner takes a more restrained and understanding view, noting that Faulkner "was a romantic and a dreamer," that Faulkner "was not the first young man who would be transformed in the eyes of others when he wore a uniform and clothed himself in tales of heroic exploits."[6] It is difficult not to have sympathy for the Blotner interpretation, in which lies are compared, seemingly rather innocuously, to clothing. This is a reading that enables Faulkner to retain a certain innocence—as a nascent artist, certainly, but also as a public figure, a media figure, a celebrity. Blotner evokes the writer as a young thespian of sorts, a budding aesthete who would naturally choose his costumes for imaginative and emotional effect. Can we imagine how a Faulkner living in the early twenty-first century would be received by the American mass media if he were found to have invented such "tales of heroic exploits" from whole cloth? Campaigning politicians in our time play fast and loose with the facts of their military service at their peril. Perhaps more pertinently, how would someone as sensitive and private as Faulkner stand up to the ridicule that today's media industry generates in an ongoing excavation of all manner of dirt? Acts of marital strife and infidelity, utterance of racial prejudice, financial ruin, poor personal bearing, or antisocial public behavior—is it going too far to speculate that Faulkner today might be either a darling of the tabloids or, in the existentialist terminology of the entertainment industry, a nobody, because the media environment today leaves such little, if indeed any, space for such a figure to develop into adolescence, let alone maturity?

Such questions cannot be answered definitively, of course, but they do invite an analytical perspective that remains mindful of the distinct cultural mores of an early-twenty-first-century media ecology marked as much by the desperation for fame as by its political fractiousness. Consider, for example, the well-known literary fraud of James Frey's memoir of addiction and recovery, *A Million Little Pieces* (2003). Frey failed to find a publisher for his fiction manuscript but eventually secured a publication contract from Random House's Doubleday imprint by recasting it as nonfiction. Here we have reason to suspect that Faulkner would have questioned Frey's judgment in publishing the work as a nonfiction memoir, and indeed that he would have had reservations about the enormous popularity of autobiography and memoir during the late twentieth and early twenty-first centuries. Faulkner spoke longingly about leaving no trace of his life behind after death except for his writings. It is worth remembering that Faulkner's famous remark that he hoped his obituary and epitaph would simply read, "He made the books, and he died," came as part of a note to Malcolm Cowley in response to the latter's 1949 *Life* profile of Ernest Hemingway. Opening with a full-page photograph of a shirtless Hemingway eating breakfast surrounded by cats in his bedroom, "A Portrait of Mister Papa" represented exactly the sort of invasive publicity and inane celebrity-worship Faulkner found so repugnant, and may explain why Faulkner told his friend Cowley he hadn't actually read the piece.[7] And in another telling exchange from several years earlier, revealing his aversion to memoir after reading Richard Wright's *Black Boy* (1945), Faulkner encouraged Wright to get back to writing fiction like *Native Son* (1940) because "the good lasting stuff comes out of one individual's imagination and sensitivity to and comprehension of the suffering of Everyman, Anyman, not out of the memory of his own grief."[8] This distaste for the autobiographical is particularly interesting coming from Faulkner, a writer for whom, in Blotner's words, "the line between reality and imagination was not as compelling . . . as it was for others."[9] David Minter, whose treatment of Faulkner's false representations of military glory shares something of Blotner's forgiving tone, likewise speaks to Faulkner's lifelong penchant for performativity, suggesting that "his authentic self was the self variously and nebulously yet definitely bodied forth by his fictions."[10] Even as he wanted to maintain a strict division between the two, Faulkner's private life and publications invite us to consider whether his own hunger for recognition from a time even earlier than his first published writings is all that different from the motives behind the machinations of James Frey and his ilk.

The photograph of Faulkner in lieutenant's uniform was produced not just in a southern context of militarism and honor, but also as an image grounded in a mass-cultural discourse of whiteness that pervaded mainstream American life during the first half of the twentieth century.[11] As a result of the conflation of race and patriotism in exactly this period of history, there emerged a clear sense among many Americans, southern or otherwise, that to be fully American was to be white. Faulkner's performance here involves not just the practical application of his strong interest in fashion (which James G. Watson explores in wonderful detail in his work on Faulkner's letters to his family from Canada, letters that included many elaborate drawings of uniforms and other types of clothing), but also a participation in the racial fashion of the day, the donning of whiteness in a widely favored and appreciated form.[12] The Britishness of the RAF uniform might be taken as an added bonus, setting Faulkner apart from the many other servicemen who returned to Oxford in more numerous and familiar American uniforms at the end of World War I. Films produced by the burgeoning Hollywood studio system about World War I over the next few years, including King Vidor's *The Big Parade* (1925); William A. Wellman's *Wings* (1927); Howard Hughes's *Hell's Angels* (1930); Frank Borzage's *A Farewell to Arms* (1929); John Ford's *The Blue Eagle* (1926), *Seas Beneath* (1931), *Pilgrimage* (1933), *The Lost Patrol* (1934), and *Submarine Patrol* (1938, for which Faulkner wrote an early version of the screenplay); Howard Hawks's *The Dawn Patrol* (1930), *Today We Live* (1933, based on Faulkner's short story "Turn About"), and *Sergeant York* (1941); among scores of other fictional and newsreel films during the war and interwar period, feature virtually no black soldiers or other characters except in minor, peripheral roles. To encounter this American film record is to see the Great War as the supreme proving ground of white masculinity, and to understand Faulkner's performance of whiteness as less narrowly regional, less southern, than our subsequent official histories of segregation and the civil rights movement would prefer to acknowledge.

Other forms of popular art and culture followed the same pattern. World War I recruiting posters, for example, displayed the same conflation of whiteness and patriotism as that on offer at the cinema. Produced by the government as well as private companies by the thousands, recruiting posters became a ubiquitous presence almost immediately upon the American entry into the war in 1917. The most famous of these, J. M. Flagg's image of Uncle Sam pointing at the viewer and declaring, "I want YOU for U.S. Army," suggested in familial terms the racial lineage imaginatively linking an entire population of military recruits to the national body. (The fact that many African Americans were eager to serve in the military during this conflict, despite these skewed representations and the reality of highly segregated armed forces, might be interpreted in a number of ways—idealistically, as a testament to black American patriotism, as a hopeful investment in a less racist future; and, perhaps simultaneously, pragmatically, as an opportunity for employment, education, travel, escape, by way of the modern war machine; and otherwise.)[13]

The uses of whiteness and blackness in constructing individual and group identities during the early decades of the twentieth century were myriad, as narratives of racial passing, perhaps the most striking literary tradition to limn the complexities of the age, amply demonstrate. Literary works such as

Nella Larsen's *Passing* (1929), George Schuyler's *Black No More* (1931), Fanny Hurst's *Imitation of Life* (1933), and several of Faulkner's works including *Light in August* (1932) and *Absalom, Absalom!* (1936) utilized the culture's common vocabulary of racial self-fashioning to widely varying effect. Different artists responded in their own ways, deploying race in subtle shades and shapes in order to respond to the challenge of forging a public persona. The American dancer and film actress Josephine Baker offers a powerful alternative to Faulkner in this context, providing a helpful extension of this discussion of the culture of whiteness into the years of Faulkner's early career, and illuminating some of the dimensions of what Frantz Fanon called the "epidermal racial schema" that transmitted the meaning of race among the various invested parties in a segregated society.[14] A St. Louis native born less than a decade after Faulkner, Baker suffered under Jim Crow segregation as a child (including her personally witnessing the 1917 East St. Louis race riot), danced her way to New York as a teenager, and expatriated to Paris as a young woman, where her international fame coincided roughly with the 1925 Exposition des Arts Décoratifs, the world's fair that brought art deco design culture, with its blending of machine-age technology and non-Western primitivism, into popular currency. Baker's naked skin became something of a trademark, her exotic yet somehow distinctly modern performances fraught and overdetermined with sexual and racial complexity. By this means Baker was a central participant in (and performer of) modernist discourses of skin that speak to race relations as well as architectural form in ways that will eventually lead us back to Faulkner's own types of racial presentation and performance. I suggest that we might see Baker, especially in her public persona, as a kind of photographic negative of Faulkner.[15]

A Danish film poster advertising the 1935 French-language film *Princesse Tam Tam* renders Baker in all her glamour—a smiling art deco goddess whose gold lamé dress and urbane hair and makeup present her as the height of sophistication, as a kind of human incarnation of the great art deco architectural monuments of the 1930s, such as the Chrysler and Empire State Buildings and Rockefeller Center, while her backlit shadow looms in blue behind her.[16] This image of Baker was also selected for a series of U.S. Postal Service stamps memorializing black cinema in 2008, an interesting choice not least because many of the posters for *Princesse Tam Tam* produced around the world presented decidedly different portraits of Baker-as–Tam Tam. Far more typical were those like the French poster presenting not the urban Baker whose skin shimmers with the same metallic glow of her dress, but another Baker, one no less modernist in her aesthetic fashioning but with entirely distinct traits: naked, faceless, designed to resemble the trunk of a banana tree rather than a skyscraper.[17] It is not difficult to apprehend why the latter portrait of Baker, an apotheosis of the primitive modern, should be passed over in favor of the more cosmopolitan, if rather sanitized, variant gazing confidently from her plush seat of mass culture. In the early twenty-first century, this regally clad art deco Josephine Baker travels better (and of course, for a postage stamp, to travel is precisely the point), and represents the ambivalent racial currents of the interwar period in a less daring fashion.

The plot of *Princesse Tam Tam* combines elements of two great modern allegories: *Pygmalion* (1912) and *King Kong* (1933). *Princesse Tam Tam* is also a narrative of passing, speaking to the performance of identity that makes racial categories elusive and quick. The bored French novelist Max de Mirecourt travels to Tunisia to seek inspiration for his writing, adopting the street urchin Alwina and grooming her for a debut in Parisian society, where she is presented as Princess Tam Tam from India. During one of the film's central sequences, Max's jealous wife plies Alwina with champagne and goads her to revel in her primitive impulses on the nightclub dance floor. Alwina emphatically strips away her shoes and tight gold dress, leaving bare feet and just a thin black slip, a breezy curtain, over her frenetically dancing body. Spurred by the percussive rhythm of African drumming, she upstages the white chorus girls in their rigidly choreographed movements, leading to a very different sort of social debut than the one the embarrassed Max had planned for his protégée. To the great surprise of Max and his scheming wife, however, Alwina's revelatory performance captivates the French elite.

The set design of this sequence evokes Busby Berkeley's geometric designs in a series of RKO musicals during the 1930s, with organic and industrial forms blending into a series of descending circular stages upon which the princess, casting aside her education, abandons herself in a vision of the primitive black body run amok in the industrial metropolis. The American musical number most comparable in architectural form, sexual sublimation, and racial politics, however, narrowly predates Berkeley's arrival at RKO, and comes instead in the 1933 musical *Flying Down to Rio,* a film perhaps best known as the first cinematic pairing of Fred Astaire and Ginger Rogers. In their own debut performance, Astaire and Rogers perform the erotic "Carioca" dance more expertly than their Brazilian hosts, inspiring their dark-skinned audience to a mass release of sexual expressiveness on the nature-themed dance floor and, implicitly, reinforcing the racial hierarchy that privileges whiteness over Brazil's numerous gradations of darkening skin. Princess Tam Tam's performance moves swiftly in the opposite direction, exposing the essential primitivism of blackness and the ultimate failure—indeed, the absurdity—of the young woman's attempt to move from her colonial African village to the heights of French society. Anne Anlin Cheng questions, in *Second Skin* (2011), her study of Baker's modernism, the nature and implications of Baker's dance of abandon:

> What exactly is it that is being exposed? Given that Alwina's "true color"—that is, her racial color—has never been a secret in the story, it cannot be the literalness of her blackness that so shocks the Parisian audience. We may say, of course, that what has been uncovered is precisely the nonliteral nature of racial difference. The account would go something like this: while the diegetic audience may know the princess is black, it has not known how black until now. So Alwina may be able to pass as a princess for a while, but her wild African nature will invariably reveal itself.[18]

What we are witnessing here is a kind of forced outing, not of sexual orientation but of racial identification. The artist formerly known as Princess Tam Tam becomes, once again, the African girl Alwina. There is a great deal more to say, as Cheng does, about this stripping away of the mask of civilization to reveal its primitivist origins, as well as the postcolonial dimensions of a such a reading of modernism, but what I want to focus on in this context is its implications for several concepts of privacy, including the one articulated by Faulkner in "On Privacy" and elsewhere.

After meeting Baker in 1928, Adolf Loos, one of the progenitors of modern architecture, designed a house for her.[19] The project ultimately went unbuilt, yet its design provides a remarkable meditation on such issues as racial performance and identification, celebrity, consumerism, and privacy swirling around the figure of Baker throughout her career. The three-story house, a rectangular block with a solid marble façade, is designed with small, deep-set windows to afford as much privacy from the outside as possible. Black and white stripes of marble stretch horizontally around the exterior of the second and third stories, perhaps alluding to the zebra pattern that was common during the time—a primitivist evocation with racial undertones, to be sure—or to tattoos and other bodily markings, which simultaneously fascinated and frightened Loos. Interior features include a café, a gesture to bring the workplace into the home, as it were—a reference to the café and nightclub scene where Baker's Parisian notoriety was forged. But the most striking feature of the Baker house design is, as Cheng describes it, "the top-lit, large, double-height (that is, two stories) swimming pool that dominates the center of the house. . . . A magnificent glass roof covers the pool to allow light to fall upon the water. The walls of the pool have thick glass windows cut into them, and low passages have been assigned to surround the pool, providing windows onto it, creating for guests of the house something of an 'underwater revue'" (51). By placing a large swimming pool with windows at the center of the house, Loos transformed Baker's domestic space into one of voyeurism, imagining this most private of structures as yet another site for the performance of Baker's varied and ambiguous public personae. Instead of fleeing the gaze of publicity, Baker, in Loos's design, welcomes this bizarrely public relation in a way that outstrips even her unclad cabaret performances. Yet the exoticizing function of the pool seems to coexist with its womblike quality, figuring its swimmer as outward performer, sexualized object, and unborn child all at once. If we consider the womb in architectural terms, it would be difficult to imagine or design a more private space (perhaps not unlike Faulkner's vision of the windowless early dwellings which represent a nascent stage of American cultural development). Loos's design imagines Baker's privacy as another form of publicity, conflating the two selves of private individual and public figure in a gesture simultaneously playful, critical, and mysterious.

Faulkner had very little interest in modern architecture as an aesthetic or intellectual movement, and may well have looked upon Loos's Baker house design as an exercise in the absurd. Yet Faulkner's personal architectural vision was devoted, in its own way, to a similar brand of public-private mediation. Comparatively flush with the earnings from his early publications, he purchased a dilapidated pre–Civil War colonial-style home on the outskirts of Oxford in 1930 and set out to restore it. The structure had no electricity or plumbing, and Faulkner's stepson Malcolm later recalled that "It looked as if it was going to collapse with the next rainstorm or high wind." Faulkner's wife, Estelle, sat down on the front steps and sobbed, "not only undone," Blotner writes, "by the condition of her new home, now that it was a reality, but also convinced that they would henceforth be beyond the pale of social life in Oxford." For Faulkner, however, this was both a refuge, nearly a mile from the center of town and amid wooded property known for its good hunting, and a bold statement of his own identity as a citizen, wage earner, and paterfamilias. The home Faulkner named Rowan Oak became, his daughter Jill later said, "the symbol in Pappy's life of being somebody . . . everybody in Oxford had remembered that Pappy's father ran a livery stable, and this was just a way of thumbing his nose at Oxford . . . a nice old house [that] had a certain substance and standing to it."[20] Beyond Oxford, Rowan Oak also existed for Faulkner in a realm between reality and fantasy, linking him to a historical chain dating back to the period before the Civil War and enabling a romanticized conception of domestic life—loyal black retainers included, of course—as part of his own identity. In the early 1940s, when his lover Meta Carpenter timidly suggested they might live together in Los Angeles, Faulkner demurred with an almost Keatsian vision of an alternative existence together in a time and place beyond the real. She described the exchange in her 1976 memoir:

> "I would like," he said, "to live in an old house with you and hear you moving about as I work. I would like to write my last words for the day and move out of my solitude to you—beautiful and quiet and untroubled."
>
> "What kind of house?"
>
> "One that is ante-bellum and stately. With a good, sound roof on it and white columns, perhaps a Georgian-style porch, and a smokehouse in back."
>
> Was he thinking of Rowan Oak or of an old sagging mansion that he had passed one day on his travels through Mississippi, tarrying for a moment to frame me in the doorway and to put himself inside the musty darkness of it?
>
> "It would be a grievous error," Faulkner said, "for us to live in Hollywood together, dear love."[21]

Such flights from reality nevertheless retained Faulkner's characteristic grounding in the actual details of real times and places. In doing so they mirrored the amalgam of public and private selves that occupied Faulkner for decades. We might thus consider some of Faulkner's methods of self-presentation and public relations management, both before his great fame and during the post–Nobel Prize years of the 1950s and early 1960s, as public performances designed to achieve a comparable sort of simultaneous concealing and revealing of himself. At the time of Faulkner's return home in the guise of a wounded, but meticulously stylish, RAF lieutenant, and through his racial performance in the fashion of the day, Faulkner's privacy became a very public mask, a self-protective retreat that depended on an audience for its fullest effects. His insistence to the contrary in "On Privacy" and other 1950s writings notwithstanding, Faulkner had long since adopted the strategy of using privacy itself as a form of publicity; he had become, in the end, famously private, and the Faulkner brand was a performance of a well-publicized privacy that shared a great deal with Josephine Baker's complex negotiations of celebrity, and with Adolf Loos's imaginative spatial rendering thereof. "Faulkner retreated into silence," biographer Frederick R. Karl writes of the novelist's behavior at his final public appearance, after receiving the Gold Medal for Fiction from the American Academy of Arts and Letters in 1962, "drawing around him that self-made wall behind which he could protect himself from faces and voices." It was a wall with which many had grown familiar, looming in Sphinx-like mystery before all who dared approach it. "Faulkner barely got through," Karl continues, "beginning in retirement and ending in that abstraction of himself which had become his signature."[22]

Indeed, Coughlan's *Life* profile served Faulkner in exactly this way, transforming the novelist's sense of violation into an attractive, if imminently extinct, cultural trait. "He dislikes publicity or public notice and any attempt to penetrate his privacy is met with an irascible and incendiary anger," Coughlan wrote somewhat hyperbolically. In fact, Faulkner had entertained Coughlan at his home and given him several leads in Oxford, contrary to Faulkner's own claim in "On Privacy" that he had neither consented to nor participated in Coughlan's work (Faulkner's rage at exposure also did not prevent him from having lunch with Coughlan and their mutual friend Robert Linscott in New York in October 1953, just weeks after the *Life* articles ran.). "Yet it is no more possible," Coughlan continued, "for Faulkner to remain inconspicuous than it would be to build a wall around the Grand Canyon. His books . . . are no longer his but have become a part of the literary landscape of his country, like Melville's and Poe's. Because he has created them, he does not belong entirely to himself."[23] Coughlan came closer to the problem of his subject later in the piece, when he noted the contradictory impulses within Faulkner himself which gave rise to such an uneven approach to his public self-presentation: "He is a self-effacing but vain man who longed for recognition and rebuffed it when it came; a man of integrity who has contributed to a false legend about himself."[24]

These are significant insights suggesting a remarkable degree of continuity in Faulkner's media relations, such as they might be understood, across his entire career from post–World War I performance artist to Nobel laureate representing American ideals in his travels on behalf of the U.S. Department of State as well as in his other public guises. More generally, however, one of the major implications of this discussion, a thread that runs through Faulkner's military attire and Loos's design of the Baker house, is that surfaces—architectural, epidermal, sartorial—are themselves media forms. Modern architecture, like modern racial construction, might more constructively be seen as process than object, network rather than fixed position, technology and tool rather than finished product. A powerful articulation of these ideas is offered by architectural historian Beatriz Colomina, who suggests in her own work on Adolf Loos and Le Corbusier, appropriately titled *Privacy and Publicity* (1994):

> It will be necessary to think of architecture as a system of representation, or rather a series of overlapping systems of representation. . . . The building should be understood in the same terms as drawings, photographs, writing, films, and advertisements; not only because these are the media in which more often we encounter it, but because the building is a mechanism of representation in its own right. The building is, after all, a "construction," in all senses of the word.[25]

Colomina states that her concern is not so much "with the relationship between architecture and the media as with the possibility of thinking of architecture as media" (15).

Turning to Faulkner's fiction at this late point in such a discussion devoted more squarely to the media history of race is admittedly an inadequate gesture. The stories are rife with powerful expressions of the mediatory qualities of architecture as well as race, often articulated simultaneously. They occur in grand designs, such as the mansion and grounds of Sutpen's Hundred in *Absalom, Absalom!* (1936), as well as small figures, such as World War I veteran and lynch mob leader John McClendon's "neat new house" in "Dry September"

(1931), "trim and fresh as a birdcage and almost as small, with its clean, green-and-white paint."[26] These deserve more thorough attention elsewhere. One of the most penetrating examples available in this context, however, comes from "The Bear" in *Go Down, Moses* (1942):

> the two brothers who as soon as their father was buried moved out of the tremendously-conceived, the almost barn-like edifice which he had not even completed, into a one-room log cabin which the two of them built themselves and added other rooms to while they lived in it, refusing to allow any slave to touch any timber of it other than the actual raising into place the logs which two men alone could not handle, and domiciled all the slaves in the big house some of the windows of which were still merely boarded up with odds and ends of plank or with the skins of bear and deer nailed over the empty frames: each sundown the brother who superintended the farming would parade the negroes as a first sergeant dismisses a company, and herd them willynilly, man woman and child, without question protest or recourse, into the tremendous abortive edifice scarcely out of embryo, as if even old Carothers McCaslin had paused aghast at the concrete indication of his own vanity's boundless conceiving: he would call his mental roll and herd them in and with a hand-wrought nail as long as a flinching-knife and suspended from a short deer-hide thong attached to the door-jamb for that purpose, he would nail to the door of that house which lacked half its windows and had no hinged back door at all, so that presently and for fifty years afterward, when the boy himself was big enough to hear and remember it, there was in the land a sort of folk-tale: of the countryside all night long full of skulking McCaslin slaves dodging the moonlit roads and the Patrol-riders to visit other plantations, and of the unspoken gentlemen's agreement between the two white men and the two dozen black ones that, after the white man had counted them and driven the home-made nail into the front door at sundown, neither of the white men would go around behind the house and look at the back door, provided that all the negroes were behind the front one when the brother who drove it drew out the nail again at daybreak.[27]

If Buck and Buddy McCaslin prefer a self-built dog-trot cabin to the mansion they have inherited, perhaps it is as much a desire for privacy from the slaves (and everyone else) as an anxiety about the morality of slavery itself that motivates them. Privacy, after all, is virtually a synonym for individualism in Faulkner's lexicon, a precious resource for the performance of whiteness and Americanness. The half-built mansion stands like a vast but empty structure on a movie set, its façade more useful for local color, to provide the background to the whites' and blacks' nightly masquerade of authority and submission, than for shelter or containment or intimacy. And as the slaves are broadcast across the countryside at night like so many telegraph or radio signals, sharing their knowledge, voices, and bodies with those they encounter on "other plantations," the larger media network they constitute, that of whole generations transmitting life itself to those who follow them, provides a model the far less reproductive brothers McCaslin, or one of them, will adopt only reluctantly.

It is not simply the point that Faulkner never transcended the racism that had been in the air, like radio waves, throughout his life, although his problematic writings and public statements on the subject late in his life make such an argument a rather easy, even facile, one to formulate. Imagining him to have done otherwise might be comparable to imagining his receptiveness to Adolf Loos's Baker house rather than his own Rowan Oak as a feasible model of his own public-private mediation. A few months before his death in 1962, Faulkner accepted an invitation to speak at West Point; the event was covered, perhaps appropriately, by *Life* magazine, with photographs by Carl Mydans. Faulkner seemed comfortable, for once, in the company of people he did not know well, flattered to read to an audience of cadets, eager to emphasize American individualism as the last best hope for the nation during the Cold War. He cut a stylish figure in his muted gray tweeds, a private man dressed nicely but in a way that doesn't seek attention or publicity. The diagonally striped navy blue, maroon, and gray tie he chose for the occasion, however, was the regimental tie of the Royal Air Force.[28] Despite his very brief and limited RAF service—179 days, all in Canada, in 1918—which Faulkner only began to acknowledge a few years after World War II, and then only partially and grudgingly, he clearly saw the West Point occasion as an opportunity to suggest, once again, four-and-a-half decades after the 1918 armistice, and in this particular way, his own military past.

The larger argument emerging from this discussion of Faulkner's lifelong recourse to early-twentieth-century American discourses of race, instead, concerns the idea that race itself functions as a medium. In my own research on early cinema and the South, I have encountered an enormous catalogue of racial representations, from fictional white elites and hillbillies in Warner Bros. dramas in the early 1930s to newsreels of white tobacco workers on strike in North Carolina; from Stepin Fetchit and Hattie McDaniel confirming crass stereotypes for cash in Hollywood to Jesse Owens winning the gold medal in Leni Riefenstahl's 1938 documentary *Olympia* and later cashing in on his celebrity by plugging Chesterfield cigarettes in early TV commercials, looking into the camera and saying: "I want you folks out there to note that when Jesse Owens smokes a cigarette, he smokes Chesterfield." There are hundreds and hundreds of others. It is important that media history should document the complicity of American film with white supremacy since their mutual emergence in the 1890s, a shared history whose roots and branches remain too little understood. In addition, though, this work might contribute to more general and theoretical efforts to explain how race travels and carries information, encodes values and ideologies, connects or divides individuals and groups; how race is radioactive, and the myth of race's determinism; how race is performed and networked and worn like clothing or, if you're a building, like cladding; how race is designed and built and maintained and demolished and recycled; and, most generally, how race presents us with a horizon of possibilities limited only by the nature of the technology and our ability to imagine its futures as different from its past.[29] Such critical work is vital in both the larger field of media ecology and in specific areas, periods, and topics within American cultural history, modernism, and Faulkner studies. That an occasional screenwriter and more-than-occasional public performer such as Faulkner might contribute to such a project, in these uneasy connections of skin and structure, should come as scant surprise to those who understand how closely veiled he kept himself despite, and amid, his worldwide travels and his own brand of overexposure.

NOTES

Epigraph: William Faulkner, *Selected Letters of William Faulkner, ed. Joseph Blotner* (New York: Random House, 1977), 48.

1. William Faulkner, "On Privacy," in *Essays, Speeches, and Public Letters*, ed. James B. Meriwether (New York: Modern Library, 2004), 72–73. Hereafter cited parenthetically.

2. Grace Elizabeth Hale and Robert Jackson, "'We're Trying Hard as Hell to Free Ourselves': Southern History and Race in the Making of William Faulkner's Literary Terrain," in *A Companion to William Faulkner*, ed. Richard C. Moreland (Oxford: Blackwell, 2007), 28–45.

3. James Baldwin, *The Price of the Ticket: Collected Non-Fiction, 1948–1985* (London: Michael Joseph, 1985), 152.

4. Joseph Blotner, *Faulkner: A Biography* (Jackson: University Press of Mississippi, 2005), 618.

5. See, for example, Daniel J. Singal, *William Faulkner: The Making of a Modernist* (Chapel Hill: University of North Carolina Press, 1997), 45–46.

6. Blotner, *Faulkner*, 67.

7. Faulkner, *Selected Letters*, 285.

8. Ibid., 201.

9. Blotner, *Faulkner*, 66–67.

10. David Minter, *William Faulkner: His Life and Work* (Baltimore: Johns Hopkins University Press, 1997), 103.

11. See, for example, Grace Elizabeth Hale, *Making Whiteness: The Culture of Segregation in the South, 1890–1940* (New York: Pantheon, 1998).

12. James G. Watson, *William Faulkner: Self-Presentation and Performance* (Austin: University of Texas Press, 2002).

13. There were, however, a few deviations from the great majority of these posters' images of white soldiers, including a privately published 1918 poster carrying the caption "Colored Man Is No Slacker." Its image of a soldier saying good-bye to his sweetheart and leaving their column-clad home as his regiment marches off to war provides one of the few images of black soldiers to read against the mainstream American convention of obscuring black military service. The Edenic quality of this domestic space, a model of marital trust and devotion, is paired with a comparably remarkable and idealistic fusion of African American military service and U.S. nationalism. For more on this poster, see Jennifer D. Keene, "Images of Racial Pride: African American Propaganda Posters in the First World War," in *Picture This: World War I Posters and Visual Culture*, ed. Pearl James (Lincoln: University of Nebraska Press, 2010), 228.

14. Frantz Fanon, *Black Skin, White Masks*, rev. ed. (New York: Grove, 2008), 92.

15. Faulkner's fiction registers a keen awareness of photographic technologies, giving my characterization of Baker as a photo negative a direct link to his imaginative explorations of race and modern media. In *Absalom, Absalom!*, for example, Mr. Compson imagines "the way in which [the racially ambiguous Charles Bon] took the innocent and negative plate of Henry's provincial soul and intellect and exposed it by slow degrees to [New Orleans], building gradually toward the picture which he desired it to retain, accept" (William Faulkner, *Absalom, Absalom!* [1936; New York: Vintage, 1990], 87).

16. See www.gettyimages.com: editorial image 147364846.

17. See www.allposters.com/-sp/Josephine-Baker-Tam-Tam-Posters_i993221_.htm?aid=39919869&LinkTypeID=1&PosterTypeID=1&DestType=7.

18. Anne Anlin Cheng, *Second Skin: Josephine Baker and the Modern Surface* (New York: Oxford University Press, 2011), 62. Hereafter cited parenthetically.

19. See www.architecture.com/LibraryDrawingsAndPhotographs/Exhibitionsandloans/AdolfLoos/Otherworks/JosephineBakerHouse.aspx#.UuGieCh6jJw.

20. Blotner, *Faulkner*, 260, 261.

21. Meta Carpenter Wilde and Orin Borsten, *A Loving Gentleman: The Love Story of William Faulkner and Meta Carpenter* (New York: Simon and Schuster, 1976), 280.

22. Frederick R. Karl, *William Faulkner: American Writer, A Biography* (New York: Weidenfeld and Nicolson, 1989), 1031.

23. Robert Coughlan, "The Private World of William Faulkner," *Life*, September 28, 1953, 122.

24. Coughlan, "Private World," 127.

25. Beatriz Colomina, *Privacy and Publicity: Modern Architecture as Mass Media* (Cambridge: MIT Press, 1996), 13–14. Hereafter cited parenthetically.

26. William Faulkner, "Dry September," in *Collected Stories* (New York: Vintage, 1995), 183.

27. William Faulkner, *Go Down, Moses*, in *Novels, 1942–1954* (New York: Library of America, 1994), 250–51.

28. See www.rafmuseumshop.com/node/4135.

29. For an introduction to some recent work in this vein, see, for example, "Feminism, Culture, and Media Studies: Race and/as Technology," special issue, *Camera Obscura* 70, vol. 24, no. 1 (2009); and W. J. T. Mitchell, *Seeing Through Race* (Cambridge: Harvard University Press, 2012).

Kodak Harlot Tricks of Light

Faulkner and Melville in the Darkroom of Race

SASCHA MORRELL

Black will make you . . . or black will unmake you.
—RALPH ELLISON, *Invisible Man*

Light though thou be, thou leapest out of darkness.
—HERMAN MELVILLE, *Moby-Dick*

What does a photographic negative imply if not the blackness of whiteness, and vice versa? William Faulkner's *Light in August* (1932) presents the startling image of Joe Christmas baring himself to the glare of approaching headlights, "watch[ing] his body grow white out of the darkness like a kodak print emerging from the liquid," then cancelling that whiteness through a performance of racial blackness, shouting "White bastards!" as the car passes.[1] Racial figurations of the photographic process recur in Faulkner's fiction, most importantly *Light in August* and *Absalom, Absalom!* (1936). Pun intended, this essay considers how Faulkner "exposes" the blackness of whiteness by "playing in the dark(room)" of photographic metaphor. Comparisons arise with the racial operations of photic conceits in nineteenth-century fiction. Nathaniel Hawthorne's *The House of the Seven Gables* (1851) may be the most prominent example of an antebellum novel using photographic symbolism to destabilize established race and class identities, but the particularly intense configurations of black-white interdependency in Herman Melville's work afford still richer precedent for Faulkner's figures.

In chapter 42 of Herman Melville's *Moby-Dick*, "The Whiteness of the Whale," Ishmael presents a dialectical conception of whiteness as its own negative, a synthesis of opposites: "not so much a color as the visible absence of color; and at the same time the concrete of all colors." Different hues are "not actually inherent in substances" but merely tricks of light, which "paints like the harlot."[2] On this logic, the hue exalted as giving "giving the white man ideal mastership over every dusky tribe" (*Moby-Dick* 201) has no real existence. Exploring Faulkner's photographic figures in connection with Melville's metaphors of paint and light not only affords a long perspective on Faulkner's black-white dialectics but may shed light on the problematic relationship between "race" and visual media technology as it persists today. In the latter part of this essay, I propose that Charles Bon's "irrevocable negation" (*Absalom* 219) of white surface images can be seen as an elaborate art of photomanipulation, anticipating the technological possibilities of the digital age.

Black and White in August

Faulkner toyed with giving *Light in August* the title "Dark House," and subsequently considered the same title for *Absalom, Absalom!*[3] Although neither work retained that dark title—*Light in August* quite the opposite—each furnishes what might be called a "darkroom of race"; they are texts in which racial imagery is incessantly developed and redeveloped to the point where black and white seem interchangeable, or indistinguishable.

The image of Joe Christmas's naked body "grow[ing] white out of the darkness like a kodak print emerging from the liquid" seems to counter a deeper process of "becoming black" that Joe experiences throughout the novel, imagined as a "black tide creeping up his legs" (339). Indeed, Joe has been so thoroughly conditioned to think of himself as a "nigger" that he adds a caption to the white image of himself that insists on his blackness. Having heard "a woman's shrill voice . . . shrieking" from the passing car, presumably shocked at his exposed genitals, Joe shouts "white bastards! . . . That's not the first of your bitches that ever saw . . ." (108).[4] Even as he "grows white," Joe defines himself in opposition to white bastards and bitches. Looking "straight into the headlights," it is unlikely Christmas could see the car's occupants, but Faulkner's third-person narrator corroborates his presumption of their whiteness: "a woman's shrill voice" becomes "the white woman's fading cry." Whether Christmas's words are equally effective as an assertion of his own blackness is more doubtful, for they go unheard: "the car was gone. There was no one to hear, to listen" (108–9).

Through the photographic metaphor, however, we comprehend that Christmas's whiteness was already cancelled, insofar as the whiteness of a "kodak print" always implies a black negative. In a photographic negative, black and white are reversed: the lightest areas appear darkest, and the darkest areas lightest. When the treated negative is "rephotographed," black becomes white in the positive prints, and vice versa. The negative is a "negation" of the object it exposes, and the positive print is a negation of that negation—a complex dialectics that, Faulkner realized, had unsettling implications when considered in the ideological context of southern racial binarism. The inner contradictions of the negative-positive development process provide Faulkner with the perfect metaphor for the indeterminacy of Christmas's racial identity.

Outside Reverend Hightower's house in Jefferson, a fading sign advertises "Art Lessons/Handpainted Xmas &. Anniversary Cards/Photographs Developed" (58, 60). The sign is disregarded by the townspeople and the service presumably defunct, but the association of Hightower's house with photographic development and Christmas cards is crucial, for the house will provide the final darkroom in the seemingly endless (re)development of Christmas's racial identity. It is here that Percy Grimm will lynch Christmas in an act of racial violence designed to code him unequivocally as "nigger." Christmas's genitals were central to his own efforts to blacken himself ("not the first of your bitches that ever saw . . ."), and when Grimm castrates Christmas, he verbally blackens his victim in a manner reminiscent of Joe's own: "Now you'll let white women alone, even in hell" (464).

It seems, however, that the print of Christmas's racial identity is no more conclusively developed here than in the earlier scene. How should we interpret the fact that, instead of fixing his blackness, the lynching is said to "release" it? As Christmas lies dying, we read:

> the pent black blood seemed to rush like a released breath . . . out of his pale body like a rush of sparks from a rising rocket; upon that black blast the man seemed to rise soaring into [the onlookers'] memories forever and ever.

Far from becoming "fixed," as in the darkroom fixing process, Christmas's blackness has become something diffuse, rising from the Kodak of his body like chemical vapor, and leaving the print—what? Blank? As he lies dying, Christmas's face is described as "empty of everything save consciousness" (466). Meanwhile, the racial identity of the white onlookers comes into question, for in haunting their memories "forever," Joe's presumptive black blood will make an appearance in the "mirroring faces" of their own progeny (466–67).[5]

Before his house provides the darkroom for the botched development of this final blank snapshot of Christmas's racial identity, Reverend Hightower himself has been photographically blackened. During the public outrage surrounding his wife's adultery and death, Hightower appeared in newsprint in a side-on photograph, looking "like Satan in the old prints" (69). The image has a dual negative function: turning a man of God into Satan, and turning an ostensibly "white" man black, as Satan was represented in medieval woodcuts. Suggestively, Christmas himself is subsequently assigned "the face of Satan" (205). Hightower's photographic blackening marks the onset of his social blackening, as rumors of miscegenation surround him after his wife's death. As a victim of racism, Hightower is shunned by the community, threatened, and even attacked by Klansmen (69–75).

Given the 1920s setting, Hightower's blackening through a newsprint photograph resonates with a contemporaneous scandal in which news photography assumed a major role in shaping racial identity, the Rhinelander trial of 1924. Kip Rhinelander sued to annul his marriage to Alice Jones Rhinelander, arguing that he was deceived about her racial background, having been told her West Indian father was Spanish when he had partial African descent (the parallels with *Absalom's* Eulalia Bon suggest Faulkner followed the trial). National newspapers reproduced photographs of Alice, with journalists variously insisting on the effectiveness of her "passing," proclaiming her obvious blackness, or insisting she had bleached her face with "acidulous lotions."[6] Highlighting the arbitrariness of racial markers, the trial coverage also made photojournalistic history as the occasion of the first newspaper "composograph." When Alice agreed to expose her breasts for the court, which (the *Daily Mirror* claimed) were "indisputable evidence of negro origin," the judge barred photographers.[7] The *New York Graphic*, however, faked an image, superimposing a rear-view image of a topless woman on a photo-collaged courtroom.[8] The apparently indecisive artist used a white model for Alice but tinted her skin darker.[9]

Christmas's resistance to his Kodak whitening is centered on his genitals; Alice's lawyers appealed to her breasts as the site of her blackness. At this peculiar juncture of sex, photography, bleaching, tinting, and female modesty, we may recall another "darkroom" in *Light in August*: the curtained corner of the dietitian's room where the young Christmas ingests then vomits toothpaste. Toothpaste cleans and whitens, but this toothpaste is a problematic pink, coiling as a "pink worm" onto Joe's finger and creating pink foam (120). Pink was not a standard toothpaste color in the 1920s and 1930s; indeed, marketers used the phrases "pink toothbrush" or "pink mouth" to suggest poor oral hygiene, referring to discoloration from bleeding gums.[10] In the context of dental care, then, pinkness represented filth. In *Light in August*, it specifically evokes "womanfilth" (132), for Joe associates the "pink worm" with something "pink-colored and surreptitious" in the dietitian's "fullbodied" femininity (120), a connection strengthened when he witnesses her submitting to a lover's unwanted advances. As Greg Forter argues, Joe's ingestion of the toothpaste "identifies him with blackness and femininity" as analogous positions of disempowerment and abjection.[11] The "pinkwomansmelling obscurity behind the curtain" accords with the rosy lighting of the 1920s darkroom,[12] and it is a space where some kind of racial "development" unmistakably takes place: Joe enters as a "shadow" with "parchmentcolored" skin and emerges to be captioned a "'little nigger bastard'" by the outraged dietitian (120, 122). In his later encounter with a young black woman in a dark shed, Joe will recall this first darkroom, feeling "something inside him trying to get out, like when he had used to think of toothpaste," even as he feels "enclosed by the womanshenegro" (156). In this context, the "liquid" from which Christmas's white "Kodak" image emerges becomes associated with his sense of immersion in racial blackness as a "lightless hot wet primogenitive Female" (115).[13]

Negatives of Labor

Holding Charles Bon's letter in the dim light of a "single globe stained and bug-fouled" in *Absalom*'s fifth chapter, Mr. Compson's hand "look[s] almost as dark as a Negro's" against his linen trousers, while the black-ink script on the paper seems a mere "shadow" (71). As in *Light in August*, racial coloration emerges here as a lighting effect, or optical illusion. It is, in Ishmael's phrase, something "laid on from without," like the harlot's paint (*Moby-Dick* 212). But in *Absalom*, Faulkner's rendering of racial ambiguity, and the photographic metaphors it attracts, are more intimately related to labor dependency in the plantation South. The photographic negative furnishes a neat metaphor for the idea, superbly elaborated by Richard Godden in relation to labor relations in Faulkner, that "white is what black makes."[14]

As Godden argues, *Absalom*'s narrators are haunted by the knowledge that the plantation South and they as its inheritors were ultimately created by black work.[15] This repressed knowledge breaches the textual surface only rarely: in the Tidewater sequence, for example, the young Thomas Sutpen recognizes that the wealthy planter's modus vivendi is made possible by "living human men [who] perform the endless repetitive personal offices, such as . . . pulling off his boots for him to go to bed," so that the master is all but relieved of "chewing and swallowing and breathing" (179–80). Effectively, the slave furnishes the master's substance. Godden compares Hegel's master-slave dialectic, in which the master comes to realize that the material abundance that manifests his mastery is produced by his slave, and thus that his mastery is slave-made.[16] The same quasi-Hegelian logic is evident in Mr. Compson's reference to the sexual servitude of "the slave girls and women *upon whom* that first caste [of white women] rested and to whom in certain cases it doubtless *owed the very fact of its virginity*" (emphases added).

As a metaphor for the "making" of "white" master by "black" slave, what is particularly interesting in the negative-positive photographic process is the priority of the negative to the positive prints. Any portrait of a "white" face has a "black" negative behind it—the black negative is the "master" from which white copies are made. With this in mind, a key moment in the "development" of whiteness from blackness in *Absalom* may be detected when Sutpen retreats into a lightless "cave" following his demoralizing encounter with the black butler at the Tidewater planter's door (185). Although not presented in overtly photographic terms, the cave provides a darkroom in which Sutpen will process his experience, and will arrive at an image of black butler as white planter. For when Sutpen reflects, "but I can shoot him," the "him" comes to refer not to the "balloon nigger" slave but the master, whose face he envisages as "looking out from within the balloon face."[17] Indeed, the black face is made to contain the white planter class as a whole—"all the human puny mortals under the sun that might lie in hammocks all afternoon with their shoes off" (189).

When Sutpen determines to "combat" the planter class by becoming a planter himself, he "chooses the oedipally-structured reproduction of slavery [rather than] . . . political resistance."[18] But to reproduce the white planter's image in himself, Sutpen needs the black negative: "you've got to have what they have," he reasons, which means land, a fine house and—indispensably—"niggers" (192). Via his (mis)adventures in Haiti, Sutpen comes by the "band of wild niggers" who, in "drag[ging]" Sutpen's Hundred out of "swamp" (28), enable Sutpen to "emerge from the liquid" of his development in the form he desires. His establishment is "even bigger and whiter" than the Tidewater mansion where he received his boyhood affront (209), yet this is the house that black built; its whiteness is, in a sense, the negative image of the black labor that produced it—or the positive print of that black negative. In Tidewater, Sutpen recognized that black labor "supported and endured [the planter's] smooth white house" (188). Like the picture of Dorian Gray, the negative lurks behind the reified positive image, and in Sutpen's case it will resurface in the person of Charles Bon—the Haitian-born, possibly mixed-race son whose presence summons up the claims of the black labor force that produced the white facade. When Quentin enters Sutpen's manor in 1909, it smells "as if . . . it was built [of] flesh" and contains a "pitch dark" so intense that "red spots" appear on Quentin's straining vision (294), linking suggestively to Charles Bon's "little spot of negro blood" (247), and to Haiti as a "spot of earth" manured with "black blood" (202)—the archetypal locus of New World slavery.[19]

Returning to Faulkner's photographic figures with this in mind, it is crucial that the very first image of the Sutpens offered in the novel's opening is expressly photographic: Quentin imagines "the four of them [Thomas, Ellen, Henry and Judith Sutpen] arranged into the conventional family group of the period, with formal and lifeless decorum . . . seen now as the fading and ancient photograph itself" (6). The image is "evoked . . . out of the airless gloom" of Rosa Coldfield's "dead house," as in a darkroom, but its "conventional" qualities lack fixity. Henry and Judith become "half-ogre children" who constitute, with their father, a "shadowy background" for Ellen, and the whole image has a "quality strange, contradictory . . . [not] quite right" (6–8). Subsequent images of Thomas Sutpen are no less contradictory. Even before the return of his negative in the person of Charles Bon, Sutpen is associated with blackness. Rosa twice calls him a "blackguard"; he presents a "black, batlike image" (139); he "should have been the same color" as the slaves he fights "chest to chest" (20–21), and so on. When Rosa recalls Sutpen's black coachman driving him and his children into Jefferson, Sutpen's face is described as "exactly like the Negro's," while his two children's faces are "replicas of his face in miniature"

(16).[20] It is as if the black coachman is the original image from which the Sutpens were reprinted—multiple prints from a single negative.

Listening to Rosa in 1909, Quentin Compson would likely have imagined photographic development in terms of the dry-plate photography popularized by Kodak, the method most widely used in his own time as in Faulkner's 1930s. However, any family photograph of the Sutpens would necessarily have been taken prior to Henry's rebellious departure in 1860, when the daguerreotype was still widely used in the United States. This photographic method does not involve printing from a negative, but produces a direct positive image on a single plate.[21]

It is unlikely Faulkner would have been overly concerned with such details, being no great stickler for minute historical accuracy. But considering the Sutpen photograph as a daguerreotype only enhances its "contradictory quality," for although not printed from a negative, it is an oddity of the daguerreotype that it simultaneously contains a positive and a negative image: because dark areas consist of highly reflective iodine silver, they appear brighter in direct light, so that "the light and the dark are reversed" depending on how an image is tilted.[22] Nathaniel Hawthorne exploits this peculiarity's symbolic potential in *Seven Gables,* in which Judge Pyncheon's dead face is photographed by Holgrave, a daguerreotypist lodging at the Pyncheon mansion, as it passes from its "singularly white" appearance through a paradoxically "swarthy whiteness" into "blackness."[23] Deriving in part from the family's implication in the national sin of slavery,[24] Judge Pyncheon's symbolic blackening accords with Holgrave's contention that a daguerreotype might not only capture surface details but expose deeper essences, "bring[ing] out the secret character."[25]

Among U.S. journalists praising the daguerreotype's extraordinary accuracy was Samuel Morse, who proclaimed in 1839 that daguerreotype images were "Rembrandt perfected."[26] If so, Rembrandt perfected was Rembrandt desaturated, for what Morse elides is the daguerreotype's reducing all colors to black and white. In light of Holgrave's suggestion that the medium might expose deeper truths, however, this reductive mode of representing the world might be said to have its own peculiar accuracy—not "true" to nature, but certainly "true" to the binaristic racial thinking of the period, in which "black" and "colored" were synonyms, with distinctions based on black and white. It is in this connection that I turn to Melville, whose representations of black-white interdependency—although rarely figured photographically—foreshadow Faulkner's photographic figures to a remarkable extent.

Leaping Out of Light

In Faulkner's library at Rowan Oak, a print of Melville's Captain Ahab hangs alongside the family portraits painted by Faulkner's mother, Maud. The print is of one of Rockwell Kent's illustrations for the 1930 Lakeside Press and Random House editions of *Moby-Dick.*[27] Traces of Ahab's portrait also appear in *Absalom*'s Thomas Sutpen. The "fixed forward dedication" of Ahab, who calls himself "more a demon than a man" (*Moby-Dick* 135, 591), accords with the "gaunt and tireless driving" of "the demon Sutpen" (*Absalom* 36). Mauled by the white whale, Ahab aims at redeeming "all the general rage and hate felt by his whole race from Adam down" (*Moby-Dick* 178). Barred at a "white door," Sutpen seeks to redeem all poor whites—past, present, and future—from existential insignificance in pursuit of his white design (*Absalom* 210). And, like Sutpen's, Ahab's racial identity is complicated by contradictions that suggest the inescapable interrelatedness—even the indistinguishability—of black and white.

There could have been no artist better suited to attempt Ahab's portrait than Rockwell Kent, in whose iconic ink illustrations black and white are at once intensely contrasted and utterly enmeshed. Images of blackness-in-whiteness and whiteness-in-blackness surround Melville's Ahab, whose "black terrific" person is split by a "lividly whitish" birthmark (165, 134). Ahab himself expressly articulates a dialectical conception of black-white interdependency in chapter 119, "The Candles." When mysterious white flames appear atop the *Pequod*'s spars in a storm, Ahab addresses them: "Light though thou be, thou leapest out of darkness; but I am darkness leaping out of light, leaping out of thee!" (551). Racial connotations arise from Ishmael's linkage of the storm to the body of the African harpooneer Daggoo, who "seem[s] the black cloud from which the thunder had come," and who looms to "thrice his real stature" before the white flames leap "to thrice their previous height" (549, 551). The Manx sailor had earlier likened Ahab's white birthmark to lightning where "all else [is] pitch black," and here, too, Daggoo supplied racial context, crying, "Who's afraid of black's afraid of me!" (191).

Ahab later establishes a curious rapport with the black ship's boy, Pip, and Pip's description of himself as the "lost leg" without which Ahab "ha[s] not a whole body" (580) affords as powerful an image of white racial dependency as any in Faulkner. Although not literally slave and slave master, Ahab and Pip are coded as such: Pip ceaselessly calls Ahab "master," and at the moment when Ahab first embraces Pip, the boy is advertising himself as a runaway slave: "One hundred pounds of clay reward for Pip; five feet high . . . !" (567). Faulkner would have been keenly attuned to such imagery, and it may be no coincidence that he hung his print of Ahab alongside the portrait of an African American man, Preacher Green Liggin.[28]

Portraiture plays a key role in Melville's subversion of racial whiteness in *Pierre; or, The Ambiguities* (1852), a novel that affords numerous parallels with *Absalom* in its deep concern with the "racial entanglement" of an aristocratic house.[29] The hero, Pierre Glendinning, is confronted by the a mysterious girl, Isabel, who identifies herself as his illegitimate half sister, and is variously described as "ebon" (314), "Nubian" (145), "dark, olive" (46) and "black" (65). Her specter flies in "the marble face of the Past" (174), leading Pierre to question "from what vile attaintings he himself had sprung" (178). Pierre's father reportedly feared having his portrait painted because he read in a work of "Physiognomy"—one of the racist "semi-sciences" lampooned in *Moby-Dick* (378)—that a painting could reveal a subject's "shadowiest" "innermost secrets" (79), and when Pierre burns his father's portrait after meeting Isabel, he watches its "blackening" and finds his own hand "blackened" (199). The sequence suggests the exposition of a "hidden character" akin to Judge Pyncheon's photographic blackening in Hawthorne's *Gables*, a hint that the Glendinnings' whiteness was already compromised prior to Isabel's advent, if not through actual racial mixture, then by virtue of racial guilt—the "patriotic historical associations" of the Glendinning land obscure a darker history of "annihilated . . . Indians" and "negro slaves" (29).[30]

As his father feared being painted, Pierre has refused to be photographed, despite being plagued with requests from publishers of his light verse. "To the devil with you and your Daguerreotype!" (254), he barks at one especially aggressive suitor. When Pierre burns his father's portrait, it suggests an "[un]bleached . . . barbaric tan" (198), and given that Pierre's own complexion "incline[s] to brown" (17), it may be that he shares his father's fears of racial exposure, although his primary objection is elitist: before the daguerreotype, only "aristocrats" could afford a "faithful portrait," but any "Tom, Dick and Harry" can now have their likeness taken (255).

Portraiture and racial definition remain closely entwined in the art gallery sequence in which Isabel and Pierre admire a copy of Guido Reni's famous painting known as "the Cenci." Depicting a "seraphically *blonde*" woman with "blue eyes and fair complexion," this picture "exactly face[s]" another portrait, depicting a "dark" young man with "crisp, curly, jetty hair," and there seems to be some "secret" connection between these "opposite" images (351, original emphasis). Even without its dark counterpart, the Cenci's ostensible whiteness is deeply suspect. Firstly, as was well known, Reni's Cenci did not depict a blue-eyed "blonde," as the narrator so emphatically asserts of the copy, but a darker-haired, brown-eyed woman.[31] Compounding this oddity, this portrait's fairness is likened to that pallor "sometimes visible in the maidens of tropical nations" with "funereally jetty hair," so that the woman's very whiteness becomes a mark of racial otherness. "Jetty hair," meanwhile, echoes the description of the dark male opposite, in which Isabel sees "shadowy traces" of herself, while Pierre sees the "resurrection" of his father's portrait. As reflections and reversals ricochet, racial identity becomes an unstable mirage.[32]

Pierre's "exactly fac[ing]" paintings have something of a sequel in Melville's collection of Civil War poems, *Battle-Pieces and Aspects of the War* (1866), in which the immediate juxtaposition of two poems suggests a positive and negative image. The first is expressly presented in photographic terms. Titled "On the Photograph of a Corps Commander," it presents a rather conventional description of a "warrior," a "manly" figure whose fame is "lighted by his soul." That "lighte[ning]" is racialized through the boast: "Trace back his lineage . . . / and you would find Normans and Templars." The commander is not identified as Union or Confederate, allowing him to function as a generic figure of war heroism.[33] But the next poem, facing opposite, troubles the first.[34] Entitled "The Swamp-Angel," and nominally describing a cannon, it introduces "a coal-black Angel / With a thick Afric lip" which is described as "*lighting* far the pale fright of the faces," with "a glaring; / That wizens, and withers, and *whitens*" (my emphases). The photograph of a hero "lightened" by his virtuous soul and by Anglo-Saxon and Norman heritage is displaced by a "coal-black" specter that "whitens" pale faces. With most Civil War photographers using the wet-plate collodion method, the negative-positive development process was now well and truly available as a metaphorical resource,[35] and Melville's twinned poems seem to represent an early engagement with its figurative potential, possibly as a suggestion of black slavery as the real matter of the war, underlying surface images of white heroism.

The idea of "white as what black makes" appears more explicitly in Melville's *The Confidence-Man* (1857), in which the superlatively "white" hands of a southern gentleman "retai[n] their spotlessness" only because the "black" hands of a "negro servant" do "most of his handling for him."[36] Another celebrated example occurs in Melville's "Benito Cereno" (1854), in which the African rebel Babo, while masquerading as a loyal slave to deceive an American captain, shaves his former master, Cereno. Unfolding in a closeted space called "the cuddy," Melville's sequence prefigures the peculiar association of toiletries with racial definition in *Light in August*, except here it is shaving foam rather than toothpaste at work: Cereno's whiteness is "heightened by the [white] lather, which lather, again, was intensified in its hue by the contrasting sootiness of the negro's body." Even as the contrast of black and white seems intensified, the former is shown to generate the latter: ministering to Cereno's person, "the negro seemed a Nubian sculptor finishing off a white statue-head," and "the servant for a moment surveyed his master, as, in toilet at least, the creature of his own tasteful hands."[37] Creative power belongs to the black servant, whose own racial identity is itself a performative mask.

Charles Bon, Photo-Editor

The photographic subjects in Faulkner's work considered so far have primarily been passive, *subjected* to processes of racial development largely beyond their control. *Absalom*'s Charles Bon is a crucial exception. At numerous points, but especially in the New Orleans sequence in chapter 4, Bon emerges as a master of photomanipulation, whose artistry blurs the boundaries between negative and positive, exposure and development, and even between different photographic techniques, with devastating consequences for white racial identity.

Before he appears in Mr. Compson's narration as a photographer, however, Bon appears as a photograph, and perhaps nothing more than a photograph. It is Rosa who claims creative control over this image. She tells Quentin: "*I never saw him. I never even saw him dead. I heard a name, I saw a photograph . . . nothing of his face but that photograph, that shadow, that picture in a young girl's bedroom.*" And yet, Rosa claims, she could have "*recognized, nay, de-*

scribed, the very face" before she saw it, leading her to wonder, "*Why did I not invent, create it?*" (117–18, italics original). Fantasizing about extending her image-making powers, Rosa imagines appropriating and mass-producing her image of Bon, inventing "*something (a machine perhaps) which would adorn the barren mirror altars of every plain girl who breathes with such* [*images as*] . . . *this pictured face*" (118). In this process, Bon is agentless; a substanceless "*shadow*" projected from female desire that "*would not even need a skull behind it*" (117). When Mr. Compson introduces Bon as photographer, however, it is Bon in creative control, and the images he produces are not the kind white maidens were supposed to be dreaming over.

In introducing Henry to the ambiguities of New Orleans's miscegenated, creolized culture, Charles Bon "took the innocent and negative plate of Henry's provincial soul and intellect and exposed it by slow degrees to this esoteric milieu, building gradually toward the picture which he desired it to retain, accept" (88). As Carol Shloss notes, early commentators on photography tended to disregard the photographer's role as "an active participant in, and shaper of, procedures and events," echoing Daguerre's original description of photography as "nature impress[ing] an image of herself."[38] Bon, however, is entirely in control of the process, "stroking onto the plate himself now the picture which he *wanted* there" (88, my emphasis). Indeed, the idea of brushstrokes in "stroking" suggests photographic retouching. At the same time, "virginity" and "stroking" are emphatically sexual—Bon, "the corruptor" (88), is engaging Henry in a kind of Kodak harlotry. Like Melville's Babo, Bon takes pleasure in creative manipulation. The image of Henry's mind as an "innocent and negative plate" is somewhat problematic, for while "innocent" suggests the photosensitive surface prior to any exposure, "negative" suggests the already exposed image from which further images are reprinted; alternatively, we might interpret it as the surface that will become the negative after exposure.

In any case, Henry, with his "heritage peculiarly Anglo-Saxon," is accustomed to a world of clear racial distinctions, and Bon's photographic tour of New Orleans introduces him to an "esoteric milieu" in which such distinctions are "dissolved." Men with "darkly swaggering" faces appear in carriages beside richly dressed women "like painted portraits"—another "mixed media" element in Bon's photographic art. Bon will "fix and then remove without obliterating" this picture, leaving "the plate prepared and innocent again" yet also somehow leaving a "background," upon which to layer further "exposures brief . . . almost staccato" (88–89). Each of these is likewise "fixed" and then removed and yet somehow retained. As patented by Henry Fox Talbot for the calotype process in 1847, fixing involved using chemical solutions "to give *increased whiteness* to photographic pictures and at the same time make them *exceedingly permanent.*"[39] In *Absalom,* by contrast, the images Bon fixes are exceedingly *impermanent,* yet curiously ineradicable. Images that contradict Henry's racial certainties (the careful separation of "provincial virgins," "Negro butlers," and so on [86]) are being palimpsestically layered to the point of indistinguishability.

If negative-process photography may be considered a "miscegenated" medium in that it requires whiteness to pass through blackness, then Bon compounds this over and over again through a process of multiple exposures (a method used in early photographic hoaxes, such as Mumler's spirit photos).[40] Indeed, in that he layers and merges and otherwise manipulates the images he produces, Bon is more like a composographer—or even, anachronistically, a Photoshop artist—than simply a photographer. There is "the picture . . . the next picture . . ." building toward a "complete picture" that will only be revealed after a passage through the "corridor of doomed and tragic flower faces" where Henry is exposed to the idea of "human flesh bred of the two races" for sexual servitude (88–89). Imagining a "Kodak harlotry" of race in this context inevitably calls to mind New Orleans's clandestine market in erotic postcards, of which Faulkner was doubtless well aware.

This is "still not it," however; rather, the corridor leads to a second gate, behind which waits the octoroon mistress Bon has married in a morganatic ceremony. Her face represents "the apotheosis of two doomed races," and her sleeping child perfectly embodies the contradictions of southern race ideology: "sleeping in silk and lace . . . yet complete chattel of him who, begetting him, owned him body and soul to sell (91). Henry's "erstwhile untroubled code in which females were ladies or whores or slaves" cannot stand. His mind has been "overexposed," forced to accept a new picture in which whores are "not whores" (93), "marriage" is "no marriage" (94), and the richly dressed, cultivated wives and children of white gentlemen are mere chattels. It is tempting to suggest that the establishment's "shuttered" façade, with its outer and interior gates, represents the shutter mechanism (89). In which case, we seem to be at once inside the camera (with Henry the "negative plate") and in the darkroom (with Bon "preparing" and "fixing" images). Different stages of different processes are collapsed, befitting the nature of Bon's project, which is the dissolution of distinctions.

Bon's starkest exposition of white racial thinking takes a simpler form, however. It is a straightforward act of photographic substitution. In chapter 4, Mr. Compson describes Judith finding a "picture of the octoroon mistress and the little boy" on Bon's corpse, in place of her own (75). In contrast, Rosa has simply assumed "*that what [Judith] held in that lax and negligent hand was the photograph, the picture of herself in its metal case which she had given him*" (114). Merging these accounts, Shreve will imagine Judith "holding the metal case she had given him with her picture in it but that didn't have her picture in it now but that of the octoroon and the kid" (286). The substitution is linked to Bon's suit for his father's recognition. Since Sutpen has given him "no sign in the eyes" (256–57), Bon has courted Sutpen's daughter as a way of "putting himself in Sutpen's way" (278), endeavoring to bring out his own latent image with Judith as chemical developer. While that project fails, Bon achieves the next best thing: abandoning his pursuit of white recognition, he himself grants recognition to his New Orleans mistress and son, putting their picture in the place reserved for a white wife. At the same time, the exchange of the "black" octoroon face for Judith's "white" face (conceivable as a "reversion" to the negative) recalls Mr. Compson's idea of white virgins "ow[ing] the very fact of their virginity" to black sex slaves.

Of course, neither mother nor child would be, tonally, the inverse of the white woman's image at all: the octoroon's complexion suggests a "magnolia," while Charles Etienne has "ivory" skin with an "olive" tint (91, 157–61). As in *Light in August*, in which the "dark complected" Joe Brown is white and the "parchmentcolored" Christmas is black (51, 123), assignations of black and white racial identities bear little relation to skin tone. In Faulkner's later novel *Wild Palms*, the character Bradley is so "sunbrowned" that his pale eyes look "almost white against his skin like a kodak negative."[41] But in the context of southern racial binarism and the "one drop" rule, Bon is effectively putting "black" in the place of "white," as negative to positive. Hence Shreve calling Bon a "black son of a bitch" as he makes the exchange (286).

This enables us to read in photographic terms the decisive moment in Quentin and Shreve's conarration in which Bon will swap his own white image for a black one. When Henry says, "You are my brother," Bon answers, "No I'm not. I'm the nigger that's going to sleep with your sister" (289). It is the unthinkable conflation of ideological opposites in this idea of "nigger" as "brother" that retrospectively explains the "contradictory" quality glimpsed in that "fading photograph" in the first chapter, and which constitutes the "irrevocable negation" (219) of Sutpen's design. Although it is Henry who ultimately "shoots" (as it were) Bon, he does not thereby halt the reproduction of Bon's racially ambiguous image. Rather, that image is "reprinted" in Bon's son, Charles Etienne, then his grandson, Jim Bond, and finally distributed en masse in the image of the Jim Bonds "bleach[ing] out" so that all Americans will be taken to have "sprung from [African] loins" (302). This is presumably not what Rosa had in mind when she dreamed of a machine that would proliferate Bon's visage.

An indirect heir to Charles Bon's project may be found in the nameless protagonist of Ralph Ellison's *Invisible Man* (1952). The novel's prologue presents the antithesis of a darkroom, a subterranean den where 1,369 electric bulbs provide "ever more and brighter light."[42] Stealing electricity from the fictional company Monopolated Light and Power, the protagonist creates what ought to be conditions of optimal visibility, if not overexposure. Instead, all the protagonist succeeds in illuminating, he tells us, is "the blackness of my invisibility—and vice versa" (13). But he also reflects on "the darkness of lightness." The "hole" in which he contemplates his invisibility is brighter than the Empire State Building "on a photographer's dream night," but its brightness has a black negative, for the Empire State Building is "among the darkest [spots] of our whole civilization" (6). The hole is located in the basement of a building inhabited exclusively by whites, which was sealed off "in the nineteenth century" (6), reflecting the white establishment's suppressed foundation in black slavery.

Ellison's boldest image of "white as what black makes" occurs when the protagonist takes employment in a paint factory where the mix for the brilliant white paint "Optic White" requires ten drops of black liquid (217–18). Oddly, Colgate-Palmolive has recently released a new line of whitening toothpaste called "Optic White," without apparent irony. We may ponder whether Joe Christmas would be able to keep it down.

Coda: Negative Advertising

The company Eastman Kodak went into administration in January 2012. Not unlike Thomas Sutpen's, the company's demise was the result of its own "creative destruction": Kodak had developed the original core technology for digital photography but failed to adequately invest in its own innovation, remaining dependent on film.[43]

In digital photography, there is no passage through a negative; electronic photodetectors register light intensity directly. But digital photography and editing have enabled a range of photomanipulative techniques that introduce a new set of complexities to the vexed field of racial representation. The visual signifiers of race can be intensified, inverted, or otherwise adjusted in ways that the photojournalists on the Rhinelander case could only dream of; a photomanipulative power like Charles Bon's is now readily available. One controversy arose in 2008 when L'Oreal was accused of digitally lightening the skin of the singer Beyoncé Knowles.

In theory, there should have been no "need" (in marketing terms) to lighten Beyoncé's complexion. For more than a decade, media commentators have been observing the prevalence of "multiracial" models in mainstream advertising, suggesting that "ambiguity is chic."[44] Through the "machine" of celebrity culture, the Charles Bons and the Jim Bonds really have come to "adorn the mirror altars" of young white women. In this context, Beyoncé's supposed lightening accords with recent suggestions that the new mixed-race ideal has its own racist strictures, limiting how dark a model can be.

Caroline Streeter observes how print-media images of "mixed-race" people purport to hail a future free of racial hierarchies, noting the 1993 *Time* magazine cover featuring a digitally created image of a "multiracial" woman, captioned as having been "created by a computer from a mix of several races."[45] *Time* magazine called her "The New Face of America." But the optimism seems misplaced. Firstly, the idea of "mix[ing] . . . several races" reinscribes the notion of distinct racial categories, reinforcing divisions it purports to be moving beyond. It is also eerily reminiscent of a "symbolic poster" in Ellison's *Invisible Man*—"a color photograph" featuring mixed-race children who represent "The Rainbow of America's Future" (385). In Ellison, the naïve image contradicts the reality of widespread racism and conflict. In representing race, today's media may simply be "stroking onto the plate" the picture it "wants there," while racist categorizations persist with real material consequences for those whose lives they circumscribe.

Following the 2008 election of President Barack Obama, another *Time* cover featured an image digitally merging the faces of Obama and Franklin D.

Roosevelt, predicting "The New New Deal." As Gerald Early observes, the putatively "postracial" election of Obama "was meant to signal a remarkable coming of racial age in the United States," but cynics are asking "what has changed, except the façade that masks the great American racial leviathan."[46] More than 150 years after *Moby-Dick*, and eighty years on from *Light in August*'s publication during the first New Deal, that question is no easier to answer.

NOTES

1. William Faulkner, *Light in August* (New York: Vintage, 1992), 82. Hereafter cited parenthetically.

2. Herman Melville, *Moby-Dick* (New York: Penguin, 2003), 212. Hereafter cited parenthetically.

3. Joseph Blotner, *Faulkner: A Biography* (Jackson: University Press of Mississippi, 2005), 326.

4. Comparably, Sutpen's Haitian wife in *Absalom* is first glimpsed "in the flash of one of the muskets" as "a white slender arm" behind a "curtain of hair," only for Quentin and Shreve to discover a "parchment-colored" woman with "raven hair coarse" behind that flash-blanched image (William Faulkner, *Absalom, Absalom!* [New York: Vintage, 1990], 203, 271; hereafter cited parenthetically).

5. Compare Joanna Burden's vision of "white children" entering the world bearing a "black shadow" (253).

6. Elizabeth M. Smith-Pryor, *Property Rites: The Rhinelander Trial, Passing, and the Protection of Whiteness* (Chapel Hill: University of North Carolina Press, 2011), 193–94.

7. Cited ibid., 203.

8. "Composographs: Faked News Pictures in the New York "Graphic" Brought US Journalism to a Half-Century Low,' *Life*, January 2, 1950, 94–96.

9. Kenneth Kobré and Betsy Brill, *Photojournalism: The Professional's Approach* (Boston: Focal, 1996), 331

10. See Kerry Segrave, *America Brushes Up* (New York: McFarland, 2010), 49–52.

11. Greg Forter, "Freud, Faulkner, Caruth: Trauma and the Politics of Literary Form," *Narrative*, 15, no. 3 (2007): 259–85, 270–72.

12. Darkroom lamps were typically dimmed through red glass or fabric (Bernard Edward Jones, *The Encyclopaedia of Early Photography* [London: Bishopsgate, 1981], 163).

13. Joe's photographic association with "womanfilth" is also apparent the night of Joanna's death, when he glances from his own "dim face" in a "shard of mirror" to a magazine containing "pictures of young women in underclothes" (110).

14. See Richard Godden, *Fictions of Labor: William Faulkner and the South's Long Revolution* (Cambridge: Cambridge University Press, 1997), 4, 55.

15. Godden, *William Faulkner: An Economy of Complex Words* (Princeton: Princeton University Press, 2007), 61–62; cf. Godden, *Fictions,* 82.

16. Godden, *Fictions,* 57.

17. Ibid., 57.

18. Forter, "Freud, Faulkner, Caruth," 275.

19. John T. Matthews also suggest this linkage in "Recalling the West Indies: From Yoknapatawpha to Haiti and Back," *American Literary History* 16.2 (Summer 2004): 257.

20. See Godden, *Fictions,* 81–82.

21. Helmut Gernsheim, *A Concise History of Photography,* 3rd rev. ed (London: Thames and Hudson, 1971), 33.

22. Cathy Davidson, "Photographs of the Dead: Sherman, Daguerre, Hawthorne," *South Atlantic Quarterly* 89, no. 4 (1990): 667–701, 681.

23. Nathaniel Hawthorne, *The House of the Seven Gables* (Oxford: Oxford University Press, 1991), 330–36.

24. See David Anthony, "Class, Culture, and the Trouble with White Skin in Hawthorne's *The House of the Seven Gables,*" *Yale Journal of Criticism* 12, no. 2 (1999): 249–68.

25. Hawthorne, *The House of the Seven Gables,* 68.

26. Cited in Marcy J. Dinius, *The Camera and the Press: American Visual and Print Culture in the Age of the Daguerreotype* (Philadelphia: University of Pennsylvania Press, 2012), 21–22.

27. According to William Griffith, the curator of Rowan Oak, Faulkner acquired the print in the 1950s. My thanks to Mr. Griffith for his assistance.

28. According to Griffith, Liggin assisted Maud Falkner following her husband's death.

29. Herman Melville, *Pierre; or, The Ambiguities (New York: Penguin, 1996).* Hereafter cited parenthetically. Robert S. Levine, "Pierre's Blackened Hand," *Leviathan* 1, no. 1 (1999): 23–44.

30. On hints of literal and symbolic miscegenation in the Glendinning past, see Levine, "Pierre's Blackened Hand,"

31. William Spengemann remarks this oddity in the notes to *Pierre,* 383n351.12.

32. Comparably, Ishmael's equation of "a white man" with "a white-washed negro" (66) makes whiteness a mere surface effect.

33. Herman Melville, *Battle-Pieces and Aspects of the War* (New York: Harper and Brothers, 1866), 105–6.

34. In the first edition, "On The Photograph" occupies pages 105–6; "The Swamp-Angel" occupies pages 107–9.

35. See "Wet-Plate Collodion Negatives," in John Hannavy, *Encyclopaedia of Nineteenth-Century Photography* (New York: Routledge, 2007).

36. Herman Melville, *The Confidence-Man: His Masquerade* (1857), ed. Hershel Parker (New York: Norton, 1971).

37. Herman Melville, "Benito Cereno," in *The Piazza Tales and Other Prose Pieces, 1839–1860,* ed. Harrison Hayford et al. (Evanston: Northwestern and Newberry, 1987), 47–117, 86–87.

38. Carol Shloss, *In Visible Light: Photography and the American Writer, 1840–1940* (New York: Oxford University Press, 2001), 32.

39. Henry Fox Talbot, "Improvement in Photographic Pictures," Patent 5171, London, June 26, 1847 (emphases added).

40. See "Spirit, Ghost and Psychic Photography," in John Hannavy, *Encyclopaedia of Nineteenth-Century Photography* (New York: Routledge, 2008), 1332–33.

41. Faulkner, *The Wild Palms* (New York: Random House, 2000), 90.

42. Ralph Ellison, *Invisible Man* (London: Penguin, 2001), 7. Hereafter cited parenthetically.

43. Rupert Neate, "Kodak Falls in the 'Creative Destruction of the Digital Age," *Guardian*, January 19, 2012, www.guardian.co.uk/business/2012/jan/19/kodak-bankruptcy-protection?INTCMP=SRCH.

44. Matthew Pratt Guteri, *Seeing Race in Modern America* (Chapel Hill: University of North Carolina Press, 2013), 182, citing fashion writer Ruth La Ferla.

45. Caroline Streeter, "The Hazards of Visibility: Biracial Women, Media Images and Narratives of Identity," in *New Faces in a Changing America: Multiracial Identity in the 21st Century*, ed. Herman DeBose and Loretta Winters (Thousand Oaks, CA: Sage, 2003), 303.

46. Gerald Early, "The Two Worlds of Race Revisited: A Meditation on Race in the Age of Obama," *Daedalus* 140, no. 1 (2011): 13.

III

Time and Space

William Faulkner's Mediated Time
Capitalism, Cinema, Syntax

MARK STEVEN

Clocks, Time, Modernism

In the opening paragraph from the second chapter of *The Sound and the Fury*, Quentin Compson narrates a half-remembered, half-imagined conversation with his father:

> When the shadow of the sash appeared on the curtains it was between seven and eight oclock and then I was in time again, hearing the watch. It was Grandfather's and when Father gave it to me he said I give you the mausoleum of all hope and desire; it's rather excruciatingly apt that you will use it to gain the reducto absurdum of all human experience which can fit your individual needs no better than it fitted his or his father's. I give it to you not that you may remember time, but that you might forget it now and then for a moment and not spend all your breath trying to conquer it. Because no battle is ever won he said. They are not even fought. The field only reveals to man his own folly and despair, and victory is an illusion of philosophers and fools.[1]

The first sentence divides itself between two mediations of time. The sash's creeping shadow, from which Quentin deduces that it is "between seven and eight oclock," functions as a makeshift sundial, registering time against the morning's diurnal transit. But as soon as the shadow's temporal index is conceptualized in chronometric units, interpolating the narrator "in time again," that natural indicator of time's passing is supplanted by mechanical mediation, the ticking of "the watch." As though it had predicted the affective intensity of this moment as well as the suicide to follow, but more likely motivated by their shared state of consciousness, the content of Quentin's analepsis describes his watch as "the mausoleum of all hope and desire," stressing that it or what it might represent will be antithetical to its conventional purpose, precipitating, for Quentin's father, an experiential paradox: "the reducto absurdum of all human experience." Multiple attempts by Compson men to "conquer" or "forget" time by measuring it out with advanced technologies only ever submits them to more and more of the punitive divisions and subdivisions of its dominion. The figural impress of time, allegorized here by the hereditary watch, thus appears to engage one of the more salient features of capitalist modernity: namely, the globally pervasive imposition of chronometric time as the measure of value, a conception that (as the Compsons all seem well aware) envelops every aspect of modern life, recasting humans as combatants who have already lost a "battle" in which they cannot begin to fight. As Georg Lukács would put it, under capitalism, time "is the frame within which a person suffers degradation. It turns into an independent and remorseless machine which flattens, levels and destroys all personal plans and wishes, all singularity, personality itself."[2]

A concern with time should be familiar to inveterate readers of William Faulkner and especially of his fourth novel; indeed, numerous commentaries have already described the book's temporal aesthetic. Jean-Paul Sartre explains his reading this way: "A novelistic technique always relates back to the novelist's metaphysics. The critic's task is to define the latter before evaluating the former. Now, it is immediately obvious that Faulkner's metaphysics is a metaphysics of time."[3] Extending Sartre's analysis into a study of the oeuvre, J. Hillis Miller suggests that, for characters in Faulkner's novels, "one does not ravel out of sequential time into eternity. One ravels out, or wishes to ravel out, *into* time."[4] That is to say, abstractly, the Faulknerian character exists through multiple temporalities coexisting within any one given moment and through which he or she will likely disperse. "To ravel out into time would be to escape the false time in which one thing seems to happen after another, in a line, by dissolving or fraying out into the all-at-onceness or always-already that is time for Faulkner."[5] The present essay agrees with these assessments, according to which some of Faulkner's technical innovations attest to his novels' metaphysical and phenomenological investments in time, but it also emphasizes the historical, economic, and above all mediated dimensions of their temporal aesthetic. Its principal claim is that one of Faulkner's stylistic signatures—specifically, his long, hypotactic sentences—is a formal reaction to literature's position within an irreducibly capitalist media ecology, and that its presentation of time is aesthetically determined by literary prose's media-ecological situation and its perceived relationship to cinema during the 1920s. Critical consensus has already confirmed that, near the end of this decade, "Faulkner passed abruptly from his novels of promise to the first achievement of his mastery, chiefly because he had found a form commensurate to his vision—a succession of grotesquely shaped fragments struggling to discover their own unity."[6] The following pages account for the inauguration of that form and its syntactically exceptional stylization of temporality by explaining how the greater totality of the book's historical and economic context is mediated through its narrative and into an assuredly modernist literary style.

It is hardly coincidental that the aesthetic ascendency of what Wyndham Lewis once described as "a sort of mystical time-cult," wherein we can undoubtedly locate Faulkner, coincided with the imposition of an increasingly technologized and regimented temporality, the intensification of which manifests an internal dynamic of the globalized mode of production.[7] Almost two decades prior to the International Prime Meridian Conference of 1884 and many more years before F. W. Taylor would publish his findings in the science of labor, Karl Marx already knew that "highly detailed specifications, which regulate, with military uniformity, the times, the limits and the pauses of work by the stroke of the clock [. . .] developed gradually out of circumstances as natural laws of the modern mode of production."[8] For Marx, the institution of "official" time as formulated and regulated by the state was, ultimately, the negative outcome of "a long class struggle."[9] In the first half of the twentieth century, humankind's refusal to accept the terms of that defeat finds itself refracted through the prose of Conrad, Joyce, Proust, and Woolf, and obtaining within the poetry of Eliot, Pound, and Stein. Given, too, that all of these names are immediately associated with modernist aesthetics, there should be no mystery as to why Fredric Jameson's metaphor for the subsequent triumph of capitalist modernity over modernism's manifest unevenness and temporal insubordination is nothing other than a giant clock:

> Ours is a more homogenously modernized condition; we no longer are encumbered with the embarrassment of non-simultaneities and non-synchronicities. Everything has reached the same hour on the great clock of

> development or rationalization (at least from the perspective of the "West"). This is the sense in which we can affirm, either that modernism is characterized by a situation of incomplete modernization, or that postmodernism is more modern than modernism itself.[10]

Squaring this periodization with the idea of a "time-cult," modernist literature ought not to be thought of as what Lewis described as an operation of "the full, instinctive indulgence and expansion of the artistic impulse [. . .] imposing its values upon the impressionable material of life,"[11] but as its negative image: the aesthetic impress of life's material, an artistic integration of time under capitalism, and a reaction to its all-subsuming rationality. Jameson's metaphor also recalls Marshall McLuhan on clocks: "As a piece of technology, the clock is a machine that produces uniform seconds, minutes, and hours on an assembly-line pattern. Processed in this uniform way," he argues, "time is separated from the rhythms of human experience. The mechanical clock, in short, helps to create the image of a numerically quantified and mechanically powered universe."[12] Though we should remain cautious of incorrectly positing organic time as utopian and chronometric time as dystopian, Jameson's metaphor and McLuhan's analogy clarify that what is at stake here is chronometric time's subsumption into capitalist production.[13] Conceived of, then, as a reaction to temporal reification through capitalist subsumption, modernism names an array of forms that collectively allow for their own temporal distortions to variously attack rectilinear time. Theirs is an aesthetic ideology whose tactical intelligence is fulfilled in the surrealist fascination with warped and distending clocks.

The determining correlation of modernist aesthetics with the regulation of time under capitalism is consistent with the fact that some of early cinema's most conspicuous clocks function as ciphers of exploited labor. To cite only the most famous of these, in Fritz Lang's *Metropolis* workers are conscripted for ten-hour shifts on the debilitating clock-machine, whose enormous, leaden arms are manually turned by an exhausted human concealed behind its face. But, given that cinema delivers on collective wish fulfillment just as earnestly as it mobilizes capitalist ideology, for every machine of industrial torture presented on celluloid, there or elsewhere appear negative reactions to the same kinds of technology. Recall, for instance, Buster Keaton's interpretation of "Punch Clock" from *The Playhouse,* in which he drives a fist through the technological apparatus designed to regulate the extraction of value from wage laborers.[14] Yet more radical than cinematic representations of time's mediation is cinema's matchless capacity to manipulate the mediation of time itself. Few writers have done more to uncover the relationship between cinematic time and capitalist temporality than Mary Anne Doane. "The significance of the cinema," she claims, "lies in its apparent capacity to perfectly represent the contingent, to provide the pure record of time," and here we should note the similarity between this medium's apparent significance and Marx's description of "official" time under capitalism. Doane's argument is that cinema isolates, preserves, and multiplies the singular contingencies of what is captured before the camera, transforming episodes of nature into technologically mediated and mechanically regulated visions of their erstwhile organic bodies. It does so, she suggests, in ways that are symptomatically homologous to capitalism, insofar as cinema's mechanical eye consistently eliminates contingency, reifying visual phenomena into temporally inflexible objectivities. "And this effort is particularly legible in the most dominant genre of the early cinema—the actuality, which appeared to capture a moment, to register and repeat 'that which happens.'"[15] Because of this homology, which implies the wholesale integration of cinema and capitalism, the principal medium of mechanical reproduction and commercial sway did not generate the means of conquering time from the exterior bounds of aesthetic autonomy, but, rather, it developed the potential to reactively transform capitalist temporality from within:

> Contingency, however, emerges as a form of resistance to rationalization which is saturated with ambivalence. Its lure is that of resistance itself—resistance to system, to structure, to meaning. Contingency proffers to the subject the appearance of absolute freedom, immediacy, directness. Time becomes heterogeneous and unpredictable and harbors the possibility of perpetual newness, difference, the marks of modernity itself. Accident and chance become productive. Their danger resides in the alliance with meaninglessness, even nonsense. The vast continuum of a nonhierarchizable contingency can overwhelm.[16]

In early cinema, commonplace techniques such as slow motion or "time-stretching" would generate new temporalities by using hand-cranked cameras to alter the flow of recorded input. Similar effects were achieved by post-production editing, whereby the insertion of parallel shots within a linear sequence would delay time's inevitable destiny. These are only the more obvious means by which time underwent formal manipulation in early cinema and so the most striking instances of how this technological medium began to provide alternative temporalities to those dictated by the "infernal machine" of capitalist modernity, revealing and reveling in its material contingencies as they are made to persist at the site of their supposed eradication.[17]

To draw these opening remarks to a close, we can now hypothesize on Faulkner's place within the capitalist media ecology and specifically in relation to cinema. According to David Trotter, "some modernist writers found in film's neutrality as a medium a stimulus to the reintroduction or re-enactment of the neutrality of literature, or in some cases of writing itself, as a medium."[18] If modernist literature reacts to cinematic formalism not with emulation but with gestures of parallel autonomy, reactively reasserting literary singularity analogously to but not necessarily in imitation of the technological medium, how might the novel match cinema's formal response to the transformation of time under capitalism? For Noel Polk, the "mechanical conventions" of Faulkner's prose "sometimes work against the words themselves, so that they reveal things other than what the characters are saying; they work, in fact, to reveal things that the narrators are incapable of saying or are specifically trying to keep from saying."[19] Here it is argued that those "mechanical conventions" also reveal the writing's sensitivity to its status as a unique medium in relation to other media, and as a form embedded within a mode of production that articulates the media ecology as a whole.

Narratography

It is widely acknowledged that Faulkner's writing engaged with the victory of capitalism over its localized alternatives and regional predecessors. For John T. Matthews, writing on *The Sound and the Fury*'s composition within its historical context, "Faulkner could not have written such sustained lamentations about the receding traditional South without witnessing its demise."[20] Richard Godden reads the Compson brothers' incestuous desire for Caddy as motivated by an unrealized need to "shore up the integrity" of their family's class, concluding that their shared impulse is "not attributable to a universal psychology (Freudian or otherwise) but to a historically specific regional psychology."[21] And, thinking specifically about the Great Migration of ex-slaves from the South to the North between 1910 and 1930, Cheryl Lester provides a comprehensive list of that protracted event's multiple avatars in the book's plot, all of which attest to an argument that "the body of the black mammy Dilsey herself serves for Faulkner as a sort of twentieth-century ruin or landmark in a South shifting from an agrarian to an industrial economy and from a rural to an urban society."[22] These patently thematic aspects of the novel direct our attention to the Compsons' grounding on a tectonically unstable economy in one of its greatest upheavals and to an understanding that the fictional family bears witness to the collision of a geopolitically specific past with the homogeneity of its historical present.

The consequences of this situation were initially felt during the postwar Reconstruction era of approximately 1865 to 1877, a period that Robin Blackburn has described as a transition from "chattel slavery" to "wage slavery," or as a failed revolution wherein the freedmen and women, as well as the members of a newly enlarged working class, were collectively integrated into a differently arranged though consistently hierarchical set of relations:

> In the post–Civil War era, the recently reunited United States was the most dynamic and soon the largest capitalist state in the world. [. . .] Great railroads spanned the continent, and vast factories sprouted up, producing steel, agricultural machinery, sewing machines. The emancipation of four million slaves, the demobilization of three million soldiers, and the arrival of a stream of new immigrants swelled the size of the most diverse laboring class in the world.[23]

The historically recent transition from one mode of economic domination to another comparably exploitative one first signals its presence in the novel's opening pages, during Luster's search for his missing quarter. "Nigger's money good as white folks, I reckon," says a travelling musician, to whom Luster replies: "White folks gives nigger money because know first white man comes along with a band going to get it all back, so nigger can go to work for some more" (888). The book's context, which presents itself here as tethered to the exchange and accumulation of money, reappears directly in relation to each of its major characters. From the necessary sale of Benjy's field; through Quentin's interactions with the working-class girl; Jason's obsessive rationalism of the "flour barrel," his gambles on the cotton market, and his ruminations on being a "slave" to business (1027, 1036, 1038–39); right down to the pivotal role played by banknotes and endowments in the final episode: all of these thematize a shared economic base, the volatility of which transfers through them and into narrative. The master trope that combines and structures these economic incursions is time, or a particularly regimented sense of time, and it is serially figured by a multitude of clocks, watches, and factory whistles.[24]

Following the provisional catalogue of narrative symptoms manifesting the novel's economic circumstances and their determining temporality, what requires demonstration is the extent to which that situation materializes through or is mediated into the formal effects of Faulkner's textual surfaces. Though it makes good theoretical sense to nominate cinema as a force that orchestrates the transfer of energies between capitalist temporality and literary form, it will also be critically rewarding to provide a more detailed context for that mediation. And, even while there is no way of proving that Faulkner had seen D. W. Griffith's *The Birth of a Nation* by the mid- to late 1920s, or that he was thinking about it when composing his fourth novel, what circumstantial evidence there is suggests that, as Peter Lurie has argued, "it is difficult to imagine the circumstances that would have prevented Faulkner from seeing the most notorious and heralded film of its time."[25] Like Faulkner's novel, Griffith's film concerns itself with the economic conditions and perceived social contradictions resulting from the Civil War, dramatizing their intrusion on its melodramatic chronicle of two families during that conflict and through the subsequent Reconstruction. While much has been written about the parallels between Griffith's revisionism and the treatment of African Americans in Faulkner's novels, for the present analysis that relationship need only register as probable cause for mediation, contributing to a claim that Faulkner may have been familiar with the film.[26] To be sure, that the film itself is dated to 1915 and that it screened for many years after this initial release allows it to retain cultural relevance during the inception and composition of Faulkner's novel—and, moreover, this film's medium-specific innovation appears to have motivated the novel's presentation of time.

In a reappraisal of Sergei Eisenstein's seminal essay, "Charles Dickens, D. W. Griffith, and Film Today," in which the logics of cinematic montage were first explained theoretically, Garrett Stewart argues that "Griffith's transfer of Dickensian technique into a different medium is only two-thirds of the story Eisenstein tells; the rest concerns the outdistancing of Hollywood craft by Soviet artistry."[27] Stewart proposes "narratography" as a means of grasping the filmic medium's immanence to its cinematic narratives, and as a means of describing Griffith's revolutionary attainment in those mutually imbricated layers of form. The "narratogram," he says, is "the smallest unit of graphic effect in a given medium, filmic or lexical, that is capable of taking a narrative charge."[28] From the perspective of narratography, Griffith's innovation was to charge individual frames with narrative significance, allowing formal instants to refract their narrative whole and simultaneously for the narrative whole to distend those formal instants. The cinematic narratogram as manifest through the individual frame thus finds its textual equivalents in "the sentence, phrase, or syllable, even the ambivalent word border," insofar as these microelements of the text might similarly refract "the junctural energy of the narrative chain itself."[29] To this we should add, emphatically, that the narratogram's ultimate purpose must be temporal: it exists to redirect the infinite expanse of narrative totality through the finite materiality of the text, dialectically folding narrative time back into the immediacy of form. Each narratogram thereby manifests an instance of temporal autonomy as seized by the subtending medium, either cinematic or literary, and from within the narrative which that medium sustains. Narratography thus defines the material apprehension and narrative reassertion of what Doane understands as contingency, the very essence of cinematic time, which she suggests is antithetical to the rectilinear and chronometric temporalities of capitalism. Perhaps unwittingly, Griffith was cinema's first narratographic craftsman, and his discovery of that form redefines cinematic time by integrating the filmic medium with cinema's narrative cruces.

Bearing in mind that Faulkner's novel is profoundly concerned with the materiality of time, Stewart's theory authorizes an argument that, if Eisenstein is cinema's major response to Griffith, then Faulkner may well be literature's answer to Eisenstein. It wouldn't be until 1939 that Faulkner would describe a subterranean zone of capitalist accumulation as "a scene like something out of an Eisenstein Dante,"[30] but we might have already encountered his own combinatorial cinematic-literary form in an episode from *The Sound and the Fury*. According to Stewart, narrative cinema derived its formal qualities from literary prose, first by Griffith, who assimilated literature's "increments and upheavals" into "shots" and "shot sequences," and then by Eisenstein who combined these "shots" and "sequences" into the "disjunctive frame advance" of montage.[31] The argument must therefore be that while Eisenstein developed the promise of Griffith's parallel editing into cinematic montage, Faulkner was more attuned to the possibilities of the individual frames, to their narratographic contingencies, whose potential was transformed by Eisenstein and redirected away from the shot and into the shot sequence. Faulkner seems to preempt this thought in accounts of his own authorship. For instance, late in his career he would claim that the writer "is like the man that's trying to carve the Lord's Prayer on the head of a pin. He's trying to put everything into one book, one page—the perfect thing would be to put all that history and anguish into one word, which you can't do."[32] Perhaps this perceived restriction on narratographic autonomy is why the novel's own iteration of a similar image takes place on the face of Jason Compson's watch-charm, as though, like Faulkner, the novel itself wants to concede literature's incapacity to construct the kind of temporal narratograms produced by cinema: "a tiny opera glass into which you squinted with one eye and saw a skyscraper, a ferris wheel all spidery, Niagara Falls on a pinhead" (938).

Perhaps Faulkner really is (in Bruce Kawin's hyperbole) "the most cinematic of novelists," but this cannot be because his novels emulate the other medium, or at least not in any conventional way.[33] Rather, the techniques that give shape to cinematic narratograms, which refuse material transfer off of the screen and onto the page, are abandoned for the specifically literary recrafting of that aesthetic object and narrative device. The narratographic impulse thus becomes a question of literary style—and, in Faulkner's case, of syntax. Despite this injunction, the narrative location of the novel's formal reaction to cinema is the chapter in which it alludes to that medium most frequently. To be sure, the reaction confines itself to the novel's fourth and final chapter, "April Eighth, 1928," and so emerges out of the book's only prolonged demonstration of a lexically "cinematic" writing—namely, a writing that makes recourse to the language of film, deploying words that cipher the mechanical technology, its apparatuses, and its aesthetic. Phrases like "gray splash" (1082), "faint dusting of wood ashes" (1087–88), "dingy windows glowed and faded in ghostly retrograde" (1104), and "his gray eyes were round and shiny" (1109) all shade the episode black-and-white. Characters enter narrative space as through iris shots and masks: Mrs. Compson sees Dilsey as "a blobby shape without depth" (1086); we know the day has begun when the "air brightened, the running shadow patches were now the obverse" (1112); and we are told that "white people in bright clumps moved churchward" (1100). Benjy uses his fingers to drum "an inaudible tune out of the dead void [...] a soundless and involved arpeggio" (1090). And Queenie, the horse, moves in a slow-motion "gait resembling a prolonged and suspended fall in forward direction" (1123). With the possible exception of Quentin's pejorative phrase "celluloid like a drummer" (948), the Compson brothers, whose thoughts circumscribe the previous three sections, do not think in the language of cinema, whereas this sampling suggests that the exceptionally omniscient narrator of the book's fourth section seems to do just that, repeatedly alluding to the medium via figuration, polysemy, and homonymy.

Provided all of this is correct—that Faulkner's preoccupation with time corresponds to an engagement with capitalism; that cinematic narratograms offer a means of renegotiating that engagement as form; and that, in its final chapter, the novel appears to be referencing cinema—then our reformulated question is this: how does that final chapter react formally to cinema and to that medium's renegotiation of their shared capitalist temporality? To answer this question, our strategy will be to narratographically map the unique styles that attend the book's temporal thematic as it develops through each chapter, emphasizing the relationship between time and sentences. To that end, the remainder of this argument accounts for the narrative presence of clocks in relation to the book's evolving syntax, which it suggests allegorize different temporalities that have occurred along the mode of production's extended history, culminating in the book's final section with a literary reaction to the cinematic medium's unique narratogram.

From Parataxis to Hypotaxis

Literary time has traditionally been allegorized in the catachresis of human sensoria. The allegory is narratographic when the dexterity of its verse or prose is used to transliterate the collusion of past events, historical progress, cosmological shifts, and chronometric regulation from character or consciousness and directly into language. One of the more canonical iterations of literary time through narratography thus takes place in those familiar lines from Shakespeare's *Macbeth,* from which Faulkner derives the title of his novel:

> Tomorrow, and tomorrow, and tomorrow
> Creeps in this petty pace from day to day
> To the last syllable of recorded time;
> And all our yesterdays have lighted fools
> The way to dusty death. Out, out, brief candle!
> Life's but a walking shadow, a poor player
> That struts and frets his hour upon the stage,
> And then is heard no more. It is a tale
> Told by an idiot, full of sound and fury,
> Signifying nothing.[34]

Time is rendered as a sequence of experiential days stretching out toward its own cessation in death. These lines seem acutely aware of a narratographic relation between their materiality and their rhetorical content, insofar as their materiality resists precisely what their content would otherwise suggest. For instance, the first line, with its triple repetition of "tomorrow," establishes a peculiar embodiment of time—its experience is slow and, rhythmically, one of falling. And, while the subsequent lines describe the player's tragic journey toward a fated death, "his hour upon the stage," that previous line both facilitates and impedes progression. Unwilling to rush headlong into fate, the recalcitrant player recognizes his situation and reluctantly stumbles. Similarly resistant, "To the last syllable of recorded time" includes one extra syllable, a syllable that remains difficult to elide and whose inexorable presence therefore disrupts the metrical flow of blank verse; not only does it make us rhythmically aware of "recorded time" itself, but it also grants the player one extra breath of life before meeting the suffocation of a "dusty death," in a line whose tetrameter cuts that rhythm short. Mindful of its own medium, time affixes itself to the conjunctive parataxis of words and is manifest in their rhythmic and metrical coordination, producing a materially contingent allegory. Narratography teaches us that the body's verbal actions are at odds with its own tragic resignation.

This is the kind of narratography we encounter within Benjy's chapter, shifted from verse to prose, where the allegorical contingency plays out neither in rhythm nor meter but as syntactic style:

> *I could hear the clock, and I could hear Caddy standing behind me, and I could hear the roof. It's still raining, Caddy said. I hate rain. I hate everything. And then her head came into my lap and she was crying, holding me, and I began to cry. Then I looked at the fire again and the bright, smooth shapes went again. I could hear the clock and the roof and Caddy.* (921)

As in *Macbeth*, the triple repetition of three syllables ("I could hear") punctuated by two conjunctions ("and") establishes a regulatory and embodied parataxis. The clock's presence in the first sentence correlates with a metronomic polysyndeton that is repeated in the sixth. Interceding between these two sentences, an encounter with Caddy lures consciousness away from the clock and its syntactical calibrations. The sentence in which the two siblings come into physical contact interrupts its parataxis to include just one hypotactic clause, "holding me," as though to indicate the experiential slowing or stretching of time, before the clock once again seizes hold of the moment and propels its narrator back into the parataxis of what Macbeth called "recorded time." That Benjy's style comprises a diminished echo of Shakespeare's narratographic capture of temporality (reducing the hero's tragic frisson to the ravings of an imbecile as he hears, smells, and sees his own fading consciousness) confirms Peter Lurie's argument that Faulkner equips Benjy with a "greater fullness of sensory activity," which ultimately reveals "the limitations of modern capitalistic abstraction," while his "mental limitations prevent reading him nostalgically and as part of an impulse for an earlier, 'purer' time or mode of being."[35] Put differently, Benjy's syntactical sensitivity to the clock registers the embodiment of chronometric time similarly to how Macbeth's dramatic verse allegorizes the temporality of tragic fate; yet both characters also experience time as mediated by the living, breathing, sensorial body, whose vitality remains the knowable horizon of temporal abstraction. These bodies momentarily assert their own alternative temporalities through literary style and against either tragic fate or the ticking clock. But, whereas Macbeth was a product of precapitalist absolutism, Benjy can only be an anachronistic avatar of modern literature's distant past—a past that cannot function in the present. The affliction of his consciousness, the object correlative to which is an interrupted parataxis, also marks the obsolescence of those differently embodied temporalities.

One of the reasons this narratographic expression of literary time is no longer a viable strategy for presentation is that, by the onset of the twentieth century, the capitalist media ecology had already standardized and rationalized time itself beyond the vitality and contingency experienced by either Macbeth or Benjy. This rationalization is what we encounter variously in Quentin and Jason's chapters. "There was a clock, high up in the sun," muses Quentin, "and I thought about how, when you dont want to do a thing, your body will try to trick you into doing it, sort of unawares" (940). Note how rapidly the cybernetic code governing this preternatural deception mutates under the radiance of that clockwork sun. Here, the nervous system's entry into the sensible reveals its own subordination to the regime of technology: "I could feel the muscles in the back of my neck, and then I could hear my watch ticking away in my pocket, and after a while I had all the other sounds shut away, leaving only the watch in my pocket" (940). At the level of prose style, the narrative has shifted its material away from a Benjy-esque parataxis to embrace syntactical minimalism, active voice, and grammatical orderliness:

> I turned back up the street, to the window. He was working at the table behind the window. He was going bald. There was a glass in his eye—a metal tube screwed into his face. I went in.
>
> The place was full of ticking, like crickets in September grass, and I could hear a big clock on the wall above his head. He looked up, his eye big and blurred and rushing beyond the glass. I took mine out and handed it to him. (940–41)

Simplistic prose capitulates to the rhythm of production, or at least to the ticking of the timepiece. What remains consistent between this chapter and Benjy's is the presence of an organic body on which chronometric time is imposed. For Quentin, however, this registers not only through syntactical narratography but also in the metaphors whose originality derives from their incompatibility with the object of comparison. The simile, "like crickets in September grass," recalls the location of Quentin's remembered night with Caddy, an organically grassy exterior that has since been replaced by the expansive realm of industrial production: "I could still see the smoke stack.

That's where the water would be, healing out to the sea and the peaceful grottoes. Tumbling peacefully they would, and when He said Rise only the flat irons" (963). Of course, Quentin's memories contain a good share of delirious and perverse hypotaxis, the book's sign of narratographic vitality, but it is also true that its hypotactic sentences are most frequently attached to encounters with the lost object, Caddy. Whereas Benjy could find solace in her presence, and that solace impacts the arrangement of his syntax, for Quentin it is already forfeited to history, maddeningly confined to distant memory: in the narrative present, his awareness of temporality and the narratographic style through which that awareness articulates are both reified into parataxis.

Thematically, the economic determinants that impose chronometric time on the erstwhile organic world of Quentin's narrative, replacing "peaceful grottoes" with "flat irons," are even more present to the section told from Jason's point of view. This becomes clear in Jason's reaction to the Parson and the infestation of pigeons in the courthouse clock. "What does he care what time it is," thinks Jason. "He pays no taxes, he doesn't have to see his money going every year to have the courthouse clock cleaned to where it'll run. They had to pay a man forty-five dollars to clean it. I counted over a hundred half-hatched pigeons on the ground" (1067). It would be tempting to argue that the preponderance of interpersonal and accusatory pronouns in Jason's discourse ironically mark the solidity of his superego or, to look at it from a different angle, his ability to shape a twistedly meaningful and consequently comical subjectivity out of the temporal wasteland that consumes his brothers. However, it is more likely this style allegorizes that, for Jason, persons are equated with time and time is equated with money, and that finance capital animates all three. "Then it struck ten," we read, when Jason first conceptualizes time as regards the stock market: "I went up to the telegraph office. It opened up a little, just like they said. I went into the corner and took out the telegram again, just to be sure. While I was looking at it a report came in. It was up two points" (1024). If Benjy marks the anachronistic obsolescence of organic time, and if Quentin bears witness to chronometric time in its ascendency, then Jason is an expression of chronometric time's subordination to the economy it is supposed to help regulate. Here, each mention of time is narratographic insofar as they all signal monetary flux: "It was three points under the opening," thinks Jason (1044); "It was down twelve points at twelve oclock," he is told (1044); "It was one point above the opening. I had already lost thirteen points" (1051);

"It has closed at 20.21, forty points down. Forty times five dollars; buy something with that if you can" (1064). For Jason, the vicissitudes of the market, though decoupled from their material referents, are what fix time with narratographic significance. "'An hour ago?' I says. 'What are we paying you for?' I says. 'Weekly reports? How do you expect a man to do anything? The whole dam top could blow off and we'd not know it'" (1051).

These readings are intended to demonstrate that between Benjy's interrupted parataxis, the syntactical simplicity of Quentin's active voice, and the calculations of Jason's financial abstraction, Faulkner performs three distinct temporal styles and that each of these styles is informed by the increased or increasing regulation of time under capitalism. Though we have already observed some of the instances in which the final chapter appeals to cinematic figuration, we can now demonstrate how it does away with all three antecedent styles in a double reaction both to capitalist temporality and to its renegotiation as cinematic time. It opens with this long sentence:

> The day dawned bleak and chill, a moving wall of gray light out of the northeast which, instead of dissolving into moisture, seemed to disintegrate into minute and venomous particles, like dust that, when Dilsey opened the door of the cabin and emerged, needled laterally into her flesh, precipitating not so much a moisture as a substance partaking of the quality of thin, not quite congealed oil. (1081)

Take note of the verbal simultaneity defining this complex image: things "dissolve" and "disintegrate," while others "emerge," "needle," and "precipitate." Note, too, the multiple tenses: the preterit past of "dawned," "seemed," "opened," "emerged," "needled," and "congealed"; the present progressive of "moving," "dissolving," "precipitating," and "partaking"; and the singular simple present of "disintegrate." The passing of time is not condensed here into the tensile composition of a "turning phrase" but is made into a literary image comprising the multiple contingencies slain by modernity's increasingly chronometric and abstracted temporalities, of those shards of apparent stasis that would ultimately be lost to cinema's narrative sequencing. The construction is tensile precisely because of the jostling verbs and competing tenses, all of which articulate within the one periodic suspension, yet each of which mark the passage of time independently from one another. In contradistinction to the temporal unfurling of Benjy's interrupted parataxis, and to the much simpler formulations of Quentin and Jason, all of which can bear narrative meaning right down to their single lexemes, this burnished hypotaxis distorts the narrative instant and suffuses its individual image with temporal heterogeneity. It is, to be sure, a uniquely literary inversion of the cinematic narratogram, an image that uses form to suspend the narrative moment and to stretch it outward into a temporally complex period. In Griffith's cinema, the narrative would reveal itself through the filmic frame, but here the form reveals itself through the narrative instant, immanently transforming that moment's temporality. In contrast to Eisenstein, who pursued collective energies through the accelerated sequence, Faulkner pursues the protracted frame and renders it in a manner that is exclusively literary. The resulting style materializes a forceful extirpation of narratographic intensity and in its absence obtains literary singularity and temporal multiplicity, manifesting through the Jamesian, Trollopesque, and even Fordian sentence that the earlier chapters had been interested in canceling. Unlike Joyce's pastiche of similar styles in the "Eumaeus" episode of *Ulysses,* which is primarily invested in the exhaustion of novelistic discourse, Faulkner's pastiche seems motivated by an almost optimistic will to redemption: within the context of the book as a whole, its narratography attains to a unique temporality; while the previous chapters allegorized capitalism's reification of time, this one appears to be doing something altogether different.

This style, which emphasizes the contradictory temporal energies coexisting within the unified narrative instant, appears all throughout the novel's fourth chapter, and its purchase on the economic context becomes evident if we pay close attention to the congregation arriving at church on Easter Sunday:

> They emerged from the cabins and struggled up the sharing levee to the road—men in staid, hard brown or black, with gold watch chains and now and then a stick; young men in cheap violent blues or stripes and swaggering hats; women a little stiffly sibilant, and children in garments bought second hand of white people, who looked at Ben with the covertness of nocturnal animals. (1101)

The collective pronoun "they" multiplies back upon itself hypotactically after the referentially thickening em-dash: it now refers to and therefore subsumes the parataxis of men, young men, women, and children, all wearing the sartorial emblems of their position within a shared economy. With this grammatical arrangement, the avatars of class are subordinated to their pronominally collective being, and reanimated through the temporal imprecision of that collective's movement as its members simultaneously "emerge" and "struggle" up the embankment, with watches conspicuously hidden from narrative perception. Sartorial detail, "garments bought second hand of white people," confirms the historical situation in which descendents of slaves as well as ex-slaves have entered into capitalism as an obviously disadvantaged class; however, the presentational subtraction of their timepieces, whose absence is nonetheless made conspicuous by "gold watch chains," renders their narrative description isomorphic with the temporal complexity of its prose—both exist somewhere outside of rectilinear time and in reaction to cinematic time. If the form is reacting to a narratographic impulse, with its syntactically binding grasp on multiple contingencies, then it may have already revealed its unconsciously perceived proximity to the cinematic medium and that medium's different mobilization of narratography.

Astonishingly, a scattering of similes all gesture toward the unseen presence of the movie studio or film set, the production zone from within which narratographic contingency would otherwise be accelerated into perceptual oblivion:

> The road rose again, to a scene like a painted backdrop. Notched into a cut of red clay crowned with oaks the road appeared to stop short off, like a cut ribbon. Beside it a weathered church lifted its crazy steeple like a painted church, and the whole scene was as flat and without perspective as a painted cardboard set upon the ultimate edge of the flat earth, against the windy sunlight of space and April and a midmorning filled with bells. Toward the church they thronged with slow sabbath deliberation, the women and children went on in, the men stopped outside and talked in quiet groups until the bell ceased ringing. Then they too entered. (1102)

Six years earlier and from several states to the north of Mississippi, William Carlos Williams composed a lyric on the supersession of churches by cinema. "The decay of cathedrals / is efflorescent," he wrote, "through the phenomenal / growth of movie houses."[36] In this passage, Faulkner seems to be tarrying in a similar efflorescence. From the description of a "scene like a painted backdrop," through a landscape made "flat and without perspective," right down to the invocation of "a painted cardboard set," the figuration implies that cinema, or at least the site of cinematic production, is what generates this charismatic setting. Specifically, though, it implies the filmic frame: a single, static image, the likes of which Griffith would successfully charge with narratographic potentiality. But, from within the narrative instant, hypotaxis distends its stalled moment and generates multiple temporalities, swelling it from within. The congregation simultaneously "thronged," "went," "stopped," and "talked," moving together and at once in a "slow sabbath deliberation" that describes both their movements and the prose that animates them. While the retroactively revealed church bell sustains the presence of chronometric time, as do the concealed watches, for just this instant it is suspended and, until the silence reminds of its inexorable presence, both persons and prose are afforded a different temporality. The congregation and its description can thus inhabit the time of slaves' descendants in religious communion—a collective being otherwise regulated by the brutal cycles of days and seasons, as well as by clocks, but who on Easter Sunday surmount that subjugation. By generating alternative temporalities for an economically particularized group of men, women, and children, and by doing so analogously to but distinct from cinema's medium-specific narratography, Faulkner's syntax acquires the insubordination of a modernist aesthetic made fully aware of its situation within the capitalist media ecology: hypotactic prose is a response both to the regulation of time under capitalism and to cinema's historically parallel renegotiation of the resulting temporality.

NOTES

1. William Faulkner, *The Sound and the Fury*, in *Novels, 1926–1929: Soldier's Pay, Mosquitoes, Flags in the Dust, The Sound and the Fury*, ed. Noel Polk and Joseph Blotner (New York: Library of America, 2006), 935. Hereafter cited parenthetically.

2. Georg Lukács, *Essays on Thomas Mann*, trans. Stanley Mitchell (New York: Grosset and Dunlap, 1965), 79.

3. Jean-Paul Sartre, "On *The Sound and the Fury:* Temporality in Faulkner," in *Critical Essays*, trans. Chris Turner (London: Seagull, 2010), 105.

4. J. Hillis Miller, "Time in Literature," *Daedalus*, 132, no. 2 (Spring 2003): 96.

5. Ibid.

6. Donald M. Kartiganer, "*The Sound and the Fury* and Faulkner's Quest for Form," *ELH* 37, no. 4 (December 1970): 613.

7. Wyndham Lewis, *Time and Western Man* (Boston: Beacon, 1957), xv.

8. Karl Marx, *Capital: A Critique of Political Economy*, trans. Ben Fowkes (London: Penguin, 1992), 394.

9. Ibid., 395.

10. Fredric Jameson, *Postmodernism: Or, The Cultural Logic of Late Capitalism* (London: Verso, 1991), 309–10.

11. Lewis, *Time and Western Man*, xv.

12. Marshal McLuhan, *Understanding Media: The Extensions of Man* (London: Routledge, 1964), 158.

13. The real utopian alternative is a temporally regulated day that allows everyone to work for shorter periods, as opposed to an organic world in which humankind conforms itself to (what Samuel Johnson would call) the "rural stupidity" of seasonal cycles and archaic schedules.

14. Fredric Jameson, *Signatures of the Visible* (New York: Routledge, 2007).

15. Mary Anne Doane, *The Emergence of Cinematic Time: Modernity, Contingency, the Archive* (Cambridge: Harvard University Press, 2002), 22.

16. Ibid., 11.

17. "Infernal machine" is from Fredric Jameson, *Representing "Capital": A Reading of Volume One* (London: Verso, 2011), 63, 87, 107, 146.

18. David Trotter, *Cinema and Modernism* (Oxford: Blackwell, 2007), 9.

19. Noel Polk, "Trying Not to Say: A Primer on the Language of *The Sound and the Fury*," in *New Essays on The Sound and the Fury*, ed. Polk (Cambridge: Cambridge University Press, 1993), 143.

20. John T. Matthews, *William Faulkner: Seeing through the South* (Sussex: Wiley-Blackwell, 2009), 9.

21. Richard Godden, *Fictions of Labor: William Faulkner and the South's Long Revolution* (Cambridge: Cambridge University Press, 2007), 25.

22. Cheryl Lester, "Racial Awareness and Arrested Development: *The Sound and the Fury* and the Great Migration (1915–1928)," in *The Cambridge Companion to William Faulkner*, ed. Philip M. Weinstein (Cambridge: Cambridge University Press, 1995), 127.

23. Robin Blackburn, *An Unfinished Revolution: Karl Marx and Abraham Lincoln* (London: Verso, 2011), 61.

24. Economic history dictates that the timepiece would serve as the objective quintessence of capitalism in the South. Echoing E. P. Thompson's observation that, in England, the distribution of watches and clocks intensified dramatically at "the exact moment when the industrial revolution demanded greater synchronization of labor," Mark Smith has detailed the relationship between the American South's consumption of timepieces and its welcoming the mode of production that both relies upon and makes them commercially available. In his words, southerners "had to import along with clocks and watches the capitalist and northern idea that time was money and that clock time could be used to regulate, measure, and exploit labor both free

and slave" (E. P. Thompson, "Time, Work-Discipline and Industrial Capitalism," *Past and Present* 38 [1967]: 69; Mark Smith, *Mastered by the Clock: Time, Slavery, and Freedom in the American South* [Chapel Hill: University of North Carolina Press, 1997], 38).

25. Peter Lurie, *Vision's Immanence: Faulkner, Film, and the Popular Imagination* (Baltimore: Johns Hopkins University Press, 2004), 184n17.

26. Anything more than this would be overreaching because of the distance between their two meticulously crafted and categorically historical settings; that the film's narrative is set during the 1860s and that the episodes of Faulkner's novel take place in either 1928 or 1910 serve up too great an anachronism to be surpassed thematically. Lurie explores relationships between Faulkner's writing and Griffith's films all throughout *Vision's Immanence*.

27. Garrett Stewart, *Framed Time: Toward a Postfilmic Cinema* (Chicago: University of Chicago Press, 2007), 250.

28. Ibid., 285.

29. Garrett Stewart, *Novel Violence: A Narratography of Victorian Fiction* (Chicago: University of Chicago Press, 2009), 231.

30. Faulkner, *If I Forget Thee, Jerusalem*, in *Novels: 1936–1940: Absalom, Absalom!, The Unvanquished, If I Forget Thee, Jerusalem, The Hamlet*, ed. Noel Polk and Joseph Blotner (New York: Library of America, 1990), 621.

31. Stewart, *Framed Time*, 250.

32. William Faulkner, "At Washington & Lee University: 15 May 1958," *Faulkner at Virginia*, ed. Stephen Railton, n.p., http://faulkner.lib.virginia.edu/display/wfaudio31.

33. Bruce F. Kawin, *Faulkner and Film* (New York: Ungar, 1977), 5.

34. William Shakespeare, *The Oxford Shakespeare: Complete Works*, ed. Stanley Wells and Gary Taylor (Oxford: Clarendon Press, 1988), 997–98.

35. Lurie, *Vision's Immanence*, 165.

36. William Carlos Williams, *The Collected Poems of William Carlos Williams*, vol. 1, *1909–1939*, ed. Christopher MacGowan and A. Walton Litz (London: New Directions, 1991), 213.

"Crossing the Junctureless Backloop of Time's Trepan"

Freedom, Indexicality, and Cinematic Time in *Go Down, Moses*

PETER LURIE

> The indexically inscribed contingency is not the embodiment of history as the mark of the real or referent, but history as the mark of what could have been otherwise.
> —MARY ANN DOANE, *The Emergence of Cinematic Time*

> I pray you, in your letters,
> When you shall these unlucky deeds relate,
> Speak of me as I am; nothing extenuate,
> Nor set down aught in malice: then must you speak
> Of one that loved not wisely but too well.
> —*Othello*

Faulkner's *Go Down, Moses* begins with a game of chance. In the novel's opening story, Uncle Buddy and Mr. Hubert play a single hand of five-card stud, the outcome of which will determine the owner of Tomey's Turl. Although the story, like other aspects of the novel, includes its ludic elements, the play in which the two white men involve themselves has serious consequences: the perpetuating of slavery (and, in this case, the necessity of marrying Sophonsiba). Instances of gambling occur elsewhere in the book, notably in the fixed, nightly crap games at the lumber mill where Rider works in "Pantaloon in Black." The same story also includes a quiet, but important reference to gaming in the rook party that the deputy sheriff's wife attends.

The poker game in "Was" is important to the book, and in several ways, as are gaming and chance to the novel generally. For while its outcome is ultimately not in question, the fact of gambling introduces a question to the economy of the region; Uncle Buck and Uncle Buddy keep slaves, but there is a chance that they won't or that something other than wealth and prior ownership will determine whose property Tomey's Turl and Tennie Beauchamp will be. (Although Mr. Hubert folds, thus giving up his hand of three kings to whatever hand Buddy is holding, we never know for certain whether or not Buddy has his four-of-a-kind.) The story is set in the slaveholding McCaslin past and offers the novel's earliest events. By the contemporary Jim Crow era in which the book's later events take place, slavery itself will no longer exist. But while *Go Down, Moses* does not narrate or relay the "peculiar institution['s]" end, it traces several objections to it and intimates African American deliverance in ways both indirect and overt. One of those alternative perspectives on race, raised by the card games and the novel's other instances of gambling, is the role of contingency in both social relations and, by implication, in a view of both history and time.

Though seemingly at a considerable remove from Faulkner's novel, recent discussion of cinema has been informed by such contingency or openness as I attribute to it. In a manner we will see, the material properties of film—particularly the classical and silent cinema of Faulkner's era—include their own strictly chance element, one that, as film theory describes it, relates closely to film's temporal dimension. As such, both *Go Down, Moses* and aspects of early film allow access to a world not contained by their own narratives, a realm of possibility or the suggestion that much of what we see in these stories—as well as the history they relay—could have unfolded differently. Moreover, as we will also see, the progression of stories in *Go Down, Moses* modifies events from earlier in the book's chronicle, including its plantation history, which, at first glance—or in certain characters' glances—appears moribund or unaccommodating of change. Such change, or even its intimation, finally, is accomplished by way of what Faulkner shares with film: an emphasis on materiality or the role of tacticity as well as form, one that we're in the process of losing in the digital age but that Faulkner's modernism, like the cinema with which it was concurrent, animates by way of a unique stress on affect—as well as on affection.

One recent study of filmic temporality raises precisely these kinds of questions. In her book *The Emergence of Cinematic Time: Modernity, Contingency, and the Archive,* Mary Ann Doane describes the way in which early film captured two distinct and opposed temporal modes. The first is the more easily recognizable: time's regimenting and standardizing, epitomized in the early twentieth century by the regularizing of railway schedules, time clocks, and industrial production, all of which imposed a rationalized and instrumental time on the bodies as well as sensibilities of modern subjects (Benjamin's "homogenous, empty time"). The second mode, which Doane claims inhered in preclassical film form, was the opposite: a sense of temporality defined by chance and ephemerality.[1] Film in fact embodied both temporal schemes. In the sequencing of discrete photograms, the individual static frame separated by a uniform gap of time (and space) and, likewise, projected at a standard rate of twenty-four frames per second, film reproduced the regularized time of industrial, commercial modernity. And, as goes without saying, in its technical aspect film itself manifests just such an outgrowth. Yet as André Bazin and other theorists point out, film, like still photography, includes another, inherent historicity. What analog film and photography capture is the momentary interaction of light on the surface of the film strip or plate, a chemical and optical process that, as Bazin describes, leaves a physical trace of a prior historical moment, a marking in time and event, like a footprint in the earth.[2] Crucially for Doane, a collateral aspect of film's indexical aspect is its capacity to capture a random moment or chance event—the fluttering of leaves in the wind, for example, in one of the Lumière brothers' famous *actualités,* or some of the random events of slapstick comedy. In this way, film seemed able to convey—or release—a sense of time's freedom. "Contingency appears to offer a vast reservoir of freedom and free play," as Doane put it, noting that, "What is critical is the production of contingency and ephemerality as graspable, representable, but nevertheless unsystematic" (11).

The other central part of Doane's historicizing of cinematic time was the emergence of the archive. Along with Philip Rosen, she describes the acute sense, beginning in the late nineteenth century and commensurate with the advent of film, of a need to preserve the past. The rise of interest in fossils, documents, "remains" of the past, Rosen argues, corresponded to a specifically historical sense of the loss of time in the present.[3] The role of the archive is to stave off such losses, manifest, as Doane describes it, in the "impulse to retrieve everything possible, driven by a temporal imperative (before it is 'too late'). . . . The fear is that of the destruction of an original object, its irretrievable loss; hence the grasping for a totalizing fullness, a refusal of the finite" (222).

Though of course not a film, a work like *Go Down, Moses* and, especially, "The Bear" may be said to manifest several of Doane's terms. Ike's relationship to the woods in the novel's wilderness stories seems, from the very start of the trilogy, to be marked by an acute anxiety over the loss of the original object: Old Ben and what he represents, such as an earlier, more pure way of life as well as the primordial forest itself. That such a time is afforded by preclassical cinema, or by modernity's impulse to archive, and through sections of "The Bear" is perhaps not surprising, given that both seem determined by a longing for or loss of origin, a past that *seems* more present, real, or ontologically "full" than the present.

But while there may be salience to considering Ike in such terms, it is not only his response to the threat of modernity that will allow us to see the value of considering *Go Down, Moses* in relation to cinema. For if this is a point of connection between Ike and film, it is also a point of departure. Ike's and the trilogy's longing toward a "totalizing fullness," one defined as a temporal "refusal of the finite," allow a clearer understanding of a different temporal order at work in the novel, one that we will see shares film's affinity with contingency and with an indexical working that, unlike both modern temporal rationalizing and Ike's historical sense, orients itself, not toward the past and a sense of history as completed, but toward a future that is still open, undefined, and free.

Before turning to the novel's versions of time and history as contingent, it is important to note how fully steeped in time's archiving are its forest scenes. The scenes in the Big Woods, for example, posit a temporal presence that equates to Ike's nostalgic longing for a past marked by "full plenitude," one that is not separate from the present or marked by difference. References to the "timeless" quality of the woods abound,[4] as do descriptions of time that show how little of its ravages are felt, as in the narrator's account of Ike feeling "as though time were merely something he walked through as he did through air, aging him no more than air did" (168). This is the "limbo" in which time does not, properly, exist, and from which at other moments figures like Ben or concepts, like mortality, emerge. This limbo occurs in another of the novel's tropes, the repeated descriptions of light and a pervasive darkness or gloom. In "The Old People," for example, on an earlier day and hunt, Sam guides Boon and Ike and Walter Ewall out of the trail. He leads them "for an hour through the gray and unmarked afternoon whose light was little different from what it had been at dawn and which would become darkness without any graduation between" (133). Here, as in the stories' several references to the unchanging, dusk-like color of light, we find an effort to fashion an arrest of time, a "junctureless" scheme in which time does not pass, and the morning, noon, and night all look and feel the same.

It is precisely this quality of description, though, that marks "The Old People" and "The Bear" as different from the novel's other stories. In their nostalgic emphasis on a period and event "restored," or one in which time is *not* marked by difference, these two pieces operate in the realm of the timeless and the mythical. Closely linked to Ike's childish consciousness, his own wish to stop the encroachments of modernity and the vanishing of the woods, both stories enact a literary version of film's archiving of time, the storing up of light and its interactions with the photosensitive surface of Ike's and the narrative's memory. Such effects of light and their interaction with the recording apparatus, as we've seen, are what for Bazin and others mark film with an indexical sense of history.

Much is "lodged" in Ike, in other words, as there is in Quentin, whom one critic recently and provocatively compared to a "great film archive" for the twentieth century, housing in his echoing melancholy a history of death and racial oppression. Julian Murphet pursues this reading through an analysis of Faulkner's use of a notable version of indexicality in *Absalom, Absalom!* Commensurate with the indexicality of examples like Charles Bon's letter to Judith, Murphet finds in this novel a lingering nostalgia for the written word versus the technologically produced novel, similar to our own digital era's longing for film. I will return to this longing, what Doane and others have identified as a renewed cinephilia in the face of digital media and imagery. Before doing so, I wish to quote from the end of Murphet's essay "Faulkner in the Histories of Film: 'Where Memory Is the Slave,'" where he describes Quentin in ways that raise important observations about the archival impulse in *Absalom* and, by implication, in other Faulkner. Referring to Quentin's failure to read Bon's letter for its content or as more than the indexical trace of southern history (as Mr. Compson puts it, "at least it would be a scratch, something, something that might make a mark on something that *was*"),[5] Murphet offers the following:

> What moves and becomes ethically compelling about these shadowy imprints of another world is not their "sense" at all, but the astonishing fact of their difference from us, their distance and their restless lack of redemption. What the novel discovers in the manuscript archive here is more or less what the cinema at the same time that these lines were written was storing up in its archive for us . . . : a "hauntology" of the present, an interruption of the seamlessness of modernity by its undead political specters, the indexical traces of slavery and the shadows of class conflict on the blank white pages of the now.[6]

This statement has much to recommend it in terms of how it positions Quentin and *Absalom* with respect to film and what Murphet elsewhere refers to as "the twentieth century's secret history" (203). For what *Go Down, Moses* and *Absalom* both show is that this history is in fact not completely secret and, what's more, is one whose effects continue to ravage the sensibilities of southerners like Ike and Quentin.

Yet what both novels also show is the inefficacy of a certain kind of filmic memory or relationship to the past. Like Quentin, Ike may be considered a "great film archive," deeply aware of the "undead political specters" of southern history. This is precisely how Ike's encounters with another indexical phenomenon, the commissary ledgers, are so often understood. Moreover, and in ways that relate to Murphet's claims about an "ethics" of time behind the filmic archive, there is a unique feature about the ledgers that further shows their affinities with film. Like the film image, and specifically the predigital, analog substrate of celluloid, the ledgers insist upon their own materiality. Dialect or phonetic alterations of speech exist elsewhere in Faulkner, as they do in many U.S. writers. The abbreviations, misspellings, and shorthand of the McCaslin ledgers are unique, though, in that they are renderings, not of speech, but of *writing.* The materiality of the letter, in other words, is insisted on in constructions like "*Dauter Tomes Turl and tenny 1862*" or, just below it, "*Child of tomes Turl and Tenny 1863*" (201). As with film, we first find sensory impressions here: the letters on the page, both that of Faulkner's novel and, in or *through* it, the imagined ledger in the commissary. This reaches a self-conscious apogee when Ike comes upon his father's notations, ones that the narrator points out are "almost indecipherable at all from the rheumatism which now crippled him" (202). Cramped and stilted, the script insists upon itself and on its having been written, primarily and before its full semantic—and historical—meaning registers. In this way, and in what that writing shows about the McCaslin plantation's past, the ledgers possess a potent indexicality. Ike's trouble with the ledgers is that they bear the palpable mark and "stain" of not only his grandfather's slave owning, but the violent effects of ownership and dehumanizing on both masters and slaves. In this respect, the "temporal archive" that we find in Quentin's relationship to history that Murphet traces appears just as urgent and importuning to Ike in his own encounter with the deaths of African Americans and their rendering in a written record.

Yet frustratingly, and rather like Quentin also, Ike does not use his relationship to southern history to much effect. Quentin does not outlive his grief over both the South's errors and his sister's loss of virginity. In *Go Down, Moses,* we find a version of Ike in his seventies who withdraws into a position removed from his contemporary scene, yet also defined by a residual racism and notions of social and natural purity. This is why Ike's vision fails. His intentions of an ethical rejoinder to his family's and the South's transgressions seem earnest, and his shock upon reading the ledgers as well as his debate with Cass are ingenuous. But what Ike manifests throughout the novel is a relationship to the past as inert, static, and, importantly, *knowable*. In his "postmortem" perspective, history as well as the future are finished, not in the process of meaningful transformation. He wishes to undo the wrongs of his family vis-à-vis property and the ownership of human beings. But Ike is not able to accommodate a view that genuinely sees the future as different. When Ike relinquishes his compass and his watch hunting Old Ben in "The Bear," he may avoid the patterning and schedules of "town time," as Ash later puts it to him (240). But just as importantly, nor does he allow for the free play of time such as that offered in film in certain of its aspects. Events for Ike—as well as their meanings—are always-already complete, not waiting to be determined in the process of their unfolding. Much of this, as we will see, has to do with Ike's messianic view of the South's history—and of himself as its predetermined savior.

A number of descriptions of Ike's temporal perspective might suggest themselves in this context. One passage in particular is notable for how it conjoins Ike's historical vision to the narrator's in order to suggest a particular quality of "fixity." After we hear of Ike's long anticipation of participating in the hunt early in the story, we read that

> His day came at last. In the surrey with his cousin and Major de Spain and General Compson he saw the wilderness through a slow drizzle of November rain just above the ice point as it seemed to him later he always saw it or at least remembered it—the tall and endless wall of dense November woods under the dissolving afternoon and the year's death . . . the surrey moving through the skeleton stalks of cotton and corn in the last open country, the last trace of man's puny gnawing at the immemorial flank, until, dwarfed by that perspective into an almost ridiculous diminishment, the surrey itself seemed to have ceased to move (this too to be completed later, years later, after he had grown to a man and had seen the sea) as a solitary small boat hangs in lonely immobility merely tossing up and down, in the infinite waste of the ocean. (142–43)

The passage begins steeped in the deeply retrospective mode of "The Bear" generally, looking back on Ike's first trip to the woods. It does so, though, through an emphasis on Ike's visual encounter with this environment: "he saw the wilderness." Such optical perception is, typically, blurred, apprehended through not only the haze of Ike's memory but the persistent "slow drizzle of November rain." This rain pervades the story, and I will return to its "dissolving" quality and function. Time itself "dissolves" or decays here too at dusk and in late fall, as the time of day and of season echo and share the approaching "year's death," a deathliness figured in the very next reference to the "skeleton stalks" of the crops. Strikingly, Ike's visual perspective—his imaging—of time and event is appropriated by the narrator, who refers to the telescoping of both space and time in the surrey's "ridiculous diminishment" seen in retrospect and "completed later, years later." Significantly, the simile of the surrey "as solitary boat" occurs after the narrator indicates that it could only appear thus once Ike "had grown to a man and had seen the sea." In other words, the narrator takes up Ike's youthful perspective and encompasses his life experience in the same utterance, spanning that lifetime and confirming an encounter (seeing the sea) that the novel itself never details. But it does so from a position anterior to these events' finishing. This is why Ike's sense of the future retards its unfolding, why it is, for example, he can only accept racial amalgamation in "*a thousand or two thousand years in America*" (266), not in the present or his family's period, as he declares in "Delta Autumn." The suppressions of which Roth's mistress accuses Ike in their exchange—"'Old

Man' she said, 'have you lived so long and forgotten so much that you dont remember anything you ever knew or heard about love" (268)—can thus be seen as true in their valance as suppressions of life but also of Ike's and the country's futurity.

Commensurately, this is one way we can understand the novel's more general treatment of its putative source: the memory of Faulkner's nurse and caregiver, Caroline Barr. Consigning her imaginatively to a realm beyond "recompense," as memorialized in the book's epigraph—or in Faulkner's well-known photograph of her—Faulkner seeks to return Mammy Callie to the same temporal order as Old Ben.

To Mammy
CAROLINE BARR
Mississippi 1840–1940

Who was born in slavery and who gave to my family
a fidelity without stint or calculation of
recompense and to my children an
immeasurable devotion and love

In its emphasis on her slavery past as well as her work for the Faulkners "without recompense," the dedication both invokes the plantation economy and suggests a perpetuating of it in the manner of Caroline's servitude. This way of "fixing" events or figures in the past is a notable property of photography, one commented on exhaustively by Frankfurt school thinkers like Benjamin and Siegfried Kracauer. In this light, it might be worth mentioning the odd compositional quality of Faulkner's photographic portrait. In addition to naturalizing Caroline's position, placed as she is within a framing set of branches and trees (while she nevertheless wears her apron, a signifier of her domestic work), the photo sets her at a somewhat precarious pitch. Leaning for support on the branch below her, which is angled upward, Caroline seems to hold herself steadily in place. If not "eternally" so, Caroline's position is one that she—like the photograph itself, like the novel's dedication—works to maintain. In its various formal and temporal modes, then, and read alongside aspects of *Go Down, Moses,* the photograph as well as the novel's dedication can be said to partake of a similar "completion" of Caroline and her past

Photograph of Caroline Barr taken by Faulkner in 1939.

that Ike attributes to the events of the South's history generally. Nothing can change for individuals like Caroline—nor, for the matter, for Ike—in a future that is already determined.

The only character in *Go Down, Moses* to impose a radical assertion of difference and futurity is the one who, contra Faulkner in his conception of Caroline, is the one who is the most mobile and, contra Ike, the one who most deeply loves: Rider, in "Pantaloon in Black." Throughout the story, and often against others' and, certainly, his white society's expectations, Rider is mobile. He walks away peremptorily from his wife's funeral and, the day after, from his job at the mill; he traverses what appears miles of countryside at night; ultimately he moves across the barriers of both the jail cell where's he's temporarily held and, quite willfully early in the story, beyond the divide that separates him and Mannie. Although he is not finally free of the racial bonds that hold him and other black characters, Rider nevertheless demonstrates qualities that mark him as both more noble, indeed more human than many of the characters in the novel—and arguably, than his author. As Judith Sensibar has demonstrated, Faulkner's denials in his earlier life of his deep familial bond to Caroline Barr resemble those of Roth Edmonds and his black caregiver in "The Fire and the Hearth."[7] This denial of humanity, even that of the most emotionally important person of his life, is what marks Faulkner's as well as Ike's limited capacity to envision a genuinely different and authentically *free* future, one in which blacks are acknowledged as more than the objects of sentimental affection (such as what we encounter in Caroline's photograph) and deserving of their own self-determining agency.

Sensibar refers to events from Faulkner's life in order to relate them to characters in his fiction. What she does not acknowledge, though, is where novels like *Go Down, Moses* offer a vision of race that extends beyond what Faulkner could manage personally (or that he mustered in the decade that followed the novel's publishing in his public remarks about segregation). Such agency and autonomy as Faulkner denied African Americans in his life appear in the novels, including if not especially *Go Down, Moses.* One way to turn more fully to such an example in Rider, whose story includes both the novel's passing reference to film and, more importantly, a temporal order that evokes a "cinematic" free play, is by way of a rather different version of photographic indexicality than that I've been discussing.

Like the role of the ledgers in "The Bear," "Pantaloon in Back" includes a kind of "writing" that bears links to an earlier event or time. Walking swiftly from Mannie's funeral, Rider stirs "the pale, powder-light, powder-dry dust of August from which the long week's marks of hoof and wheel had been blotted by the strolling and unhurried Sunday shoes, with somewhere beneath them, vanished *but not gone,* fixed and held in the annealing dust, the narrow, splay-toed prints of his wife's bare feet . . . himself, his own prints, setting the period now" (103, emphasis added). The rising dust here, as elsewhere in Faulkner, provides a palpable index of past events, one in which Rider can "read" both Mannie's earlier presence and his effort to mark it with his own trace or "sentence" (to which he places the "period"). A similar reference to dust attends the very first appearance of Sutpen in *Absalom, Absalom!* Sitting in Rosa's office in the novel's opening pages, Quentin first encounters a vision of Sutpen that emerges "out of the biding and dreamy and victorious dust" (5). Like the characteristically long sentence that only finishes here—the stylistic trope that to many readers evokes Bergson's notion of duration and its links to the past—the dust surrounding Sutpen bears his image and presence forward in both space and time.[8]

References to the dust here and in "Pantaloon in Black" can return us, however briefly, to the Wilderness stories and their pervasive, damp gloom, noted earlier. (In addition to an unchanging light in the November forest scenes in the Big Woods, it is always raining.) The rain in the trilogy, we might say, washes out the dust that elsewhere figures an indexical relation to history and the past, whether of Sutpen or Mannie, coming back in these tiny particles, or in the narrator of *Absalom*'s description of Rosa's parlor as "mote-palpitant" (17) points of contact with earlier events and bodies. What is left in the Wilderness stories, rather, is a "pure" image, soundless, still, in which Ike and the narrator fashion a space that, like the photograph—or we might say, the digital image—is time*less*, bereft of history and what it ordinarily connotes of change.

With these reflections I do not mean to suggest that Faulkner is a kind of film theorist manqué or that Rider's and other characters' dusty historical tracings amount to some kind of para-cinematic expression. Rather, what I wish to suggest is that Faulkner's novels, and *Go Down, Moses* in particular, register a contact with the past that, like film in certain of its temporal aspects, retains a trace of history. The dust that swirls evocatively throughout his fiction, we know, is always redolent of an earlier period in Yoknapatawpha and in characters' (and readers') imaginative encounters with it. More important to this sense of the indexical in Faulkner's prose, as in cinema, is what it also retains by way of its unwitting accommodating of contingency, the random moment or unplanned event that film allows—along with its patterning of time and its seeming regimenting of sequential, static images.

It is at this point that we need to turn to Rider and the very different sense of time that his story evokes and that, among other reasons, distinguishes it from other portions of the novel. For several critics, the anomalous quality of "Pantaloon" is due to the fact that the story's protagonist is not related directly to the McCaslins, like nearly all of the book's other characters, black or white. It is also true, however, that the story's events are markedly different in their emphasis on a kind of African American experience than we see elsewhere in the novel and, commensurate with it, a temporal sense at variance with the surrounding stories as well. This temporality, while not fully consonant with the kind of freedom inherent in cinematic time such as Doane and others describe, nevertheless posits the freedom everywhere else denied Rider and characters like him.

Rider himself, as we know, is ultimately circumscribed by the law and by white vigilante violence, as were countless African Americans during Jim Crow. Yet his story includes several details that suggest, if not a full emancipation, then a meaningful impulse toward racial and personal autonomy, one that, in the story's emphasis on Rider's *movement*, recalls both earlier Faulkner racial narratives like *The Unvanquished*, with its emphasis on African Americans' collective journey northward after the Civil War, and historical and demographic events like the Great Migration.[9] Importantly, that motility registers a uniquely cinematic temporality, one that registers its own intimations of freedom.

Rider's grief for his wife, Mannie, is what drives him through the story's events and space. Having settled into a quiet, even staid, domesticity in their marriage, Rider finds himself compelled back onto his aggressive, wandering actions after she dies. Unable or unwilling to stop himself immediately following her funeral, Rider carries his rageful mourning through the next several days, including his encounter with her ghost—a passage that suggests its own alternative, unbounded temporal sway. Later in the story, after his ferocious binge and arriving at the mill where he works, Rider hesitates before entering the backroom where he knows an after-hours dice game is being played. Describing Rider's approach to the clearing where the mill is located, the narrator indicates, as he has throughout the story, "And now he [Rider] was moving" (114). In the following sentence the narrator offers one of the novel's signature passages, one that implies an even more encompassing temporality: "He crossed the clearing and entered the boiler shed and went through it, crossing the junctureless backloop of time's trepan, to the door of the tool-room, the faint glow of the lantern beyond the plank-joints" (114).

Faulkner's locution bears considering on several levels. And this is true both in the immediate context of its potential meanings and in connection with other events in the novel. In describing Rider "crossing the junctureless backloop," Faulkner uses one of his characteristic oxymoronic constructions; the very act of crossing implies a juncture or at least a span. Just prior to this moment Rider had performed another juncture crossing: when he greets Mannie from across the divide of death in their rented cabin. Effecting another crossing here, Rider seems to step into—or, rather, across—"time's trepan," the hole bored into time or the saw used to cut into the cranium, here perhaps Rider's own skull or the encasing of a mental time. Evoking that hole or cavity, the "backloop" referred to here may connote the way in which the event that follows Rider entering the shed—his cutting Birdsong's throat with his razor—recalls or "loops back" back to a similar event from the previous story: Lucas holding his razor to Zack Edmonds's throat when he threatens to kill him in "The Fire and the Hearth." Looking back in the novel and to an earlier historical time, this moment in "Pantaloon" then returns to its present event of Rider and Birdsong. Importantly, however, it does so by way of altering the nature of events or of the racial terms involved in the book previously. In the earlier story Lucas could not bring himself to kill Edmonds—a fact that his cousin seems to anticipate. Here, later, in a moment both bound to the earlier confrontation but also advancing and changing it in the future, Rider does follow through with the threatened action, pursued, as would have been Lucas's, as an act of racial self-assertion. What this echo and change imply, then, is that the novel envisions a different future for men like Lucas Beauchamp than what they manage in life. "Crossing the junctureless backloop of time's trepan" means, in this view, finding and then filling gaps in temporality, showing junctures that become connected and—importantly—progressively modified.

An aspect of the story that bears mentioning here is that, like "Was," "Pantaloon in Black" evokes the variable, unpredictable outcomes of gambling and its own implication of a different, nonroutinized temporality. Although Birdsong has fixed the dice game, what Rider insists on in challenging him is the aspect of chance—contingency, that is, and the opportunities or outcomes it does not guarantee but at least makes possible. In another potential example of "backlooping," Rider recalls Tomey's Turl and what Thadious Davis describes as his consistent efforts, described in "Was," to use gaming—his regular running away from the McCaslin plantation and the chase that ensues—as the opportunity for self-expression and a freedom denied him as property. Like the modifications of Lucas's threat to Zack in "The Fire in the Hearth" I described above, "Pantaloon in Black" also extends the earlier story of Tomey's Turl but with a more powerful outcome. As Davis puts it, "[Rider] resists accepting the 'rules' of the game that signify the barriers preventing his union with his dead wife, and that very resistance defies the logic of race in his society. Rider's story thus achieves what Tomey's Turl's cannot: It names the misreading underlying racial stereotyping"[10]

Breaking out of such containment as stereotyping is only one of the many constraints against which Rider strikes—and in this respect, his "uncontainable" nature serves for many readers as a synecdoche for a novel that itself refuses to cohere. This formal quality is key, and it returns us to temporality and film. After Rider's death and in its ending, "Pantaloon in Black" offers the book's only mention of cinema. But its context is instructive. Following the scene of Rider at the mill, Faulkner shifts to a frame narrative in which the deputy sheriff tells his wife the story of Rider's apprehension and ultimate lynching. Several aspects of the narrative arrest his attention, perhaps above all the elemental quality of grieving that he seems fascinated to find in a black man. While the deputy sheriff is hardly sympathetic, critics have noted that he evinces a white interest in African American consciousness that is unusual, at least by comparison to his wife's more sharply articulated impatience with him and his act of telling. (She insists he finish talking and eating dinner so that she can go to the pictures [120].) We might say that, like many moviegoers, his wife has a strong impulse toward the narrative cinema's escapism, its capacity, as Roland Barthes describes, to subsume individual reflection and insist on a sense of shared, "public" time. In *Camera Lucida* Barthes offers a view of cinematic temporality that is relevant to how I'm reading the coda of "Pantaloon in Black." There Barthes refers to the fact that the still photograph allows for a freer set of associations for the viewer, private contemplations that do not need to follow the "public," discursive time of images organized (in cinema) in the service of narrative.[11] Like Doane, Barthes sees in film a version of time that is ordered and instrumental versus the freer, imaginative play afforded by photography. But Barthes's distinction between film and photography offers a way to approach the seemingly casual mention of filmgoing in "Pantaloon," namely the deputy-sheriff's wife's urge to use the picture show as a stop to hearing (or thinking) about Rider. Such a quality seems to obtain in other depictions of filmgoing in Faulkner, including the sustained attention to the picture show he pays in "Dry September" as well as the passing reference to the exiting movie crowd the weekend of Joe's murder in *Light in August.* Both instances, moreover, like "Pantaloon in Black," connect the public events of lynching with the communal experience of (southern) moviegoing.[12]

The fact of giving over to the crowd—whether in the shape of the standardized narrative temporality of the movies or the violent ministrations of the lynch mob—stands out, though, against the private act of contemplation we find in the deputy sheriff, however briefly, or that is afforded by modes of perception and affect that offer the contingent play of meaning. This is not to suggest that the deputy sheriff offers a model for a particular effect of film or a full awareness of Rider's suffering. Such alternative temporalities as we find in the story, however, and that Rider's actions (like certain aspects of film) enable, allow a way to consider the story's ending and Rider's death differently from what the deputy sheriff's wife evinces. Such differences also point to a way to read *Go Down, Moses* generally as historical, but in a manner that is at odds with many understandings of the novel, indeed, of Faulkner's historicity generally.

This approach is suggested in David Evans's recent book *William Faulkner, William James, and the American Pragmatic Tradition.*[13] In it, Evans is at pains to encourage a new approach to Faulkner's historical novels, in particular the critical tradition that reads works such as *Absalom, Absalom!* and *Go Down, Moses* for their revelations of closely guarded "secrets" about the South's past. Evans lodges his critique in what he considers a structural error in historicist readings of Faulkner, an approach that takes the view that the past and its singular truth can be determined. While this may be already a well-known antiexegetical turn,[14] it is particularly apposite to moments in Faulkner that suggest their own seeming expository power.

One of the most emblematic of these is the paradigmatic, many find climatic, moment in *Go Down, Moses* of Ike reading the ledgers—what Evans describes as a scene of "spectacularly successful reading" (214). Evans finds Ike's response to the information he finds there to be based, not in his naïve belief in the efficacy of his renouncement, or his ability to fashion a text's meaning, but in Ike's providential view of his family's and the South's history. Ike sees his native region as "cursed" (206). But he also sees it waiting to be redeemed—with himself in the role of redeemer. Ike's interpretation of his family chronicle is a variation on Sacvan Bercovitch's *American Jeremiad,* a story that proceeds through an original sin—in Ike's view, that of property and ownership of the land—but that ultimately is optimistic in its redemptive ends (211). Evans's suggestion is to read Faulkner "pragmatically," that is, with an eye not on his work's at times burdensome relationship to the past, but with the sense that the past and our understanding of it is best understood as a still-unfolding process, a continuum of event in which the "answers" to history or any postulate of truth are yet to be revealed.

One other feature of the novel that allows for an open contingency and an understanding of its historical vision as unfinished is its structure. As readers have long acknowledged, more than any of Faulkner's modernist texts, *Go Down, Moses* refuses to cohere. Even works as seemingly disjointed as *The Sound and the Fury* and *As I Lay Dying* lack what Evans (clearly recalling Rider) calls the "sullen resistance" of *Go Down, Moses* to integrating (228). In addition to its thematic use of gambling and chance—the poker game in "Was," the dice game in "Pantaloon"—the novel's narrative gaps allow for an unpredictable, unmanageable sequencing, one in which anomaly, even chance, might be said to obtain over and above any clear patterning. While its fragmentation is a common modernist characteristic, the particularly "unruly" structure of *Go Down, Moses* marks it as possessing features in common with an important dimension of preclassical film, namely its incorporating of contingency or an unfinished, "open" quality. As such, events in *Go Down, Moses* may be said to avoid succumbing to the heavily nostalgic mode of other Faulkner and modernist works, and of characters like Ike who share film's felt need to archive history or "store" time against modernity and its losses.

At this stage of media history, one of those losses includes film itself, and the indexical traces of history it includes as well as its intimations of a non-instrumental time. In an effort to gather the lines of this discussion, I would like to refer to a suggestion offered by Joseph Urgo that we read Faulkner's writing "performatively." Like other founding texts of national meaning, Urgo suggests, Faulkner's novels offer a way to "think America."[15] If, as Gilles Deleuze suggested, the postwar cinema offered a new way to image thought—in particular the skeptical, detached attitude of modern philosophy—what I'm calling Faulkner's cinematic modernism *in Go Down, Moses* offers a way to "think" the nation.[16] Like the civil rights struggles that would follow in the decades after the publication of this novel, and that Faulkner anticipates a few years later in *Intruder in the Dust, Go Down, Moses* offers a way to think about the country in ways that, unlike Faulkner's earlier modernism, encourage us to look forward and ahead as much as, or more, than back.

To make this case about *Go Down, Moses,* we might do well to turn to a final indexical aspect of both the novel and film, one that is facilitated by a renewed expression of cinephilia. Several film scholars have described this phenomenon and the consonance of its appearance in the era of increasing digital imagery. Against the encroachments of the digital, what remains is the ineluctable aspect to film that is understood as uniquely physical, sensuous even—but equally indeterminate or unknown. David Rodowick describes this aspect of film as our historical relationship to the medium: "The renewed interest of film theory in indexicality is characteristic of how, in the era of digital simulation, we are becoming resensitized to the powers of photography and cinema, especially since this experience is now practically lost—it is already *historical.*"[17] In our sustained interest in Faulkner, but also in a renewed interest in his fiction's own affinity with film and with cinema's indexical relationship to history, we might consider how his work itself contributes to our "resensitizing" to the powers of media other than Faulkner's own. While we might view this affinity by way of the shared nostalgia in Faulkner and in film for a time lost, I think we can better—or more hopefully—consider what analog film shares with a novel like *Go Down, Moses,* one that, more than his other modernist works, has an eye on the future and in ways that follow from our attention to its indexical elements as well as its varied temporality. Part of the unique indexicality of film, as we've seen, is its open-ended quality. As Rodowick puts it, "The causal or indexical power of photography and film have sense for us, but their *meaning* is always incomplete, open-ended, and ambiguous" (75). In his own discussion of cinephilia, Mark Betz described one of the bases for a love of film in the same terms. Yet to Rodowick's accent on a salutary temporal deferral, Betz offers another quality to film that distinguishes it from the digital: "What emerges, in the end, is the overwhelming physical disposition of film, how it figures bodies, machines, rooms, landscapes, and their relation as forms of deferral beyond the space and time of the film itself, leaving it for us to rescue, to explore, to articulate—though not to complete—their moments of inscrutable pleasure."[18] In addition to the notably open-ended quality to *Go Down, Moses,* we might add what I earlier called the uniquely material, sensuous aspect of Faulkner's prose and its own "overwhelming physical disposition": the dust on the road that Rider inadvertently stirs, the dirt he shovels onto Mannie's grave, the nearly palpable lettering of the ledgers' script.

This is why, at this historical moment, it may be worth mentioning a defense of medial nostalgia. Like Betz, Doane refers to cinephilia as a phenomenon that reflects a nostalgia for the pleasures and properties of film. It is a nostalgia, though, that we are well able to historicize, given the passing of not only a certain kind of moving image and aesthetic encounter, but a particular conception of time. As Doane puts it in the passage cited in my epigraph, "The indexically inscribed contingency is . . . history as the mark of what could have been otherwise" (231). The ability for time to *feel* unsystematized in film, the capacity of the medium to capture seemingly random events, allows for a temporal sense that remains noninstrumental, irrational—and thus, free. Other versions of visual culture and contemporary narrative like digital media, in their lack of physical indexical traces and thus, of a certain kind of contingency, fail to evoke both this sense of possibility, what Doane freely extols as cinema's "utopian" dimension, and any commensurate feeling of "excessive" passion, devotion, or love—terms central to understanding the cinephile and that are apposite to certain characters like Rider. If a character like Ike fails to realize or "redeem" the future for his region, this is so in part because he fails to embrace a sense of temporality that allows for a nonordered, nonprovidential sense of history as well as because, as we have seen, Ike fails to love anyone at all.

A final example from the novel offers a helpful way for me to end my discussion. At the close of the book's final story, "Go Down, Moses," Gavin Stevens hears from his friend, notably a newspaper editor, that Butch Beauchamp's aunt wanted him to print Butch's story in his paper. We never know if the editor grants Mollie her wish. We do know that the editor shares with Stevens his consternation that an elderly, illiterate black woman would want such a story to appear, and the two men consign her to their disbelief and Gavin's patronizing summation that "*It doesn't matter to her now . . . She wanted that casket and those flowers and the hearse and she wanted to ride through town behind it in a car*" (281). Molly's request, however, is meaningful in ways that clearly lie beyond the ken of Stevens and the editor. What she stresses is that she wants the paper to include "all" of Butch's story. What the novel suggests in its efforts to reach back through history and backloop to slavery, the McCaslin plantation, and the Big Woods, as well as forward to Rider and Butch's contemporary execution in Chicago, is that telling "all of hit," as Mollie puts it (280), would require a much fuller accounting than the newspaper could realistically provide—or that its writers and editor would allow, even if they fathomed what Mollie is urging. (In a poignant observation, Evans notes that Mollie's phrasing implies the violence to which Butch, like countless African Americans, including Rider, is subject, an element of the story or the "history" of men like them she wants told. Print "All of *hit*," she twice urges [202].)

In closing, it might be worth noting another quality to the story Mollie beseeches. In her stress on its sprawling, inclusive quality—"All of hit"—she hints at a kind of narrative that editors, by definition (as well as some critics), are unwilling to allow. Including "all" of the story of her nephew, such a story would of necessity evade editorial excisings and manipulations, would, then, tell more of the story than Stevens or the editor wants to hear. That freer openness itself suggests allowing contingency or disorder, a resistance to containing that we've seen distinguishes Rider's movement as well as the "movement" and structure of the novel generally. Yet it also true that what Mollie seeks is not only a full-bodied narrative of African American suffering. She intuits, that is, that her own contemporary media—the newspaper—amounts to an indexical tracing. Despite the fact that she cannot read the story, she nevertheless wants it to appear in the paper, where others can not only read it, but for whom the events of Butch's life might make their own historical mark. Here we may be reminded of Doane's emphasis on the capacity of the indexical to suggest a measure of indeterminacy, not only in how we perceive events in the past, but then the hope or possibility for a different outcome of events in futurity. We may not be content with history and events as they have transpired. But if a mode of rendering them retains an indexical openness and proleptic charge, the sense that the turn of a card can hold meaning or that a drawn blade can, after all, prove lethal, then perhaps that rendering can include the capacity to believe that events could *have* changed. Or could change yet. In her own effort to produce an indexical mark on time with Butch's story, Mollie Beauchamp—unlike Quentin and Ike—seeks to effect history not as providential or redemptive, nor as a lamentable archive of loss, but more freely, if also more dolefully, "as the mark of what could have been otherwise."

NOTES

I would like to thank Tyler Schintzus for discussion of *Go Down, Moses* and the novel's temporality in the early stages of conceiving this essay.

1. Mary Ann Doane, *The Emergence of Cinematic Time: Modernity, Contingency, the Archive* (Cambridge: Harvard University Press, 2002). Hereafter cited parenthetically.

2. André Bazin, "The Ontology of the Photographic Image," in *What Is Cinema?*, trans. Hugh Gray (Berkeley: University of California Press, 1967).

3. Philip Rosen, *Change Mummified: Cinema, Historicity, Theory* (Minneapolis: University of Minnesota Press, 2001).

4. William Faulkner, *Go Down, Moses*, in *Novels, 1942–1954* (New York: Library of America, 1994), 200. Hereafter cited parenthetically.

5. William Faulkner, *Absalom, Absalom!*, in *Novels, 1936–1940* (New York: Library of America, 1990), 105. Hereafter cited parenthetically.

6. Julian Murphet, "Faulkner in the Histories of Film: 'Where Memory Is the Slave,'" in *Faulkner and Film: Faulkner and Yoknapatawpha 2010*, ed. Peter Lurie and Ann J. Abadie (Jackson: University Press of Mississippi, 2014), 216. Hereafter cited parenthetically.

7. Judith Sensibar, *Faulkner and Love: The Women Who Shaped His Art* (New Haven: Yale University Press, 2009), 102.

8. See, for example, Aaron Nyerges, "Immemorial Cinema," in *Faulkner and Film*, ed. Peter Lurie and Ann J. Abadie (Oxford: University Press of Mississippi, 2014), in which Nyerges avers the links between Faulkner's prose and a conception of film temporality as fluid, continuous, and as a series of linked moments of becoming. There are many readings of Faulkner's putative Bergsonianism; among the more recent, as well as compelling, accounts of that relation is Marjorie Pryse's "Textual Duration against Chronological Time: Graphing Memory in Faulkner's Benjy Section" (*Faulkner Journal* 25, no. 1 [Fall 2009]).

9. Not only Rider's movement, but the fact of his *speed* matters to some: "In a world where black people were told for a century to go slow on their march to freedom and equality, this is one negro who does everything fast" (John T. Matthews, *Faulkner: Seeing Through the South* [Oxford: Blackwell-Wiley, 2009], 178). For scholarship on Faulkner and the Great Migration, see Cheryl Lester, "As They Lay Dying: Rural Depopulation and Social Dislocation as a Structure of Feeling, *Faulkner Journal* 21, nos. 1–2 (2005): 28–50.

10. Thadious Davis, *Games of Property: Law, Race, Gender and Faulkner's "Go Down, Moses"* (Durham: Duke University Press, 2003), 142.

11. Roland Barthes, *Camera Lucida: Reflections on Photography*, trans. Richard Howard (New York: Hill and Wang, 1981), 89–90; 97–98.

12. I have commented elsewhere on the affinities between lynching and southern moviegoing. See Peter Lurie, "Inside and Outside Southern Whiteness: Film Viewing, the Frame, and the Racing of Space in Yoknapatawpha," *Faulkner and Whiteness*, ed. Jay Watson (Jackson: University Press of Mississippi, 2011).

13. David H. Evans, *William Faulkner, William James, and the American Pragmatic Tradition* (Baton Rouge: Louisiana State University Press, 2008). Hereafter cited parenthetically.

14. See Philip Weinstein, *Unknowing: The Work of Modernist Fiction* (Ithaca, NY: Cornell University Press, 2005); and Catherine Gunther Kodat, "Unhistoricizing Faulkner," in *Faulkner's Sexualities: Faulkner and Yoknapatawpha 2007*, ed. Ann Trefzer and Ann J. Abadie (Oxford: University Press of Mississippi, 2010).

15. Joseph R. Urgo, "Where Was That Bird? Thinking America through Faulkner," in *Faulkner in America*, ed. Urgo and Ann J. Abadie (Oxford: University Press of Mississippi 2001), 98–115.

16. Gilles Deleuze, *Cinema 2: The Time-Image*, trans. Hugh Tomlinson and Richard Galeta (Minneapolis: University of Minnesota Press, 1989).

17. David Rodowick, *The Virtual Life of Film* (Cambridge: Harvard University Press, 2007), 74. Hereafter cited parenthetically.

18. Mark Betz, introduction to "In Focus: Cinephilia," special issue, *Cinema Journal* 49, no. 2 (2010): 132.

Mired Mediations

As I Lay Dying, a Horse, a Fish, Telepathy, and Economics

RICHARD GODDEN

I thought it apt, when addressing a novel famously consisting of fifty-nine sections, to make a paper from bits.

Bit 1: Darl's "little spy-glass" that "he got in France at the war"[1]: Prior to his aside, late in his last and nineteenth section, and only seven pages from the novel's close, the reader can have scant idea that Darl served in the American Expeditionary Force. Surprise may only be compounded by Faulkner's use of a pornographic device to trigger the abrupt dislocation in time and space, from "here" (Jefferson, Mississippi) to "over there" (the Great War), and from now (circa 1927) to then (1917–18). Grasping what the spy-glass lets us see will depend upon an adequate contextualizing of the image. Darl, given up by the Bundrens to two Jackson Asylum guards and taken by them to the Jackson train, observes himself:

> They [the guards] pulled two seats together so Darl could sit by the window to laugh. One of them sat beside him, the other sat on the seat facing him, riding backward. One of them had to ride backward because the state's money has a face to each backside and a backside to each face, and they are riding on the state's money which is incest. A nickel has a woman on one side and a buffalo on the other; two faces and no back. I dont know what that is. Darl had a little spy-glass he got in France at the war. In it it had a woman and a pig with two backs and no face. I know what that is. "Is that why you are laughing Darl?" (254)

The positioning of the guards (waged by the state), one "facing him," one "riding backward," prompts Darl to a skid of associations that may be said to generate and annotate the contents of the glass. "[B]ackward" elicits "backside," which in turn requires "face"; a conjunction that yields a "coin," incestuously earned, since the state's agents ride on the state's money, and "ride" (as in, "ride me down," African American slang used severally by Faulkner)[2] constitutes a sexual union; though, strictly speaking, the incest specified is oral and homosexual, involving a hint of putting money where the mouth or anus is. Having coined an impossible coin, Darl considers the nickel, "a woman on one side and a buffalo on the other"; the absence of "back," despite the earlier prevalence of "backward" and "backside," defies his comprehension until (enabled by the buffalo) he recalls the spy-glass with its image, "a pig with two backs and no face." Faulkner presumably intends an annotative echo as, care of *Othello*, he darkens the image by taking it from Iago's mouth, "Your daughter and the Moor are now making the beast with two backs,"[3] though the compounding of "back," in conjunction with sexual activity, serves to call into the provenance of the glass, Darl's own conception, according to Addie:

> Then I found that I had Darl. At first I would not believe it. Then I believed that I would kill Anse. It was as though he had tricked me, hidden within a word like within a paper screen and struck me in the *back* through it. (172, italics mine)

Cunning penetration from behind, perceived as murderous. The associative range of the spy-glass extends, as far as I am aware, to one further usage: Tull, looking back across the swollen and finally forded stream, regards his mule, not as a beast in a glass, but as the glass itself:

> it was like he [the mule] was one of these here spy-glasses and I could look at him standing there and see all the broad land and my house sweated outen it like it was the more the sweat, the broader the land; the more the sweat, the tighter the house. (139)

When is a mule not a mule, but a spy-glass? A mule is not a mule when it is "sweat" or coagulated labor; so perceived, the mule as labor power allows the additional perception that agricultural land (extended through labor) and a house (ditto) are sweat that the swollen river, swollen by the floods of 1927, threatens quite literally to wash away. (As Tull puts it earlier, "*I be durn if I like to see my work washed outen the ground, work I sweat over*" [90]). The beast, as the glass that turns itself and the land that it works into labor, earns an associative place—"back" or no "back"—beside Darl's conception, both connotatively packed into his "little spy-glass": not least because Addie resents Anse's attentions in large part because she—"the mule of [his] world"[4]—recognizes herself as the generative source of the Bundren labor force. Addie's reproductive capacity ensures the family's productive capacity.

I have come a long way from the Great War, to which I intend to return in Bit 3, but not before, nudged by "the Moor" (Othello) in the spy-glass, engaging with why Faulkner blackens the Bundrens.

Bit 2: The blackened Bundrens: Darl burns Gillespie's barn ostensibly to burn Addie's much-decayed body within it, though his purpose may be thought to shift once it is recognized that to burn a barn in Mississippi, anywhere between 1880 and 1930, was to engage in an overtly political and covertly racial act. Black sharecroppers, trapped at the foot of tenancy's one-runged agricultural ladder, might, in desperation, burn the property of their landowner.[5] Faulkner's "Barn Burning" (published in 1938; set in the 1890s; recollected in the 1910s) acknowledges that white croppers—in this instance Ab Snopes, for whom "the element of fire spoke to some deep mainspring of his . . . being"[6]—might adopt African American means of resistance. Ab's reasoning runs: if de Spain's great white house amounts to "nigger sweat," and de Spain "wants to mix some white sweat with it," then a white tenant may be justified in taking his "niggard . . . shrewd fire" to the property in which his landlord stores the stolen sweat of tenantry.[7] The Bundrens are *not* tenants, yet Darl's arson collectively blackens them. In Vardaman's section, immediately following the fire, Cash's leg, held in its concrete case, "turned black" (224), complementing Jewel's burned back, treated with "butter and soot"; to Vardaman, "a nigger's foot," "a nigger's back" (224). Inversion extends to Jefferson, where on entry, and incited by the reaction of passersby to the smell, Jewel, "as though blind for the moment," mistakes white for black (229–30).

Whether or not one reads the burning of Gillespie's barn as a racialized act (and I find it difficult not to do so), one cannot escape the presence of two fires within one: the barn loft "explode[s] . . . as though it had been stuffed with powder" (218–19); "the hallway looks like a searchlight turned into rain" (221); the mouth and eyes of Mack Gillespie resemble "three round holes" in a face whose freckles "look like English peas on a plate" (220), while "a rain of burning hay" falls "like a portière of flaming beads" (222). Such detail, care of Darl's "spy-glass," draws the trenches from the barn, ensuring that two places exist in one. Moreover, Darl's conscription (and subsequent passage to France) allows us to read his crime of arson as an extension of an earlier crime associated with his drafting, a crime of regional disaffiliation.

Put tersely, the draft takes the land out of Darl's eyes. In his diatribe against the road, Anse intimates initial and considerable resistance to the drafting of his son, resistance sufficient to bring "the law" along the road, "to threaten me out of him" (37), "talking me out of him" (36), "trying to short-hand me with the law" (36). Anse's case against the draft was that Darl "was alright at first, with his eyes full of the land all the time . . . he tends to his own business" (36). One can only imagine that Anse's locution appeals to the farmer's exemption clause of the Selective Draft Act (1917), whereby essential farm labor might be exempt (Darl "tends to his business . . . the land"). However, federal promises to the contrary, agricultural exemptions under selective service regulations were permitted only to those who produced substantially for the market: semi-subsistence producers (like the Bundrens) were not exempt. Anse's complaints reflect a regionwide unrest, turning on the perception that county draft boards—drawn from local elites—exhibited sustained class and racial bias, "persistently exempting rich men's sons," town dwellers, and "drafting African-American men in disproportionate number."[8] As Jeanette Keith puts it in her study of the politics of southern draft resistance, "poor men of both races . . . [finding] that the government regulation did not respect their status as farmers . . . [were] pushed to rebellion by the implementation of the draft in the region."[9] She adds that allocation of exemptions, "under regulations intrinsically prejudicial to the poor," drove "nominally dominant white men" to deploy "the same methods of protest used by disenfranchised blacks . . . evasion, foot-dragging and desertion."[10] Ergo, Anse's evasive mumbling drags a slightly darkened political foot.

Anse's feet are memorable, "splayed . . . cramped . . . bent . . . warped . . . with no toenail at all on his little toes," suited to brogans that Darl describes as "hacked with a blunt axe out of pig-iron" (11), whose "clumping," to Tull's ears, sounds "like they was iron shoes" (32). Anse, wanting men off the road and "up-and-down ways like a tree" (36), has an arboreal pedicure: he is an autochthon, or "one sprung from the soil he inhabits." Adam (made from mud) and Oedipus (club-footed) are autochthonic heroes, as was Darl *before* the draft, "all right *at first*, with . . . his eyes *still* full of the land" (36–37, italics mine). The "land," owned by the Bundrens, as the means to their substance, and coterminous with their lifework, necessarily fills their eyes, even as it congeals from their sweat. Anse protests Darl's conscription as "the law," "[t]alking me out of him, durn them" (36), adding, "they begun to threaten me out of him" (37): his phrasing, idiomatically understood, simply describes the removal of Darl from Anse (a "short-hand[ing]" or dismemberment of the collective body of subsistence labor). Read against the idiomatic grain, the phrasing equally describes "the talking of Anse ('me') out of Darl ('him')," or an excision of the father's mode of labor from the son. Anse retains the land in his eyes, where Darl, returned from the Great War, proves empty-eyed: Dewey Dell notes: "Darl . . . sits at the supper table with his eyes gone further than the food and the lamp, full of the land dug out of his skull and the holes filled with distance beyond the land" (26–27). But why should France effect such an evacuation?

Bit 3: The Great War: Given that Faulkner did not experience war, I am loath to "go down the trauma route," locating a recurrent, inassimilable trench experience in the texture of Mississippi mud, so frequently encountered in ditch and flood by Darl. Yet John Liman is surely right to identify the prevalence of mud in *As I Lay Dying* as originating in Faulkner's preoccupation with World War I (else why the French "spy-glass"?).[11] Mud is literally "land" in malleable form, though the novel's mud most typically stogs:

> *The tilted lumber gleams dull yellow, water-soaked and heavy as lead, tilted at a steep angle into the ditch above the broken wheel; about the shattered spokes and about Jewel's ankles a runnel of yellow neither water nor earth swirls, curving with the yellow road neither of earth nor water, down the hill dissolving into a streaming mass of dark green neither of earth nor sky.* (49)

Categories collapse, only to be held in place by chiasmus: that which is "neither water nor earth" cannot go far where formally constrained to recur as "neither of earth nor water"; further, one chiasmus implies another, ensuring that "earth" and "sky," as "sky" and "earth," will retain their distinctions, albeit tacitly, no matter what the "stream" or "dissolution." One should add, of Darl's italicized account of his failure, with Jewel, to deliver a load of timber (and presumably to realize the three dollars for their labor), that Darl offers it as an interjection at the very moment of his mother's death. The passage, of which I have quoted half, occurs in Darl's fifth section as Vardaman "begins to move slowly backward from the bed, his eyes round," above which Anse "leans," and just before "Cash comes to the door, carrying the saw" (49). Even as the wagon blocks the road, so Darl's account of it blocks his account of the "dying"; one might say that, like the novel's title, the incident so used sets the reader up to be impeded. Indeed, the stogged wagon functions primarily to impede transition, from work to wage; from dying to death; its broken wheel slows the Bundrens' departure, setting a precedent for motion as all but stasis. Nine days ... some forty plus miles ... to adapt Addie, the Bundrens "go" so "terribly ... along, the earth, clinging to it" (173) that they barely "go" at all. Mud, flood, and fire impede them to a point at which they most resemble their attendant buzzards, "circles of not-moving" (194).

It might be objected that since I appear to have taken the mud entirely out of the trenches, how might such "stogging" be said to originate there? In response, I offer Walter Benjamin: at the close of "The Work of Art in the Age of Mechanical Reproduction" (1936), Benjamin turns to war. Although he addresses fascism and the anticipation of war, in 1936 his locus classicus for modern warfare necessarily remains (as for Marinetti whom he later quotes) the Great War: "War, and war only, makes it possible to give mass movements on a colossal scale a goal, while retaining the traditional ownership structure. ... Only war makes it possible to mobilize all the technological resources of the present day while retaining the ownership structure."[12] Benjamin's case would seem to be that even as war mobilizes masses, in what is in effect an enforced proletarianization, exposing those men to technological modernity in extremis, it does so precisely to preserve the ownership structures that violated and will continue to violate the masses. Witness African American draftees returning to the South from France with the expectation of enhanced citizenship rights—denied. Witness conscripted southern subsistence farmers, dependent for cash on their peripheral relation to plantation agriculture, returning to a mode of production changed only insofar as the value of the cotton cash crop had fallen, and would continue to fall for more than a decade (so that the floods of '27 washed only "sweat," not value, "outen the ground" [90]). Witness Darl, who having encountered modernity in France, returns not simply to an unchanged "ownership structure," but to a premodern regime of accumulation associated with semi-subsistence agriculture. It should be remembered that Darl went to France linked by resisted conscription to a degree of "rebellion" and "protest" that readied him to commit a black crime in defense of his mother's body. As a result, at his return, he becomes, in effect, a split sign; one whose "here" and "now" (archaism in Mississippi) will always be subject to "there" and "then" (modernity in France). Note, for example, the contradiction between the form and content of Darl's "little spy-glass." The glass, a pornographic purchase, might be thought to join Cash's "graphophone" as a figure for commercialized modernity, yet its content remains insistently autochthonous: an image of the passage of an agricultural beast into a human, prior to entry into the earth,[13] the image joins the fish and the horse in an autochthonic series, albeit technologically developed. The little glass, like its owner, caught between economic regimes, exhibits "morbid symptoms": the phrase is Gramsci's, drawn from his definition of "interregnum," a term relevant to *As I Lay Dying* not least because Faulkner writes the novel's first draft in the six weeks of October and November 1929, during which Wall Street crashed. Through Darl, Faulkner articulates a conjunction of incompatible economies. Here is Gramsci on the "interregnum," whose crisis consists "precisely in the fact that the old is dying and the new cannot be born: in this interregnum a great variety of morbid symptoms appear."[14]

Bit 4: Darl's telepathy as "morbid symptom": "Telepathy," from the Greek "tele" ("far off") and "pathy" ("suffering; feeling"); "felt communication across distance by impalpable means." The telepath knows what he cannot know, in a manner that links times and places whose linkage appears beyond reason. We are back with "there" as "here," and "then" as "now," but one should add that whether or not the symptom originates with the war, understood as a disjunctive experience of labor (whereby a subsistence farmer meets a proletarian in a military factory),[15] its exacerbated expression takes form through local antagonisms. Whatever their origins, Darl's powers remain partial: for example, despite his seeming capacity to loiter at the edge of Jewel's or Dewey Dell's consciousness, he exhibits no anticipation of their connivance in his apprehension by the asylum guards. Faulkner offers clues both to the source and specificity of Darl's telepathy; the clues gather around Jewel's horse and his gaining of it by means of labor stolen from the collective body of the Bundren workforce. Jewel gains the horse, from Quick, by working nights for five months to clear forty acres of Quick's "new ground" (135). Although "money" is mentioned ("the horse cost," "it was my money," "he earned the money" [135]), we see no money exchanged or saved prior to exchange: labor simply accumulates. Anse charges that Jewel has "[t]aken the work from your flesh and blood and bought a horse with it" (136). Note the ambiguity of "your," at once the substance of Jewel himself ("your" singular) and that of his family ("your" plural). The shifting of the pronoun catches exactly how, under subsistence conditions, the one *is* the other, the individual being inseparable from the collective in the matter of labor. Furthermore, Darl's account of the long theft emphasizes loss of "flesh" and compensatory "milk" and "nurture," in a manner that ties shared physical work to maternal gestation. Jewel's exhaustion is typified by his inability to complete the daily task of milking: Darl finds him, "the bucket in place and half full and his hands up to the wrists in milk and his head against the cow's flank" (129); Addie "got Dewey Dell to do his milking" (130), and fixes Jewel "special things to eat," which she "hide[s]" about the house because, "losing flesh" (130) and "gaunt as a bean pole" (131), Jewel "falls asleep in his plate . . . his jaws still chewing" (130). Addie's furtive feeding (itself based on a redistribution of tasks among the Bundren siblings) enables Jewel's labor, which yields a horse. Darl, witness to her secret mothering, extrapolates from the hidden food ("And that may have been when I first found it out" [130]) to a hidden conception; that is, to his recognition that Jewel is Addie's child, but not by Anse. Confronted with Addie's extreme reaction to Jewel's arrival with the horse, Darl identifies the first instance of his telepathic ability with his own discovery of her deceitful conception:

> That night I found ma sitting beside the bed where he [Jewel] was sleeping, in the dark. She cried hard, maybe because she had to cry so quiet; maybe because she felt the same way about tears she did about deceit, hating herself for doing it, hating him because she had to. And then I knew that I

> knew. I knew that as plain on that day as I knew about Dewey Dell on that day. (136)[16]

Presumably, the degree of Addie's equine reaction stems from her realization that Jewel's deceitful labor in the matter of the horse mirrors her deceitful labor in the matter of Jewel; a recognition that implies a silent metaphor in which her gestative labor on behalf of her son and his manual labor on behalf of the horse merge, and from which, in a huge but logical "semantic impertinence,"[17] steps the horse as both mother and son. To adapt Aristotle on metaphor as seeing the likeness through the difference,[18] labor here provides the likeness in (and in spite of) the equine and maternal difference, from which laborious resemblance the horse and Darl's telepathic sensitivity to it emerge. Darl seems unerringly accurate in his reiterated variants on "Jewel's mother is a horse" (95). That Darl "knew that [he] knew" about Dewey Dell, "plain . . . as [he] knew" about Addie, and on specified days, serves to confirm that his telepathic ability originates in, and attends to, maternal conception as labor provision. What he knows about Dewey Dell is that Lafe impregnates her while they work: Lafe, picking cotton (cash crop and semen) into her "sack"; their hands (instruments of labor) "touching"; her sack (a means of production) "half full" and "full," in a projection of pregnancy.

But my recovery of an origin story for Darl's telepathy leaves me with a key problem: why should Faulkner derive that telepathic capacity from secret or deceitful conceptions, and date those conceptions in relation to the activity of labor? Put schematically, gestative labor in the provision of future labor power, under conditions of archaic semi-subsistence production, and at a time of pending modernization, *is* a deception. Addie knows it: she has no desire to go on "chapping" (173), and forced to do so, famously discounts her children (176). Dewey Dell knows it: she seeks to abort a child who will be raised, like Vardaman, to be another hand in a valueless field. Darl knows it, but only as a contradiction. Caught up by war (or modernity in extremis) and returned to peasant production (perceived, by way of contrast, as archaism in extremis), he finds himself subject to the monsters of his own divided perception: the cotton house as cubist canvas (3–4); his sister's leg, "coming long from under her dress" as a "calliper" (104), where callipers were first deployed to measure the caliber of bullet and shell; the flooded river as no-man's-land (141–49); the coin as "incest" spun toward endogamous perversity (homosexual fellation) . . . not to mention the horse as mother and son, and Vardaman's fish.

One way to catch what I would call monsters of the interregnum (a corpse that cannot die; a conception that must not be born) as they materialize primarily from Darl's telepathic perception (itself a form of knowledge half-born), would be to compare them with a creature that is more complete, and more completely linked to the emergent system of commodity production.

Bit 5: Marx's dancing table: Famously discussing "the commodity and its secret," Marx causes a table to all but dance. Noting that wood, self-evidently, is "altered if a table is made out of it," and adding that said table nonetheless "continues to be wood, an ordinary, sensuous thing," Marx observes a subsequent and extreme mutation should the table go to market: "As soon as it emerges as a commodity, it changes into a thing which transcends sensuousness. It not only stands with its feet on the ground, but, in relation to all other commodities, it stands on its head, and evolves out of its wooden brain grotesque ideas, far more wonderful than if it were to begin dancing of its own free will."[19] The table, under the sign of "commodity," has multiple reasons for exuberance. Taken to market, it loses its particularity in exchange for "a relation to all other commodities." To gain as much, it must be priced, or represented by money. Money, for Marx, "obliterates" and renders "invisible" the "specific attributes" and "real elements" of the production that it represents, doing so in the cause of commensurability.[20] Without money as price, and therefore equivalence, goods could simply not go to market: the linen could not become the coat; the coat could not buy the Bible, and the table would "stand in relation" to none of them. It follows that money, commodity's strange sign, liberates the table from its "ordinary . . . sensuousness." Marx comments that considered as an item of exchange, "not an atom of matter enters into the objectivity of the commodity."[21] Since the table owes its "coarsely sensuous objectivity"[22] to wood and to the worker in wood, the carpenter and his materials are set aside in the table's monetary dance; not least because, from the viewpoint of exchange, the table will sell better if the conditions of its production are expunged. Production involves producers drawn together in social relations, but the table, inverted and about to dance, insists on its own agency; in due deference to which, persons conform to things and makers vanish into that which they make.

Yet work cannot be so readily forgotten, even in the marketplace, since it gives substance to all that appears there. If, however, under market imperatives, labor itself becomes a saleable item, it, too, will be subject to comparability: a high degree of abstraction attends the subsequent translation of unlike into like labor. For labor power to become price it must be subsumed within abstract labor (the substance and chief form of capital), or else its qualitatively diverse occasions could not be quantitatively compared. By which means, abstract labor (a generic entity) displaces labor power (as various and specific as those who deploy it), in the cause of a "socially average" and "necessary" quantity of time, which temporal quantity ("socially average labor time") emerges, for Marx, as the basic comparator, in relation to which price may be assessed and surplus value extracted.[23]

I offer Marx's terms merely to explore what table and labor power share in going to market as price; each tending to opacity in the matter of its matter; or, better, each growing obscure in relation to what makes its concreteness concrete. As the carpenter's labor power recedes, care of the abstraction of his work, so the matter of the table, drawn toward equivalency, grows spectral. Can one see, touch, hear, or smell "equivalence" within the thing become commodity en route toward exchange value? Derrida speaks of the table come to market as caught within a "spectral movement" through "secret, mystique, enigma, fetish" toward "a bodiless body" resembling "a prosthesis of itself," from which perspective, the case of the dancing table turns on the transformative and problematic passage of labor power through the veil of capital toward duplicity, or a double body, at once concrete and abstract.[24] If the table had half a brain, it might desist from its balletic purpose, appreciating the collateral damage inherent in its movement through equivalence and toward abstraction.

Bit 6: A three-dollar load, or "[i]t means three dollars" (17):

> In a strange room you must empty yourself for sleep. And before you are emptied for sleep, what are you. And when you are emptied for sleep, you are

> not. And when you are filled with sleep, you never were. I dont know what I am. I dont know if I am or not. Jewel knows he is, because he does not know that he does not know whether he is or not. He cannot empty himself for sleep because he is not what he is and he is what he is not. Beyond the unlamped wall I can hear the rain shaping the wagon that is ours, the load that is no longer theirs that felled and sawed it nor yet theirs that bought it and which is not ours either, lie on the wagon though it does, since only the wind and the rain shape it only to Jewel and me, that are not asleep. And since sleep is is-not and rain and wind are *was*, it is not. (80)

Darl adopts lumber as an analytic means to self-shaping. Jewel, he claims, "knows" himself ("knows he is") because, presumably, he is his horse, that which he both "is . . . , and is not," care of the sweat that he put into it. As a coextensive body—workingman, horse, and mother—his inability to sleep extends not from existential failure, but from mourning and missing parts of himself—mother and horse. Darl, in contradistinction, knows that "he is not," his self-absence finding form in timber exposed to wind and rain. He can no more "shape" himself than he can allocate ownership to the wagon's load: the wood, separated from those who "felled and sawed it," is not theirs by right of work or use, "nor yet theirs that bought it," by right of exchange. Its distribution incomplete, and stuck between failing economic categories, it lapses in outline (since "only . . . the wind and the rain shape it"). What matters here is that the timber anomaly strikes Darl as an apt equivalent for himself. If he were Jewel, though unable to sleep, he would know who and where he was. As Darl, alienated from labor power and not yet realized through price (the three-dollar portage fee remains unpaid), he casts himself as the phenomenal equivalent of mal-distribution, in a double sense: the lumber is not delivered, the coins are not received. What he *does* know is that he has often "lain beneath rain on a strange roof, thinking of home" (81); a concluding remark to his sixth section that, care of mud as seen through the "spy-glass," relocates him in the trenches. Ergo, in two places and times at once, yet equivalent to neither, he loses his body because grown double-bodied: despite abstractions, insufficiently abstracted to be exchange value; despite concreteness, unable to cohere through labor power. In effect, representing himself by way of "tilted lumber" "angled into [a] ditch" (49), Darl proves himself more functionally dryadic than Benjamin Compson's Caddy (she who repeatedly smells like trees).

As a man who problematically passes into problematic timber, Darl grows opaque to himself and mysterious to us. I would stress that my account of the load should not be understood as rendering opacity transparent; rather, I have sought to expose the conditions from which opacity forms. But some objects in *As I Lay Dying*, produced outside market imperatives, may be experienced not as opaque, but as transparent to the work that goes into them.

Bit 7: Vardaman's fish: In his third section, consisting only of the statement, "My mother is a fish" (84), Vardaman intends no metaphor. He will bore holes in the coffin so that the fish may breathe. When the coffin is swept from the wagon by the flooded stream, Darl, being "the best grabbler," should "hold her under water" but fails; "[y]ou knew she was a fish but you let her get away" (151). Coffin restored, Vardaman doubts that Addie can be in it since, "*My mother does not smell like that. My mother is a fish*" (196). Yet subsequently, in Gillespie's barn, he will go to the coffin, to "hear her inside the wood," displacing a cat, drawn there before him, perhaps as to a fish (214). Vardaman sustains the reembodiment because it keeps Addie alive, but his trick works only because of the work he puts into it, work transparently related to the regime of subsistence labor from which he derives.

From the first, the fish has been instrumental in Vardaman's bid for working status; he caught it, carried it, cleaned it, and sought to give his labors heroic status by showing the fish to his mother. In the process, he "grunts" and "spits . . . like a man" (30); objects to cleaning the fish since that is woman's work ("Why cant Dewey Dell clean it?" [31]), and required to do so, "cusses," again "like a grown man," before "toting it [the fish] in both arms. . . . On around the house . . . like a armful of wood" (31), necessary household labor but boy's work. Just as Cash labors over the coffin, so Vardaman labors over the fish, indeed the extended fraternal tasks intersect, for Vardaman, in the coffined fish, both offerings remaining incomplete at the point of Addie's death.

To substitute a dead fish for a dead mother could not resurrect the mother, but because Vardaman has sweated into that fish, "nigh long as he is" (30), that fish is not dead; as congealed labor power, it lives and allows Addie to live. The afterlife of Addie in the labor-life of the fish proves lengthy, undergoing extraordinary transformations, each of them inseparable from Vardaman's use of the word "it":

> Then I begin to run. I run toward the back and come to the edge of the porch and stop. Then I begin to cry. I can feel where the fish was in the dust. It is cut up into pieces of not-fish now, not-blood on my hands and overalls. Then it wasn't so. It hadn't happened then. And now she is getting so far ahead I cannot catch her. (53)

The first "it" in the first paragraph of Vardaman's first section ("It is cut up") refers to the fish, gutted and cleaned, allowing the "not-fish" tacitly to elide the "not-mother." A second "it" ("Then it wasn't so") effects a temporal reversal, restoring integrity to the fish, which, in any case, Vardaman "can [still] feel . . . in the dust," but, as it does so, splitting to refer also to Addie's death, recast, care of the persistence of the felt-fish, as "not having happened." A claim compounded by a third usage ("It hadn't happened then"), in which "then," prompted by its adjacency to "so" (the last word in the previous sentence), slips from temporal adverb to point of emphasis, as in "so, it hadn't happened then." As the subject of an assertion rather than a question, "it," liberated from "then" understood temporally, operates to link the undead mother to the uncut fish, both lodged in the pronoun and released from temporal sequence by the felt persistence of the fish, a persistence dependent on Vardaman's labor. I grow convoluted in pursuit of Vardaman's syntactical adjustments, as his abuse of syntax (the "so" that jumps the full-stop) and of time (the "then" that ceases to function adverbially) serves the higher purposes of "it," rendering that pronoun densely but transparently complex.

The progress of Vardaman's first two sections amounts centrally to an iteration of "it"s, as the "it" draws to itself, through rhythm and alliteration, linked terms: "stick," "hit," "hitch," "gittin," "kilt," "et." How readily the "it" sound, dominant in certain sentences and paragraphs of the initial sections, and doubled in particular phrases, slips its phonemic exceptions to produce iteration. Listen to, "vomiting it. It makes a lot of noise" (54), or "I strike. I can hear the stick striking. I can see it hitting" (54), where a doubling and trebling of "it" in the company of related sounds yields "itting it" and "it itting," so that Vardaman's actions—here, vomiting tears, hitting Peabody's team—seem secondary, not to language, but to sound as a resounding of the coffined fish held living by labor in the "it."

It might be objected that I conduct a sound experiment while Vardaman grieves, except that in the resonance of "it" Vardaman finds and manages his grief. During his first two sections, in effect a detailed account of his immediate response to loss, Vardaman stretches both his own and our ears toward non sense because for him and at this time, making sense amounts to a dead mother. To avoid which, through "it," he makes himself a body that "sounds"; here, I borrow from Jean-Luc Nancy on "listening": "To sound . . . is not only for the sonorous body to emit a sound but it is also to stretch out, to carry itself to be resolved into vibrations that both return to itself and place it [the sonorous body] outside itself."[25] The manner of the "return," in what I am calling Vardaman's "iteration," is that of the echo in a rhyme, where rhyme expects the recovery of a sound, accompanied by an inference of eternity, insofar as the rhyme opens toward potential endlessness. The resonance of rhyme therefore implies a particular temporality whereby a sound anticipates the return of the very thing that it recalls. In the sonority of Vardaman's "it," so glossed, Addie may come, and go, and come again, continuing to exist as a fish in the physical vibrancy of "it," as it re-sounds in her son's ear and throat. Small wonder that Vardaman longs to hear "it" again, and finds satisfaction in "vomiting it" or in "hear[ing] the stick striking . . . hitting" as he cries "kilt" (54).

Having beaten and driven Peabody's team away with a stick found in the barn, Vardaman takes his weighty "it" back to the barn and, more particularly, to a stall holding Jewel's horse. Called to the house by Dewey Dell, he remains with the horse:

> I can cry quiet now, feeling and hearing my tears.
>
> "Then hit want. Hit hadn't happened then. Hit was a-layin right there on the ground. And now she's gittin ready to cook hit."
>
> It is dark. I can hear wood, silence: I know them. But not living sounds, not even him. It is as though the dark were resolving him out of his integrity, into an unrelated scattering of components—snuffings and stampings; smells of cooling flesh and ammoniac hair; an illusion of a co-ordinated whole of splotched hide and strong bones within which, detached and secret and familiar, an *is* different from my *is*. I see him dissolve—legs, a rolling eye, a gaudy splotching like cold flames—and float upon the dark in fading solution: all one yet neither; all either yet none. I can see hearing coil toward him, caressing, shaping his hard shape—fetlock, hip, shoulder and head; smell and sound. I am not afraid.
>
> "Cooked and et. Cooked and et" (56–57)

Listening, and primed to hear his own tears, Vardaman speaks aloud to himself as though to put "hit" severally into the air, along with "gittin," as a prelude to "*It* is dark" (italics mine), though the pronoun seems only inadequately to counter his image of the fish, removed from the ground and taken to the stove. As though listening for a revival of "it" by way of "hitting," Vardaman lists what he *can* hear in the dark: "wood" (the barn timber, cooling) and silence (that of the horse), "I know them." In addition, and by way of contrast, he notes sounds that he does not know, "not living sounds": through *t*, released from "not" by the more likely and therefore antonymically present phrase "no living sound," I posit "it" (briefly emptied of Addie) listened for, and sounded again, though with limited relief in, "*It* is as though the dark were resolving him again out of *his* integrity" (italics mine). Given that within five lines Vardaman will use the word "dissolve," "resolving" seems a risky choice (since darkness tends to "dissolve" the integrity of those forms that stand within it), though it might be added that the effort of the straining eye to pull an equine form from the cloaking dark tugs "to solve" from "to resolve" and thereby posits "solving" within "dissolving," to counter, or at least to modify, the force of the subsequent "scattering." Vardaman replicates the "resolve"/"dissolve" tension in his choice of the pronoun "his"; initially a reference to the outline of the horse, under possible erasure by the dark, "his" will yield to the at least as likely "its," only if the dark subsumes "his" into "its" integrity. Antonymically, triggered tensions, within "resolving" and "his," provide a measure of Vardaman's distress in the barn: all but lost for the integrity of his fish, soon to be "[c]ooked and et," he cannot, at this exact point, afford to accept the dissolution of Jewel's horse. He knows the family story of what went into the horse, five months' work by night. He doubtless senses the force of Darl's charge against Jewel, "Your mother is a horse." Jewel's horse, like his own fish and Cash's coffin, coagulated labor power offered as a living substitute for Addie, cannot be allowed to go to pieces. Straining his ear for "snuffings and stampings," his nose for ammonia in horse hair, his touch for bone under hide, he recovers "an *is* different from my *is*," where the present tense of the verb "to be," twice repeated, announces an essence or integrity, and the integrity of the horse, by dint of difference, further preserves the integrity of the child. Having "resolv[ed]" so much, Vardaman can literally let the horse go to pieces—"legs," "eye," "splotch"—confident that "hearing" will allow him to put it together again. "Not horse," "not fish," "not Addie" cease to trouble him because through "sound" (the resonance of "it" in an equine "is" and a repetition of "et"), he can extend himself through the barn as stored "sweat," returning to himself accompanied by horse and fish and coffin as objects of a shared labor that guarantee Addie's continuance and confirm, "My mother is a fish." Hence, "I am not afraid" (57).[26]

Language remains problematic here. As Eric Sundquist put it, in a remarkable account of the novel as "obsessively concerned with problems of disembodiment," Vardaman's "utterance seems disembodied from the conscious identity of character on the one hand and author on the other."[27] Plainly, many of the words do not derive from Vardaman's vocabulary. Equally, any notion of authorial narration stands at odds with the physiological acuity of the passage as it traces the rhythm of Vardaman's responses. From where, then, might the words be said to derive, if not from Vardaman's or Faulkner's consciousness? Or, more bluntly, if identity does not reside in consciousness, wherein might it be held to reside? My reading of Vardaman's fish has foregrounded not the materiality of language but the materiality of sound as an index to a particular form of labor. Vardaman works the sound of a word ("it") only because that sound grants him access to his prior work on a fish; which work, in contrast to Marx's table or Sundquist's "disembodiment," embodies Addie through him. Faulkner emphasized audition, sonority, rhythm, pause, timbre, or language as "agitated . . . air,"[28] foregrounding externality in an effort to take thought outside the subject. The Vardaman sections, as read, offer scant interiority (one cannot speak of "subjectivity," as one might perhaps of the Quentin Compson section of *The Sound and the Fury*) since what Vardaman offers does not consist of more and less conscious ideas, or of verbal condensations and displacements whose pursuit and elaboration constructs an "inside." Those associative patterns that do exist prove simple (fish, horse, coffin, mother), tending beyond him into the barn and toward the ground: they constitute an "outside" of worked objects toward which his sounds grope.[29]

Of course, *pace* Sundquist, *As I Lay Dying* centers on a body in a state of decomposition. But I would suggest that one needs to set Addie's "disembodiment" (and her children's responses to it) within a context arguably defined by Addie's relation to her own body both as productive of labor, and of a labor force that she perceives as at once forced labor and labor without usefulness, on land without value. Addie's body, put slowly into the ground, takes its historical form from a particular moment in regional land use.

* * *

Bit 8: Two versions of land and how to use it: The Bundrens own their poor land, but do so under particular conditions that I have been describing as semi-subsistence production. Eric Wolf, historian of twentieth-century peasantry, might call the Bundrens "middle peasants," working in a "peripheral economy."[30] The ethnography of Michael Taussig would yield "peasant proprietors" or "semi-proletarians," whose culture resists "market organization" despite being "market dominated":[31] that is to say, for whom the market exists as a demanding option though not as an imperative.[32] So defined, the codependent subsistence unit "produces for its own use" things that confront it "as products of collective labor . . . [and not] as commodities."[33] Under such generic conditions, Vardaman's fish proves typical rather than exceptional insofar as its transparency to the process of its own making bespeaks "a situation in which the collective labor stored in a given [thing] . . . is always and everywhere visible to its consumers and users."[34] Put reductively, the Bundrens as "peasants," or "semi-subsistence producers," for the most part produce use values rather than exchange values: where "use" should not be understood to entail nostalgia for a simpler past somehow prior to the market but as a structurally specific form of transparency to labor, through which land becomes "sweat" and an extension of the collective body, lodged necessarily in the eyes of its owners.

None of which is to say that the Bundrens don't go to market—Vardaman's bananas, Anse's teeth, Cash's graphophone stand in ample evidence of market presence—merely that they don't *have* to go to market.[35] Money certainly appears in *As I Lay Dying*, but its passage toward exchange proves frequently blocked: I have space only to nominate examples. Cora's cakes remain unsold. Although as a trainee accountant, Cora grasps credit and debit, the notion that adequate accountancy would require her to price her own labor power proves entirely inconceivable (6–8). Cash purchases his tools from a catalogue, but the flood, and the elaborated collective labor of their redemption from the flood, repurposes them: as offerings made to one who lies on his own offering to his mother, the tools cease to be opaque to the work that went into them. Moreover, Cash himself, who Anse fears may take his craft skills independently to market (thereby "short-hand[ing] [36] the Bundrens), proves conspicuously unable to sell himself: injuries combine to hobble him.

Jewel's horse, made with work stolen from shared labor, is stolen back for the collective: Anse takes the horse as a means to barter, whereby the Bundrens gain a team. At very many points, therefore, Bundren monetary exchange proves neither systematic nor systemic. As Taussig argues concerning "peasant proprietors," the peasant who owns his own land, as his primary means of production, does not treat that land as a commodity; nor does he treat his body, and the goods made by his body from the land, primarily as that which goes to market. Peasant land remains matter made for use by way of shared work, and arguably, therefore, the Bundrens are all more and less autochthonous, springing from the soil they inhabit, undermediated by money and its opacities.

Bit 9: The Silent Crash: We know that Faulkner drafted *As I Lay Dying* between October 25, 1929, and January 12, 1930, doing so, apparently and in large part, by night in the boiler house of the University of Mississippi, Oxford, while supervising African American labor. As he wrote, U.S. finance capital famously crashed. It will be my contention that to read *As I Lay Dying* with no reference to the Crash, though it contains no reference to the Crash, would involve a limitation of understanding. One reads Fitzgerald's *Tender Is the Night* (1934), Book 3 of which is set in 1929 (though prior to the Crash) and from which the Crash is omitted, as subject to the Crash. Likewise, one cannot read *The Age of Innocence,* largely set in the 1870s, and at its close reaching toward 1911, without recognizing that the shadow of the Great War falls across its high Victorian leisure-class world. Wharton published *The Age of Innocence* in 1920. Similarly, I have trouble believing that an author who starts a manuscript on the day after Black Thursday (October 24, 1929) in which he has a character called Cash (possessed of scant cash, and that taken from him) fall "twenty-eight foot, four and a half inches, about" (90), does so with no intent to allude. What, then, might be the function of that allusion?

The abyssal fall of U.S. finance toward the close of 1929 should not be divorced from a particular use of land. During the Florida real-estate boom of 1925, investors who purchased lots did not in any real sense buy land, many of the lots being marginal, unusable, or nonexistent. Rather, in an expectation of rapidly rising prices, they bought to resell, thereby gaining profit that involved neither labor nor capital investment in the underlying asset.[36] Monies, so made, seemingly exhibit "self-expanding value."[37] Strictly speaking, purchasers purchased their own euphoria, which, added to the euphoria of others, drove the ascendant price curve. "Irrational exuberance"[38] made land from price volatility, where there was no land: such lands amount to lands made from language, or, more accurately, from exorbitant paper and tape, issuing in celebration of price and its expansion. Likewise, when the bubble burst, what investors sold (if they had time) was not land but panic, adding to the panic of others, and realized through the paper on which it was not worth printing the falling prices. Liquidity and text, in their jointly materializing passage through mood, prove inextricable from financialization. As J. K. Galbraith puts it, in his study on 1929, "by the summer . . . the market not only dominated the news. It also dominated the culture," in the form of market talk involving, "abstraction associated not with the fact or reality, but with the man who asserts it and the manner of its assertion."[39] Jason Compson knows that cotton is made from "hump[ed] back[s]" and "red neck[s]"[40] but he knows equally and better that a short trade in cotton futures transforms a staple into paper. His day, April 6, 1928, is littered with checks, telegrams, and money orders, about which he has much to say ("I say. I say")[41] as he loses perhaps four thousand dollars in the short sale of a single cotton futures contract.[42] Galbraith catches exactly the degree to which Finance, as a cultural dominant, appears "self-expanding," not least in the matter of its own vocal assertions, and not least in relation to land.

Money made nominally in Florida (though actually "in money" and talk of it), after 1925, most typically went in search of compound growth to the stock market, where it might engage, for example, in selling short. The short sell involves an investor (or his broker) borrowing a security (for a fee to its lender) in the expectation that its price will fall. Prior to that fall, the borrower sells the security. When the market drops (as anticipated), he rebuys that which he sold, handing it back to the lender. He gains the difference between the high sale price and the low buy-back price (minus the fee). His risk, however, can be unlimited, since he is obliged to return that which he has borrowed (at a designated date), whatever the price of the borrowed security. Should the price rise rather than fall (no matter what its elevation), he must rebuy that which he merely borrowed. Since he may well have borrowed additionally to cover the anticipated buy-back price, his losses will compound. He who shorts, whether successfully or unsuccessfully, trades in an asset that is no more than a locus of price variation; or, of money made through volatility from borrowed money. The referent of the short trade might be figured as $M\text{-}M^1$, where M equals money; M^1, money plus some; and the dash equates with risk, which risk amounts to a conjunction of anxiety and exuberance, mediated through price and small print. The trader trades less in a "substance" than in the peculiar materialization of affect through the textualized rhythm of market movements. In such transactions text is vital; Christian Marazzi, theorist of finance capital, speaks of the "linguification"[43] of the real within the financial. J. K. Galbraith, less given to neologism, observes that during the months prior to the Crash, "incantation"[44] materialized as ascendant value on the New York Stock Exchange. I have briefly sought to lodge such "incantation" over stocks in a prior "linguification" of Florida lands.

Bit 10: Addie Bundren and the land's body: Caught within the interregnum that split Darl, Addie—a perambulated "morbid symptom"—cannot die until she has removed her labor from the land, doing so in response to what John T. Matthews aptly describes as "the coloniz[ation of her] most intimate space by male command."[45] Her means are incantatory. For all her dismissal of words as "quick as harmless" (173), she exorbitates the sign, rendering it a productive force that displaces sweat as the ground's ground for being ground. I grow gnomic in my effort to sketch a case that I have yet to make. The case follows: Peabody, called to attend her dying, observes that Addie—"no more than a bundle of rotten sticks" (44)—has been "wore out" by Anse (41). Addie knows as much: her section details the systemic abuse of her gestative labor in the provision of a workforce whose sweat has made the Bundren land mean. In her dying, and with equal systematicality, she cancels Anse (seminal source of labor), as a prelude to cancelling her children:

> He did not know that he was dead, then. Sometimes I would lie by him in the dark, hearing the land that was now of my blood and flesh, and I would think: Anse. Why Anse. Why are you Anse. I would think about his name until after a while I could see the word as a shape, a vessel, and I would watch him liquefy and flow into it like cold molasses flowing out of the darkness into the

> vessel, until the jar stood full and motionless: a significant shape profoundly without life like an empty door frame; and then I would find that I had forgotten the name of the jar. I would think: The shape of my body where I used to be a virgin is in the shape of a   and I couldn't think *Anse*, couldn't remember *Anse*. It was not that I could think of myself as no longer unvirgin, because I was three now. And when I would think *Cash* and *Darl* that way until their names would die and solidify into a shape and then fade away, I would say, All right. It doesn't matter. It doesn't matter what they call them. (173)

Addie forgets names in order to forget the persons and things to which those names refer. Her logic runs: Anse (person) into *Anse* (word); proper noun into "vessel" plus liquid ("cold molasses"); "full jar" into "empty door frame"; frame into "   ", which space functions as an iconic analogue to vaginal space (fingered by Addie as she dies); vagina (or textual space) prior to entry by *Anse*, which, care of italic, proves to be not Anse as phallus but *Anse* as word, when that word has already been erased. Ergo, the space in the text, white on the page, retains hymeneal form, allowing Addie to be "three now" and yet "virgin." Addie linguistically regrows her hymen, a trick that counters her earlier impregnation with Darl. Then, Anse, "hidden within a word like within a paper screen," had "struck [her] in the back" through the inscribed and screening page (172). Accordingly, Addie erases the inscription (*Anse*), cleansing the "paper screen." Likewise, she will insist that carrying Cash to full term amounted to a "violation" of her body, "made whole again by [that] violation: time, Anse, love, what you will, outside the circle" (172). One might understand the circle as anticipating the blank, both signs murderous in the extent of their erasure. "And . . . I would think *Cash* and *Darl* that way until their names would die and solidify into a shape and fade away": italic serves to signal the subsumption of the sons, like the father, into an immaculate *un*conception whereby Addie may at last begin to hear "the land" as no longer "of my blood and flesh."

The space on the page finds a further and logical correlate in Addie's choice of resting place: she "asked Anse to promise to take me back to Jefferson when I died" (173), presumably so that she may be buried in her family plot under her maiden name, a name that, since we do not have it, remains blank. Anse's "word," requested and given, triggers the journey. Few words could be less "quick" or "harmless." Consider only the most harmful impediments to Bundren haste, flood and fire. The flood, we are repeatedly told, washes work out of the ground. The fire, as Cash puts it, "burn[s] up . . . the value of the horse" traded "to get [Addie] nigh to town" (233)—five months' work by night—not to mention Gillespie's sweat stored within the burned barn. Labor erasure punctuates Addie's progress toward her unspecified maiden name. I would stress that Addie's means to the retraction of her gestative labor from a labor force, and so, by extension, of their labor power from its "terrible doing" on the land, is language. Which begs the question: from what does Addie's language derive its considerable capacity for harm?

On the face of it, Addie speaks with a revivalist voice, honed in the tradition of itinerant evangelism. Her casting of words as "spiders" (172) borrows directly from Jonathan Edwards's sermon "Sinners in the Hands of an Angry God."[46] Her choice of lover, Whitfield, recalls George Whitefield (his name often written Whitfield), a friend to Edwards, famed open-air preacher, and founder of America's oldest extant charity (Bethesda Orphanage). Addie moves from "spiders" to "orphans" (174) in her efforts to image the alienated work of words. Yet her words remain those of a schoolteacher married to a middle-peasant: of both, Eric Wolf notes that, "caught between [an] understanding of how the world ought properly to be ordered and the realities of a mundane existence," they tend to transmute social unrest into millennial terms.[47] He adds that teachers to the peasantry—dissatisfied intellectuals in an "undeveloped country"[48]—may well dream of "miraculous intervention" by a "Son of Heaven."[49] Hence, Whitfield; where Whitfield functions as little more than Addie's mode of access to a divine word.

Addie takes Whitfield as emphatically as she "took Anse" (170), though for an entirely different purpose. Disillusioned with Anse's words ("love," "motherhood"), which "dont ever fit what they are trying to say at" (171), Addie seeks to restore ontological vehemence to language through her adultery with a minister. Certain that she can "hear . . . the dark land talking of God's love and His beauty and His sin" (174), she finds in Whitfield an analogue to the specified trinity of terms that she has overheard in the land. Whitfield, as a talker "ordained [or loved] by God," may be supposed capable of "talking of God's love," moreover she considers him "beautiful" in "his secret coming" (175) and as "dressed in sin" (174). Their adultery "in the woods" (174) "shape[s] and coerce[s] the terrible blood to the forlorn echo of the dead word high in the air" (175). What that word might be matters less than Addie's conviction that her little and adulterous death on unworked ground elicits, from her own and

Whitfield's coerced blood, a sound that summons (as an echo recalls its origin) a word from "high in the air," which word quickens from the "dead" into the living as Jewel, son of God and Addie. Cora is right to accuse Addie of "sacrilege" (168), when Addie assures her that, "He [Jewel] is my cross and he will be my salvation. He will save me from the water and from the fire" (168), where water and fire seem to emerge, theodically on cue, from the "word" drawn by Addie from Anse, doing so to validate Jewel, an all-but-immaculate conception, who, as the echo of a word, all but amounts to the Johaninne "Word . . . made flesh." In effect, and for Addie, her language has "become an instrument in the production of [a] real fact,"[50] or of Jewel, understood as both textual figment and millennial vanguard, tasked with responsibility for the withdrawal of her worked-out body from the laborious land.

I exaggerate in order to outline the nature of Addie's linguistic work. Words exert agency throughout her section, her famed and contradicted diagram notwithstanding.[51] Addie imbues Bundren land with failed communication ("forlorn echo," "dead word," "dark voicelessness") so that she may disabuse it of subsistence labor. I modify a formulation borrowed from Christian Marazzi's *Capital and Language.* What Marazzi says about contemporary financialization and its crunch accords with the conditions of the crash in 1929: "The New Economy has [a] peculiar element: it is a mode of production imbued with communication . . . [and subject to] the productive force of language in the monetary and financial sphere."[52] Just as linguistic assertion took land from land in Florida (circa 1925) in order that it might go to Wall Street, so—as Cash and U.S. finance crash in '29—Addie translates land into a linguistic event, whose destination proves to be land (a grave) without name or substance, beyond a severally ruined corpse.

Bit 11: Why the bits cannot join up: In *As I Lay Dying,* anomalous economic realities—peasant production, the commodity market, finance capital—are thrown into contrastive definition by the emergency of the Crash. Arguably, Faulkner does the Bundrens in different voices in order to articulate incompatible labor imperatives as they structure single vocal features (Darl's telepathy; the divided trajectory of Addie's revivalist lexicon), or as they ally voice with voice (Vardaman as the vocal extension of his father's autochthony), or, indeed, set voice against voice (Addie versus Anse). At no point are the economic options reconciled, though each moves toward figuration as a form of labor on Bundren land. The land consequently divides, operating as an irremediably split sign, locus of what might usefully (and in conclusion) be called a structure of mixed feeling. I borrow the phrase "structure of feeling" from Raymond Williams, for whom such structures most typically "take place at the very edge of semantic availability."[53] By "form," "figure," "structure," I refer not to "fixed" or "finished" entities (whether as "labor," "land," or "language"), but to "formations in process,"[54] forming from contradictory usage (whether of "labor," "land," or "language"). *As I Lay Dying* would be so much simpler if one could identify "peasant," "commodity producer," or "speculator" as extant entities possessed of separate voices. Identification cannot occur because each occurs at the other's edge, yielding overlap, disturbance, latency, trouble (for which Darl's telepathy is simply the most overt expression). Yet a focal figure for *As I Lay Dying* may be said to emerge in "1929," understood as the silent and precipitative crash from which the novel takes the full range of its substantial instabilities.

NOTES

1. William Faulkner, *As I Lay Dying* (New York: Modern Library Edition, 1992), 254. Hereafter cited parenthetically.

2. In *If I Forget Thee, Jerusalem* (1939), Faulkner has Charlotte seduce Harry into his abortive incision with, "We've done this lots of ways but not with knives have we?"; she adds, "what was it you told me nigger women say? Ride me down, Harry" (New York: Library of America, 1990), 644–45. Aptly, in "Pantaloon in Black" (1942), Faulkner names his African American labor hero and former sexual athlete, Rider.

3. William Shakespeare, *Othello* 1.1.115–17.

4. Zora Neale Hurston, *Their Eyes Were Watching God* (London: Virago, 1987), 29.

5. See Albert C. Smith, "Southern Violence" Reconsidered: Arson as Protest in Black Belt Georgia, 1865–1910," *Journal of Southern History* 51, no. 4 (November 1985): 527–64.

6. William Faulkner, "Barn Burning," in *Collected Stories of William Faulkner* (New York: Random House, 1977), 7.

7. Ibid., 7, 12. "Niggard," repeated three times within the space of a page, suggests that the narrator may hear, within its latencies, the phrase "nigger fire," thereby identifying (albeit in occluded form) the ethnic "blackness" of his father's "mainspring."

8. Jeanette Keith, "The Politics of Southern Draft Resistance," *Journal of American History*, 87, no. 4 (March 2001): 1345.

9. Ibid., 1349.

10. Ibid., 1352, 1346, 1352.

11. John Liman, "Addie in No-Man's Land," in *Faulkner and War*, ed. Noel Polk and Ann Abadie (Jackson: University Press of Mississippi, 2004), 36–54.

12. Walter Benjamin, *One Way Street and Other Writings*, trans. J. A. Underwood (London: Penguin, 2009), 257.

13. I am aware that I put earth into the glass, where there is no earth, doing so in an extension of the autochthonic (or bestial) imperative. In *The Hamlet*, Ike Snopes consummates his love for Houston's cow in the place where he milks her. Faulkner specifies and celebrates the passage of white liquids into the ground (see Richard Godden, *William Faulkner: An Economy of Complex Words* [Princeton: Princeton University Press, 2007], 52–53).

14. Antonio Gramsci, *Selections from the Prison Notebooks*, ed. and trans. Quintin Hoare and Geoffrey Nowell Smith (New York: International, 1971), 276. For Gramsci, amelioration of the "symptoms" of the "interregnum" remains "blocked" for as long as the rift between "popular masses" and "ruling ideologies" persists. *As I Lay Dying* might be understood as recasting Gramsci's sticking point as an experience of contradiction occurring when incompatible economic relations—peasant production, capitalist marketplace, and finance capital—crash together in 1929.

15. The allusion to industrial production is not casual: regarding the flooded river, as its "surface" seems to "sever" the "torsos" of Jewel and Vernon, Darl notes, "[i]t looks peaceful, like machinery does after you have watched it and listened to it for a long time" (163).

16. Darl's four uses of "that" fix the inception and quality of his telepathy: "that" times four, or four directional imperatives, are insistent in their pointing toward, and equally insistent in their non-nomination of that toward which they point. Darl's reiterated "that" mimes the quality of his telepathic knowledge—material through its performativity, yet immaterial as to its referent—real *and* abstracted, or a real phantom.

17. Paul Ricoeur, "The Metaphoric Process as Cognition, Imagination and Feeling," *Critical Inquiry* 5, no.1 (Autumn 1978): 145.

18. Ibid., 148.

19. Quotations concerning the dancing table, up to this point, are drawn from Karl Marx, *Capital*, vol. 1, trans. Ben Fowkes (Harmondsworth: Penguin, 1978), 163–64.

20. Marx, *Capital*, vol. 3 (London: Lawrence and Wishart, 1984), 393.

21. Marx, *Capital*, 1:138.

22. Ibid.

23. Ibid., 1:150–51. For a useful account of the abstractive passage of labor power into "socially average labor time," see Moishe Postone, *Time, Labor and Social Domination* (Cambridge: Cambridge University Press, 1993), 123–85.

24. Marx speaks of the "double form" of commodities (see *Capital*, 1:138).

25. Jean-Luc Nancy, *Listening*, trans. Charlotte Mandell (New York: Fordham University Press, 2007), 8.

26. The call remains close: witness the delicacy of the balance between *dis*solution and *re*solution in "all one yet neither, all either yet none"—a near-perfect chiasmus (addressing *dis*-integrity), yet momentarily made perfect in the phonemic transposition of an *n*, en route from

"*n*either" to "*n*one." Minus the *n* the chiasmus forms correctly, "all one yet either, all either yet one" (addressing *in*tegrity). Vardaman learns his *n*'s from his *t*'s, and more particularly from the work of "it." He strains to "see hearing" (or the sound of a letter as that letter moves through the air), in order that sound shall ensure the integrity of the horse. If the horse holds together, so too will the fish and, within both, the mother.

27. Eric Sundquist, *Faulkner: The House Divided* (Baltimore: Johns Hopkins University Press, 1983), 30, 29. See also Erin E. Edwards, "Extremities of the Body: The Anoptic Corporeality of *As I Lay Dying*," *Modern Fiction Studies* 55, no. 4 (Winter 2009): 739–64.

28. "[L]anguage is practical consciousness . . . burdened with matter . . . which here makes its appearance in the form of agitated layers of air, sound" (Karl Marx, and Friedrich Engels, *The German Ideology*, ed. C. J. Arthur [London: Lawrence and Wishart, 2004], 50–51).

29. My reading of sound, as a route to an externality from which the subject derives, and wherein he may lodge, owes much to Fredric Jameson. See his *Valences of the Dialectic* (London: Verso, 2009), 120–24.

30. Eric Wolf, *Peasant Wars of the Twentieth Century* (Norman: University of Oklahoma Press, 1999), 291.

31. Michael Taussig, *The Devil and Commodity Fetishism in South America* (Chapel Hill: University of North Carolina Press, 1980), 9, 10, 99. For Taussig, such groups "[on] the threshold of capitalist development . . . [retain] pre-capitalist beliefs and practices" (11).

32. Ellen Meiksins Wood, *The Origin of Capitalism: A Longer View* (London: Verso, 2002), 101.

33. Marx, *Capital*, 1:171.

34. Jameson, *Valences of the Dialectic*, 170.

35. The emphasis here differs markedly from a grouping of essays concerning *As I Lay Dying* and the commodity form; nonetheless, this essay would not have been possible without that work. See Cheryl Lester, "*As I Lay Dying*: Rural Depopulation and Social Dislocation as a Structure of Feeling," *Faulkner Journal* 21, no. 12 (Fall 2005/6): 28–52; John T. Matthews, "*As I Lay Dying* in the Machine Age," *boundary 2* 19, no. 1 (Spring 1992): 69–94; and Susan Willis, "Learning from the Banana," *American Quarterly* 39, no. 4 (Winter 1987): 586–600.

36. J. K. Galbraith comments: "[A]t some point in the growth of a boom all aspects of property ownership become irrelevant except the prospect of an early rise in price. Income from property or enjoyment of its use, or even its long-run worth, is now academic. As in the case of the more repulsive Florida lots . . . [w]hat is important is that tomorrow or next week market values will rise—as they did yesterday and last week—and a profit can be realized" (*The Great Crash* [London: Penguin, 2009], 46).

37. Marx, *Capital*, 3:394.

38. Alan Greenspan (former chair of the Federal Reserve Board) used this phrase in 1996, immediately prior to a precipitous drop in stock market prices. Robert J. Shiller took Greenspan's words as the title for his study of market activity, emphasizing the degree to which "information cascades" (159) and "unsubstantial whispers" (xiii) produced market volatility. (*Irrational Exuberance* [Princeton: Princeton University Press, 2005]).

39. Galbraith, *The Great Crash*, 99.

40. Faulkner, *The Sound and the Fury* (New York: Norton, 1994), 120.

41. Ibid., 113.

42. For the fullest accounting, see Wayne W. Westbrook, "Skunked on the New York Cotton Exchange: What Really Happens to Jason Compson in *The Sound and the Fury*," *Southern Literary Journal* 41, no. 2 (Spring 2009): 53–86.

43. Christian Marazzi, *Capital and Language*, trans. Gregory Conti (Los Angeles: Semiotext[e], 2002), 40.

44. Galbraith, *The Great Crash*, 111.

45. John T. Matthews, *William Faulkner: Seeing Through the South* (Chichester: Wiley-Blackwell, 2009), 151.

46. Jonathan Edwards, "Sinners in the Hands of an Angry God," in *The Heath Anthology of American Literature*, vol. A, *Colonial Period to 1800* (New York: Houghton Mifflin, 2006), 672.

47. Wolf, *Peasant Wars of the Twentieth Century*, 292.

48. Ibid., 288.

49. Ibid., 292.

50. Marazzi, *Capital and Language*, 33.

51. The diagram: "I would think how words go straight up in a thin line, quick and harmless, and how terribly doing goes along the earth, clinging to it, so that after a while the two lines are too far apart for the same person to straddle from one to the other" (173).

52. Marazzi, *Capital and Language*, 140.

53. Raymond Williams, *Marxism and Literature* (Oxford: Oxford University Press, 1977), 134.

54. Ibid., 132.

Contributors

Sarah Gleeson-White is senior lecturer in American Literature at the University of Sydney. She has published widely in the field of southern literature, and is completing an edition of Faulkner's Twentieth Century-Fox screenplays. Her current project concerns regionalism and mass culture.

Richard Godden teaches in the English Department at the University of California, Irvine. He is the author of *Fictions of Capital* (1990), *Fictions of Labor: William Faulkner and the South's Long Revolution* (1997), and *William Faulkner: An Economy of Complex Words* (2007). He currently works on the relation between narrative poetics and finance capital.

Robert Jackson is associate professor and director of graduate studies in English at the University of Tulsa. He is the author of *Seeking the Region in American Literature and Culture: Modernity, Dissidence, Innovation* (2005); his current book project considers the complex and varied relations between black and white southerners and the motion picture medium from the silent era to World War II.

Donald M. Kartiganer is Howry Professor of Faulkner Studies Emeritus at the University of Mississippi (1991–2009), and former director of the Faulkner and Yoknapatawpha Conference (1994–2011). He is the author of *The Fragile Thread: The Meaning of Form in Faulkner's Novels*, coeditor of *Theories of American Literature* and seven collections of Faulkner criticism, and author of more than forty essays on, in addition to Faulkner, Kierkegaard, Freud, Conrad, T. S. Eliot, W. C. Williams, Kafka, Welty, Hemingway, Philip Roth, and the critic Murray Krieger.

Catherine Gunther Kodat is dean of the Division of Liberal Arts and professor of humanities at the University of the Arts in Philadelphia. Her essays on twentieth-century U.S. film, dance, music, and literature have appeared in journals such as *American Quarterly, American Literary History, Representations, Salmagundi,* and the *Boston Review* and in several edited collections. She is the author of a forthcoming book on the metapolitics of Cold War culture.

Peter Lurie is associate professor of English and film studies at the University of Richmond. He is the author of *Vision's Immanence: Faulkner, Film, and the Popular Imagination* (2004) and of a forthcoming work on history and the visual in American literature and film. He is also the editor, with Ann J. Abadie, of the forthcoming *Faulkner and Film: Faulkner and Yoknapatawpha 2010.*

John T. Matthews is most recently the author of *William Faulkner: Seeing Through the South* and editor of *A Companion to the Modern American Novel 1900–1950* (both 2009). He has also written *The Play of Faulkner's Language; "The Sound and the Fury": Faulkner and the Lost Cause;* and articles on Faulkner, southern literature, and modern American fiction. His present projects are a book on the disavowal of the South in American literature, and two forthcoming edited volumes on Faulkner. He teaches in the Department of English at Boston University.

Sascha Morrell is lecturer in English at the University of New England, Australia (UNE). She completed her Ph.D. at Trinity College, Cambridge. Her current research concerns include the dialectics of race and class identity in American literature; continuities between nineteenth- and twentieth-century modernisms; the comparison of literary "zombies" and "robots"; and symbolic invocations of Haitian and other Caribbean histories in Anglophone literature.

Julian Murphet is Scientia Professor in English and Film Studies at UNSW Australia, where he also directs the Centre for Modernism Studies in Australia. He is the author of *Multimedia Modernism* (2009), and the coeditor of *Modernism and Masculinity* (2014) and *Flann O'Brien and Modernism* (2014). He edits a new journal in modernism studies, *Affirmations: of the modern.*

Stefan Solomon is a Visiting Fellow in the School of Literature, Languages, and Linguistics at the Australian National University. He has written on the intersections of film, literature, and new media, and is now completing a book on William Faulkner's career as a screenwriter.

Mark Steven completed doctoral research at the University of New South Wales and is now a Research Fellow in Film at the Centre for Modernism Studies in Australia. His thesis was titled "Red Modernism: Poetry, Communism, and the American Avant-Garde." He has published on literature and film, and has coedited *Styles of Extinction: Cormac McCarthy's* The Road (2012) and a forthcoming collection on the cinema of Theo Angelopoulos with Edinburgh University Press.

Jay Watson is Howry Professor of Faulkner Studies and professor of English at the University of Mississippi, where he is also director of the annual Faulkner and Yoknapatawpha conference. He is the author of *Forensic Fictions: The Lawyer Figure in Faulkner* (1993) and *Reading for the Body: The Recalcitrant Materiality of Southern Fiction, 1893–1985* (2012), which received Honorable Mention for the 2013 C. Hugh Holman Award for the year's outstanding publication in southern literary studies. He is the editor of *Conversations with Larry Brown* (2007) and *Faulkner and Whiteness* (2011), and coeditor of three forthcoming volumes in the Faulkner and Yoknapatawpha series. From 2009 to 2012, he served as president of the William Faulkner Society, and he spent the 2002–3 academic year in Turku, Finland, as Visiting Fulbright Professor of American Studies at the University of Turku and Åbo Akademi University.

Michael Zeitlin is associate professor in the English Department, University of British Columbia. He is the author of essays and chapters on Faulkner, former coeditor of the *Faulkner Journal* (2003–8), and editor of *Misrecognition, Race, and the Real in Faulkner's Fiction* (2004). He has written essays and chapters on Freud, Lacan, Donald Barthelme, and the American wars in Vietnam, Iraq, and Afghanistan. With Paul Budra, he is the editor of *Soldier Talk: The Vietnam War in Oral Narrative* (2004).

Index